Foreign Military Sales Customer Financial Management Handbook (Billing)

Jointly Developed by

Defense Institute of Security Assistance Management

Defense Finance and Accounting Service

Tenth Edition

Library of Congress Catalog Card No. 96-71924

Acknowledgements

Defense Institute of Security Assistance Management

Defense Finance and Accounting Service Directorate, For Security Assistance

Dr. Ronald H. Reynolds
Commandant

Alfred S. Graham
Director

Authors and Contributors

Chris M. Krolikowski, DISAM
2475 K Street
Wright-Patterson Air Force Base, Ohio 45433

> **Phone Commercial (937) 255-5850**
> **DSN 785-5850**
> **Commercial Fax (937) 656-4685**
> **DSN 986-4685**

DFAS-Indianapolis (DFAS-IN/JAXBC)
8899 East 56th Street
Indianapolis, Indiana 46249

> **Phone Commercial (317) 510-7208**
> **DSN   699-7208**
> **Commercial Fax (317) 510-7278**
> **DSN   699-7278**

Editorial Assistant
Patricia Vocke, DISAM

Graphics
Danny Palmer, DISAM

PREFACE

The Foreign Military Sales (FMS) Customer Financial Management Handbook (Billing) is intended to provide an explanation of the financial aspects of the U.S. foreign military sales program, with emphasis on Foreign Military Sales billing and reporting. This publication describes "how" the Foreign Military Sales financial system works and, in many instances, delineates "why" this financial system is designed to function as it does. While the U.S. Department of Defense (DoD) is always receptive to suggestions to improve Foreign Military Sales financial procedures, readers of this publication should observe that many such procedures are followed because of legal requirements contained in U.S. Public Law. As a result, DoD very often has little flexibility in the financial administration of the Foreign Military Sales Program. This publication does not take precedence over officially published U.S. government directives, instructions, or manuals and is intended as a guide only. Additionally, this publication goes to press in a time of dynamic changes in the security assistance arena. Some changes may even occur while this handbook is being printed.

Any requests for clarification or suggestions for improvement or content should be addressed to the following:

Defense Finance and Accounting Service (DFAS-IN/JAXBC)
East 56th Street
Indianapolis, Indiana 46249-8901
     Telephone - DSN 699-7208
     Telephone Commercial - (317) 510-7208
     Fax - DSN 699-7278
     Fax Commercial - (317) 510-7278

Or

The Defense Institute of Security Assistance Management (DISAM/DR)
2475 K Street, Building 52
Wright-Patterson AFB, Ohio 45433-7641
     Telephone - DSN 785-5850
     Telephone Commercial - (937) 255-5850
     Data Fax - DSN 785-4685
     Data Fax Commercial - (937) 986-4685

6

Table of Contents

Part I
General Overview

*"The next best thing to knowing something
is knowing where to find it."*

Samuel Johnson

Chapter 1
An Introduction to the Foreign Military Sales Program

Purpose

The purpose of this chapter is to acquaint the reader with selected terminology, legislative provisions, and policies associated with the management of the foreign military sales (FMS) program. These laws and policies - most of which have their foundation in the *Arms Export Control Act* (AECA), as amended - form the foundation for the procedural aspects of the FMS financial management and billing system and the role of Defense Finance and Accounting Service, Indianapolis, Indiana, DFAS-IN.

The What, Why, When, and How of Foreign Military Sales

What

Just what is FMS? FMS is the largest program element of the overall U.S. security assistance program. Other program elements include the following:

- International Military Education and Training Program (IMETP)

- Commercial exports licensed under the AECA

- Economic Support Fund (ESF)

- Peacekeeping Operations (PKO)

The Foreign Military Sales Financing Program may be used to finance FMS agreements, United States of America Letter of Offer and Acceptance (LOA) and in some instances, to finance commercially licensed exports.

FMS is a process through which eligible foreign governments and international organizations may purchase defense articles and services from the United States Government (USG). The FMS government-to-government agreement is documented on an LOA. FMS is accomplished in two basic ways, as follows:

- FMS cash purchases whereby the purchaser pays in cash (U.S. dollars) all costs that may be associated with a sale.

- Foreign military financing (FMF) wherein USG grants/non-repayable and repayable loans are involved. These credit or loan arrangements are negotiated by the foreign government and the U.S. government.

- In either situation–cash purchases or financing - the funds that are required to implement the LOA must be paid or transferred to DFAS-IN where they are closely accounted for in the FMS Trust Fund.

Why

Why does the USG have an FMS program? There are many reasons. Since World War II, the United States has provided various forms of security assistance to other nations in furtherance of the principle of collective security. In furtherance of this principle, Section 1 of the AECA establishes the rationale for FMS:

The Congress recognizes . . . that the United States and other free and independent countries continue to have valid requirements for effective and mutually beneficial defense relationships. Because of the growing cost and complexity of defense equipment, it is increasingly difficult and uneconomic for any country, particularly a developing country to fill all of its legitimate defense requirements from its own design and production base.

There are many benefits that accrue to the FMS purchasing country and the United States as a result of FMS. Some of these benefits include:

- Lowered unit production costs and shared research and development costs.

- Progress toward standardization and interoperability of equipment between the United States and friendly foreign nations.

- Utilization of Cooperative Logistics Supply Support Arrangements (CLSSA) by selected countries, which permits support of the foreign nation's equipment from U.S. stocks on an equal basis with comparable U.S. forces having a similar mission.

When

When (or under what circumstances) is an FMS agreement approved? Again, Section 1 of the AECA applies:

It is the sense of the Congress that all such sales be approved only when they are consistent with the foreign policy interests of the United States, the purposes of the foreign assistance program of the United States as embodied in the *Foreign Assistance Act of 1961* (FAA), as amended. . . .

How

How is the FMS program administered? The overall security assistance program is under the supervision and general direction of the U.S. Secretary of State. However, the Secretary of Defense is responsible for administering certain security assistance program elements, one of which is FMS. In accordance with Section 42(d) of the AECA, the Secretary of Defense has primary responsibility for:

- The determination of military end-item requirements.

- The procurement of military equipment in a manner which permits its integration with service programs.

- The supervision of the training of foreign military personnel.

- The movement and delivery of military end items.

- Within the Department of Defense (DoD), the performance of any other functions with respect to sales and guarantees.

Basic Foreign Military Sales Policies

There are several policies, many of which have their roots in the AECA, which affect the conduct of the FMS program. Other policies are found in the *Security Assistance Management Manual* (SAMM) or DoD directives/instructions. The ones listed herein are considered to be the more pertinent in providing a background to the FMS financial management and billing system from the perspective of the FMS customer.

- **FMS Agreement.** The AECA, in the absence of a country-accepted LOA, effectively prohibits the advance procurement of FMS articles and services. Accordingly, it is important in country acceptance of the LOA that all necessary copies be signed and returned, including the copies destined for DFAS-IN. DFAS-IN receipt of the signed LOA and the initial deposit specified, is prerequisite to proper implementation of the LOA (generally referred to as an (FMS case).

- **Standardized Documentation.** The LOA is used for all foreign military sales of defense articles and services, including training, by the military departments (MILDEPs) and defense agencies. DD Form 645 Foreign Military Sales Billing Statement is used to report deliveries, work in process, and the amounts due. The DD Form 645 is prepared on a quarterly basis by DFAS-IN.

- **Pricing.** FMS pricing policy is addressed in Sections 21 and 22 of the AECA. The various pricing factors involved, many of which specifically show up in FMS billing documentation, are addressed in Chapter 3. Unless otherwise specified, all prices indicated on the LOA are estimates and final costs may vary from these estimated amounts.

- **Advance Collection.** The normal method of collection shall be in advance of performance or delivery. Advance collection is accomplished in two general ways:

  - Through receipt of an initial deposit upon acceptance of the LOA.

  - Through payment of amounts billed on the DD Form 645.

- **Interest on Arrearages.** Both the AECA and the LOA, Standard Terms and Conditions, specify that interest must be paid by the FMS customer on any net amount by which it is in arrears on payments.

- **Country Administrative Self-Sufficiency.** Countries purchasing under the FMS program are expected to attain a high degree of administrative self-sufficiency, to include:

  - Establishment of a purchasing mission in the Continental United States (CONUS), or the vesting of adequate purchasing authority with the attaché or embassy staff in the United States.

  - Establishment of a freight forwarder, so that the DoD transportation system (DTS) is used only in rare circumstances when specifically agreed upon by the USG.

- Establishment of communications channels, regarding FMS, directly between country representatives and appropriate U.S. government activities in the CONUS.

- Establishment of country records required to follow the progress of orders placed under FMS.

It is this latter aspect, i.e., establishment and maintenance of country records, that DFAS-IN billing and performance reporting documentation can be highly useful to the FMS customer. As part of the documentation, as shall be seen in subsequent chapters, detailed information is provided with respect to the delivery of equipment and services on a transaction-by-transaction basis. Furthermore, in addition to receiving a performance status document, the FMS customer is provided with an invoice which supports the expenditure of country funds.

- DoD Management. The U.S. government, in accordance with the LOA standard terms and conditions, is responsible for acquiring (and, under certain circumstances, delivering) the desired article and service. In this regard, the FMS customer benefits from the management expertise of DoD, who often must contract with industry. The LOA Standard Terms and Conditions specifically states:

> When procuring for the Purchaser, the DoD will, in general, employ the same contract clauses, the same contract administration, and the same quality and audit inspection procedures as would be used in procuring for itself, except as otherwise requested by the Purchaser and as agreed to by the DoD. . . .

FMS, involves billions of dollars of new orders annually, is no small effort in terms of the impact on the DoD work force. In fact, the DoD expends thousands of man years of effort annually managing the FMS program. FMS is a big program that requires intensive management. In this regard, it is DoD policy, as delineated in DoD Directive 5132.3, that:

> The development and execution of the [security assistance] program shall be accorded the same high degree of attention and efficiency as other DoD programs. To the extent practical, security assistance requirements shall be integrated with other DoD requirements and implemented through the same DoD systems, facilities, and procedures.

Summary

The FMS program is governed by law and executive branch policy. Some of the basic FMS policies include:

- FMS is documented on a signed copy of the LOA. Receipt of the LOA, together with the requisite initial deposit, is necessary for implementation of the FMS agreement.

- The FMS customer is expected to attain administrative self-sufficiency in many areas, to include the establishment of communications channels and country records.

- Pricing of FMS is mandated by the AECA, as amended.

- Payment for FMS shall normally be in advance.

- Interest must be collected in the event that the country is in arrears on payments.

- It is DoD policy that the FMS program be managed with the same attention and care as other DoD programs.

The FMS process is described in the next chapter, together with the USG organizations which interface with DFAS-IN.

Chapter 2
Foreign Military Sales: Organizations and Processes

Purpose

An awareness of the U.S. government organizations involved in foreign military sales (FMS), their interrelationships, and the FMS process is a prerequisite to understanding the FMS financial management and billing system. This chapter will provide that awareness through descriptions of the organizations and the processes, together with flow charts to illustrate the relationships.

United States Government Organizations for Foreign Military Sales

FMS is a large, complex program, which cuts across several U.S. government organizational lines. In the discussion, which follows, an effort is made to highlight the functions of those organizations, which have a substantial role in the FMS process, with an emphasis on financial management.

Department of State

Secretary of State

In accordance with Section 2 of the *Arms Export Control Act* (AECA), as amended, the Secretary of State is responsible for:

- The continuous supervision and general direction of FMS and commercial exports licensed under the AECA.
- Determining whether there shall be a sale to a country and the amount.

Under Secretary of State

The Under Secretary of State for Arms Control and International Security is the principal adviser to the Secretary of State and focal point for security cooperation (including FMS) matters within the Department of State (DoS).

Bureau of Political-Military Affairs

The Director, Bureau of Political-Military Affairs serves as the principal channel of liaison and contact between the DoS and the DoD. Two offices within this Bureau are specifically concerned with security assistance.

- The Office of Regional Security and Arms Transfer Policy promulgates and oversees export control policy and coordinates arms transfer authorization/denial decisions for the Secretary of State.
- The Office of Defense Trade Control is responsible for the licensing of exports or arms and materiel on the *U.S. Munitions List*, contained in the *International Traffic in Arms Regulations* (ITAR).

Department of Treasury

The Department of Treasury is involved in FMS in the following ways:

- Receiving and reviewing periodic reports of accountability from DFAS-IN.
- Overseeing the functions of the Federal Financing Bank (FFB) which (in coordination with the Defense Security Cooperation Agency (DSCA) provides guaranteed loans to finance FMS and commercial export sales.
- Setting the rate of interest in the event of FMS payment arrearages on the part of the foreign government.

Department of Commerce

The Department of Commerce, through the Maritime Administration, has a responsibility to determine if foreign countries (through their freight forwarder agents) are properly utilizing U.S. flag shipping for items financed under the U.S. government credit/loan program.

Department of Defense

Secretary of Defense

The legal responsibilities of the Secretary of Defense are as noted in Chapter 1 of this Handbook. Many of these responsibilities have been delegated; DoD Directive 5132.3 is a primary source in this regard.

Office of the Secretary of Defense

Under Secretary of Defense for Policy [USD(P)]. This official serves as the principal adviser and assistant to the Secretary of Defense for all matters concerned with the integration of departmental plans and policies with overall national security objectives.

Assistant Secretary of Defense (International Security Affairs) [ASD(ISA)]. The office within the DoD which is responsible for supervising security cooperation programs (except those of the New Independent States of the Former Soviet Union and Latin America) is the ASD/ISA.

Under Secretary of Defense (Acquisition, Technology and Logistics) [USD(AT&L)]. This office promulgates policy and procedures on a variety of security assistance functional areas, to include cooperative logistics supply support arrangements and international co-production agreements. The Defense Threat Reduction Agency reports to this office adding responsibilities for reducing the threat to the U.S. and its allies from weapons of mass destruction and special weapons.

Under Secretary of Defense (Comptroller). It is the responsibility of this office to establish policy and procedures involving financial management, fiscal matters, accounting, pricing, auditing, and international balance of payments as these matters relate to security assistance. Within this office the DoD 2140 and 7000 series of directives/instructions applicable to the FMS pricing and billing are published.

Joint Chiefs of Staff, Combatant Commands, and Overseas Activities

Joint Chiefs of Staff. The Chairman of the Joint Chiefs of Staff (JCS) is the principal military adviser to the President. The Joint Staff constitutes the immediate military staff of the Secretary of Defense, serving in the chain of command that extends from the President to the Secretary of Defense, through the JCS, to the commanders of unified and specified commands.

JCS is a key participant in the security cooperation program development and review process. The following security assistance functions are performed by JCS:

- Coordinating security assistance with U.S. military plans and programs and providing the Secretary of Defense with military advice concerning security cooperation programs, actions, and activities to include:
  - Recommending military force objectives, requirements, and priorities for actual or potential security assistance recipients.
  - Determining the impact of security cooperation programs on U.S. programs and defense readiness.
  - Recommend security assistance organizational and manpower requirements for overseas Security Cooperation Organizations (SCOs) and security cooperation

personnel augmentations to Defense Attaché Offices.

    •• Assign Force/Activity Designators to determine priorities in the allocation of defense articles among recipient nations and between recipient nations and the U.S. Armed Forces within guidelines established by the Office of the Secretary of Defense in DoD Directive 4410.6, and recommend priorities of allocation of materiel and equipment when competing requirements cannot be resolved.

Combatant Commands. Six of the combatant commands (COCOMS) have responsibilities for the conduct of the U.S. security cooperation program within their respective geographical regions. They are listed below.

- United States European Command (USEUCOM)
- United States Southern Command (USSOUTHCOM)
- United States Pacific Command (USPACOM)
- United States Central Command (USCENTCOM).
- United States Northern Command (USNORTHCOM)
- United States Africa Command (USAFRICOM)

With regard to security assistance, the functions of the COCOMs include (among many others):

- Making recommendations to the Joint Staff and the Secretary of Defense on any aspect of security assistance programs, projections or activities.
- Commanding, supervising, and supporting the SCOs in matters that are not functions or responsibilities of the Chiefs of the U.S. Diplomatic Missions, including the provision of necessary technical assistance and administrative support to SCOs.

Security Cooperation Organizations. Functions of SCOs (among many others) are FMS case management, training program management, and security cooperation program monitoring. In performing these functions, each SCO maintains liaison between DoD components, the appropriate elements of the U.S. Diplomatic Mission, and the foreign defense organization.

Defense Agencies

Defense Security Cooperation Agency. As prescribed by DoD Directive 5105.38, DSCA is established as a separate agency of the DoD under the direction, authority, and control of the ASD/GSA. Some of the functions of DSCA are:

- Administering and supervising security assistance planning and programs
- Conducting international logistics and sales negotiations with foreign countries
- Serve as the DoD focal point for liaison with U.S. industry with regard to security assistance activities
- Managing the credit financing program
- Developing and promulgating security assistance procedures, such as the *Security Assistance Management Manual* (SAMM) (DoD 5105.38-M)

Defense Finance and Accounting Service (DFAS). As prescribed by DoD Directive 5118.5, DFAS was established January 15, 1991, under the direction, authority, and control of the DoD Comptroller to perform finance and accounting services for the DoD. As part of the DFAS Indianapolis, Indiana, Security Assistance (DFAS-IN) performs finance and accounting services for specific DSCA security assistance programs. Some key functions of DFAS-IN include:

- Serving as the central point of contact within DoD for FMS Trust Fund accounting and/or billing inquiries from U.S. government activities and foreign governments.

- Preparing and reviewing all DoD FMS bills, and calculate and assess interest due on delinquent debts.
- Maintaining a centralized, automated FMS financial data system.
- Managing each FMS customer Trust Fund account to include timely recording of customer deposits, control of cash expenditure authority, recording disbursements, and identifying developing customer Trust Fund cash flow problems.
- Developing and promulgating finance and accounting policy and procedures through the *DoD Financial Management Regulation* (DoD 7000.14-R).

Defense Logistics Agency (DLA). DLA is a DoD activity whose mission is to provide support to the military services, other DoD components, Federal civil agencies, and foreign governments. Such support includes the providing of assigned materiel commodities and items of supply, logistics services, contract administration services, and other support services.

Defense Contract Audit Agency (DCAA). DCAA is a separate agency under the control of the Assistant Secretary of Defense (Comptroller). Through its field audit offices, it provides audit services for many FMS-related contracts.

Defense Language Institute English Language Center (DLIELC), located at Lackland Air Force Base, Texas, operates under the command and control of Headquarters, Air Education and Training Command. The Center is tasked by the Army, Navy, and Air Force, under provisions of a joint regulation. It is responsible for the conduct, supervision, and technical control of English language training programs for non-English speaking foreign and U.S. service personnel.

National Geospatial - Intelligence Agency (NGA). NGA offers support on matters of mapping, charting, and geodesy to foreign countries under the U.S. security cooperation program.

Defense Institute of Security Assistance Management (DISAM). In accordance with DoD Directive 2140.5, the DISAM shall:

- Conduct courses of study that will prepare military (U.S. and foreign) and civilian (USG, foreign, and U.S. contractor) personnel for assignments in security assistance management positions.
- Conduct research, consultations, or special studies directed toward improving the curricula in security assistance management.
- Disseminate security assistance information.

DISAM is organized as part of the DSCA. The U.S. Air Force, as the executive agent provides logistics and administrative support to DISAM with reimbursement from DSCA.

Secretaries of Military Departments

Functions. The Secretaries of the MILDEPs serve as advisers to the Secretary of Defense on all matters of security assistance impacting on, or related to, their department and shall act for the Secretary of Defense where responsibility for actions is delegated. In carrying out their responsibilities, the Secretaries:

- Provide the Secretary of Defense recommendations considered appropriate and necessary to ensure the successful conduct of security assistance, including its interface with and support of military department policies, objectives, plans, and programs.
- Provide data, upon request, pertaining to price, source, availability and lead time for use in developing and reviewing security cooperation programs, including FMS cases.
- Provide to elements of the Office of the Secretary of Defense, JCS, COCOMs, and SCOs, as appropriate, technical information as to weapons systems, tactics and doctrine,

training, and pertinent logistic support.

- Conduct training, and acquire and deliver defense articles and services included in approved programs.
- Coordinate and establish delivery schedules and necessary internal procedures for follow-up, expediting, and related actions during implementation of approved programs.
- Within policies and criteria established by the Assistant Secretary of Defense (ISA), and under direction of the Director, DSCA, make sales of defense articles and services to eligible countries and international organizations.

Military Department Subordinate Organizations. A discussion as to how each MILDEP is organized for FMS is almost a handbook unto itself. Suffice to say that numerous major/ subordinate commands and field activities are involved. In a general sense, the following types of organizational components have a role in FMS:

- **Systems/Logistics/Training Commands.** Prepare the LOA and LOA data studies. Acquire defense articles and services, once an LOA is implemented.
- **International Logistics Control Offices (ILCOs).** Maintain the detailed case records for accounting and logistics reporting.

The Foreign Military Sales Process

Many of the organizations discussed above will now be further addressed in the context of the basic FMS process (Figure 2-1). This process, of course, can be viewed in terms of various phases, depending on what is being emphasized. For the purpose of this Handbook, the FMS process is divided into three supporting processes (or sub-processes):

- The LOR Process
- The LOA/Implementation Process
- The Execution/Performance Reporting Process

Letter of Request and Offer Process

This process (illustrated in Figure 2-2) sets the stage for subsequent financial transactions. The customer initiated LOR for defense articles/services is submitted to the implementing agency (IA) for action; however, all LORs must be approved by the DoS and DSCA. The IA (e.g., U.S. Army, U.S. Navy, U.S. Air Force, etc.) definitizes the purchaser's requirements in the form of an LOA which is submitted through review channels to the DSCA, the DoS, and, in some instances, the U.S. Congress.

> [**Note:** The channels are determined by the dollar amount and type of articles/ services being offered. Under Section 36(b)(1) of the AECA (million or more, design and construction services for $200 million or more, or major defense equipment for $14 million or more, must be presented to the U.S. Congress for review.]

The LOA, once approved, is signed by the IA, countersigned by DSCA Comptroller, and then forwarded to the purchaser for acceptance. The DFAS-IN records the LOA in its computer system.

It is during this initial process that the IA prepares an estimate of the LOA data for the article or service requested. The price is developed in accordance with current pricing practice and is based upon the IA's understanding of the customer's requirements. The price will have two essential elements:

- A base price
- Applicable surcharges

At least four events, among others, can make a difference between the price quoted in the LOA and the ultimate price to the customer. First, if the foreign purchaser changes any item/specification/ quantity during the life of the program, costs will most likely be impacted. Second, if the inflation rates predicted for the life of the program change, prices may be different particularly for programs which span several years. Third, if the rate of production for procurement items is altered in a contractor's plant, either by the foreign purchaser or by the USG (for systems for U.S. military use), the overhead rates and attendant costs could be different. Finally, procurements involving research and development or high level technology (with the attendant risks and cost sharing contractual instruments) may result in different prices than originally quoted. The Purchaser, in accordance with the standard terms and conditions of the LOA, agrees to pay all costs once determined.

Letter of Offer and Acceptance and Implementation Process

Once the FMS Purchaser accepts/signs the LOA, it constitutes the agreement and with applicable funding completes the contract. Upon receipt of the signed LOA and, if required, an initial deposit DFAS-IN is in position to issue obligational authority (OA) to the IA. OA enables the IA to prepare requisitions that will result in Material Release Orders (MROs), work requests for services, or purchase requests for any contracts that may ensue. Most FMS cases are implemented by means of an IA implementing directive (e.g., case directive, program/project directive, etc.) which is distributed to the performing activities and further allocates the required obligational authorities. The performing activities will prepare/route the necessary requisitions, work requests, etc., and, in the case of new contracts, start the procurement cycle with requests for proposals (RFPs) or invitations for bid (IFBs) sent to appropriate defense contractors. The LOA/implementation process is illustrated in Figure 2-3.

Execution and Performance Reporting Process

Performance on an FMS case is demonstrated to the FMS purchaser through receipt of status data or the quarterly requisition report (QRR) from the IA, receipt of the ordered articles/services, or the reporting of the performance/delivery in the delivery listing accompanying each quarterly FMS Billing Statement (DD Form 645). Any event may occur first depending on the nature of the item or service and other factors. In theory, however, the impending release of the materiel should be accompanied by *Military Standard Requisition and Issue Procedures* (MILSTRIP) shipment status (AS_), followed next by physical delivery, and finally by the FMS billing documentation (including an FK_ document identifier–FMS Materiel/Service Transaction). This process is illustrated in Figure 2-4.

Flow of Funds

Figures 2-1 through 2-4 provided an overview of the entire FMS process. Figure 2-5 depicts a portion of the entire process from a "Flow of Funds" perspective. This flow works as follows:

- Monies (in U.S. dollars) are received from the foreign customer in response to:
- The initial deposit requirement associated with LOA acceptance
- Quarterly Billing Statements (DD Form 645) from DFAS-IN
- Supplemental billing arrangements. The monies are deposited into the FMS Trust Fund Account or the Federal Reserve Bank Accounts
- OA is provided by DFAS-IN to the IA/disbursing organization at time of case implementation. Under reimbursable financing the IA/disbursing organization cites its performing appropriation as the funding source and this appropriation is subsequently reimbursed by DFAS-IN following performance. Under direct citation financing, the IA/disbursing organization cites the FMS Trust Fund Account on a

DoD contract; no reimbursement is required.

- Expenditure authority (EA) is a DFAS-IN reservation of funds and the release to the IA of authority to disburse, either for direct cite or self-reimbursement purposes. DFAS-IN issues expenditure authority at country and implementing agency level and reduces the customer country's available cash balance. The IA is limited to the EA issued dollar amount for disbursements for progress payments to contractors or other funds supporting the FMS Trust Fund. IAs have the authority, within DFAS-IN issuance, to disburse and record expenditures at FMS case level.

Data Sources for DD Form 645

Figure 2-6 serves as a summary of portions of the earlier processes figures and provides a concentrated perspective of the types of documents which are consolidated and referenced in the FMS Billing Statement (DD Form 645) and its supporting listings. Some of these source documents are distributed to the Purchaser i.e., processed:

- Supply Discrepancy Report (SDR)
- LOA
- Payment Schedule
- ULO Report

Other source documents are retained by the DoD for its internal use the following:

- Material Release Order (MRO)
- Interdepartmental Bill (IDB)
- Voucher for Transfers between Appropriations and/or Funds (SF-1080)
- Contractor's Request for Progress Payment (DD-1195)
- Material Inspection and Receiving Report (DD-250)
- Delivery Transaction
- The Committed Values for Requisition Cases Report

Summary

The FMS process involves several USG organizations. Although FMS is under the general direction of the Secretary of State, the DoD is responsible for administering the program.

The overall FMS process involves a series of sub-processes. For purposes of this Handbook, the three sub-processes are:

- The Letter of Request/Letter of Offer and Acceptance Process
- The Letter of Offer and/Implementation Process
- The Execution/Performance Reporting Process

Figure 2-1
Foreign Military Sales Processes - Overview

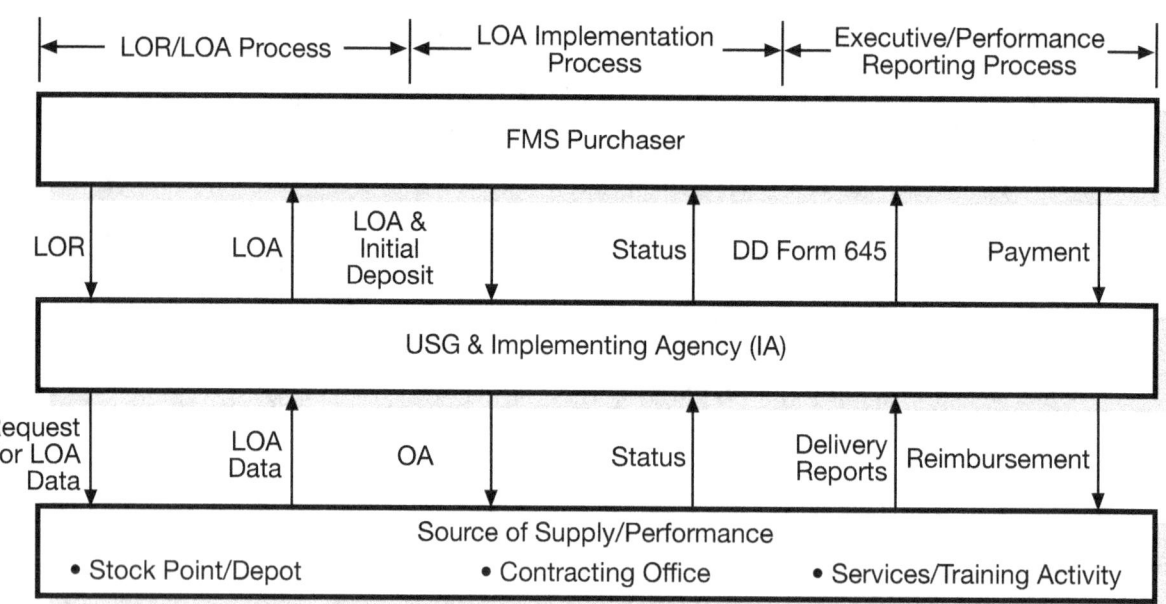

Figure 2-2
Letter of Request/Offer Processes

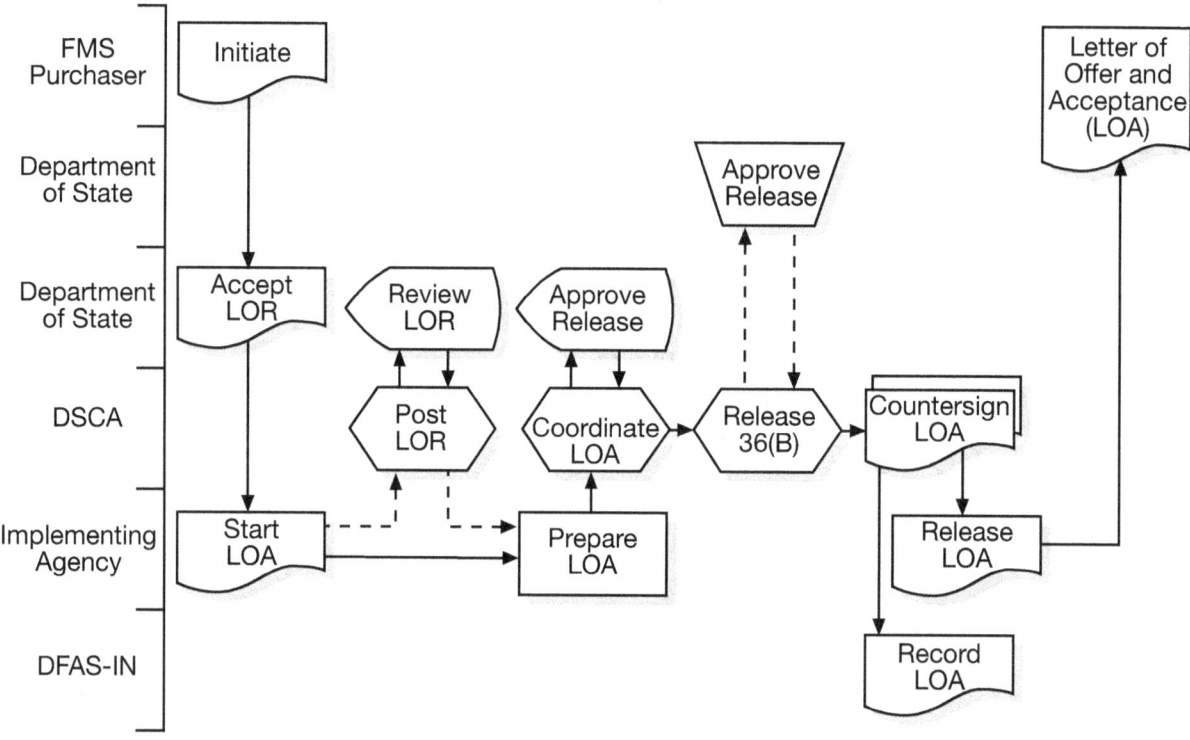

Figure 2-3
Letter of Offer and Acceptance (LOA)/Implementation Process

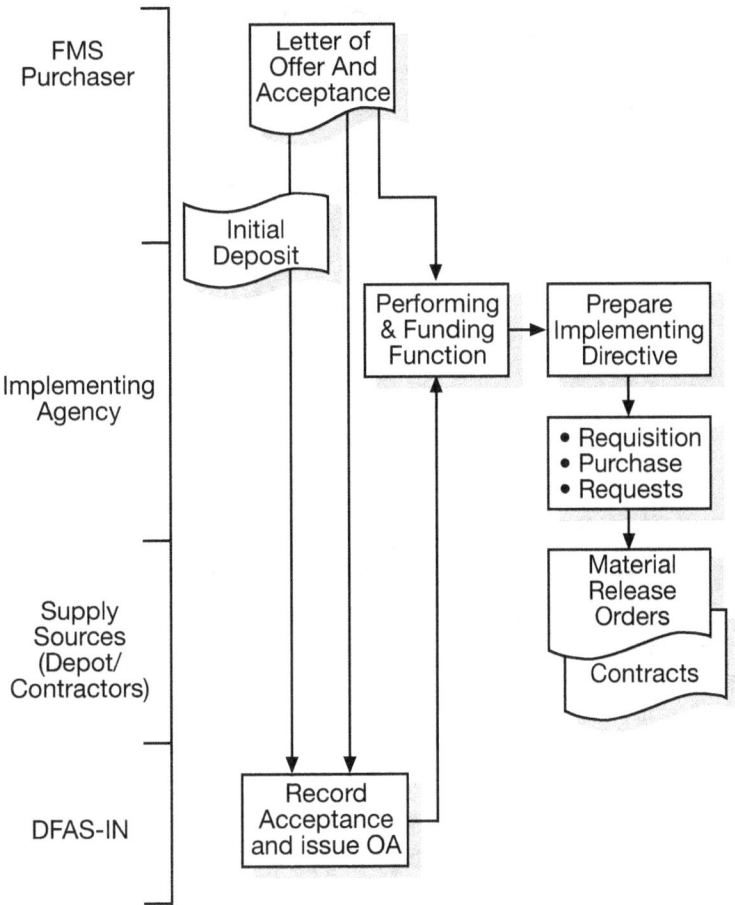

Figure 2-4
Execution and Performance Reporting Process

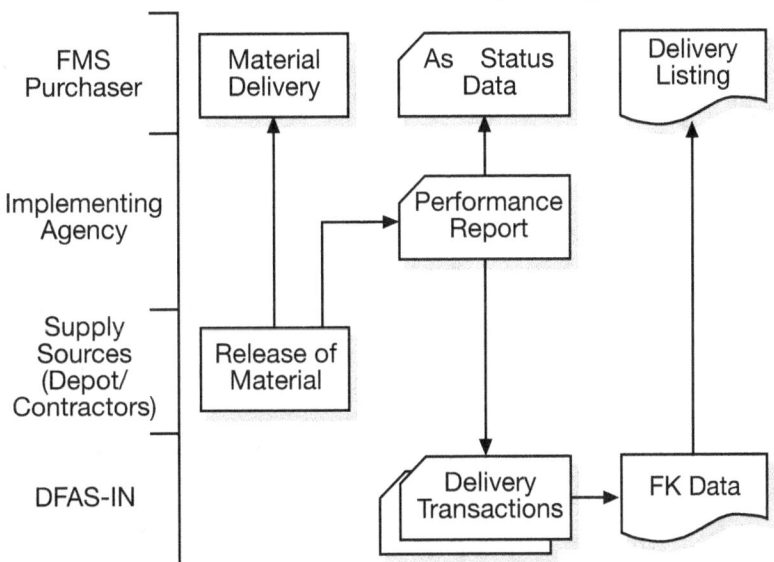

Figure 2-5
Flow of Funds

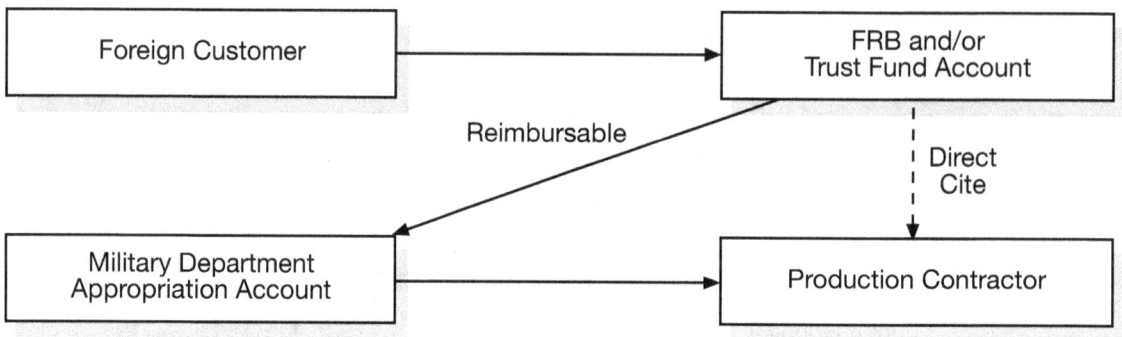

Figure 2-6
Data Sources for Foreign Military Billing Statements

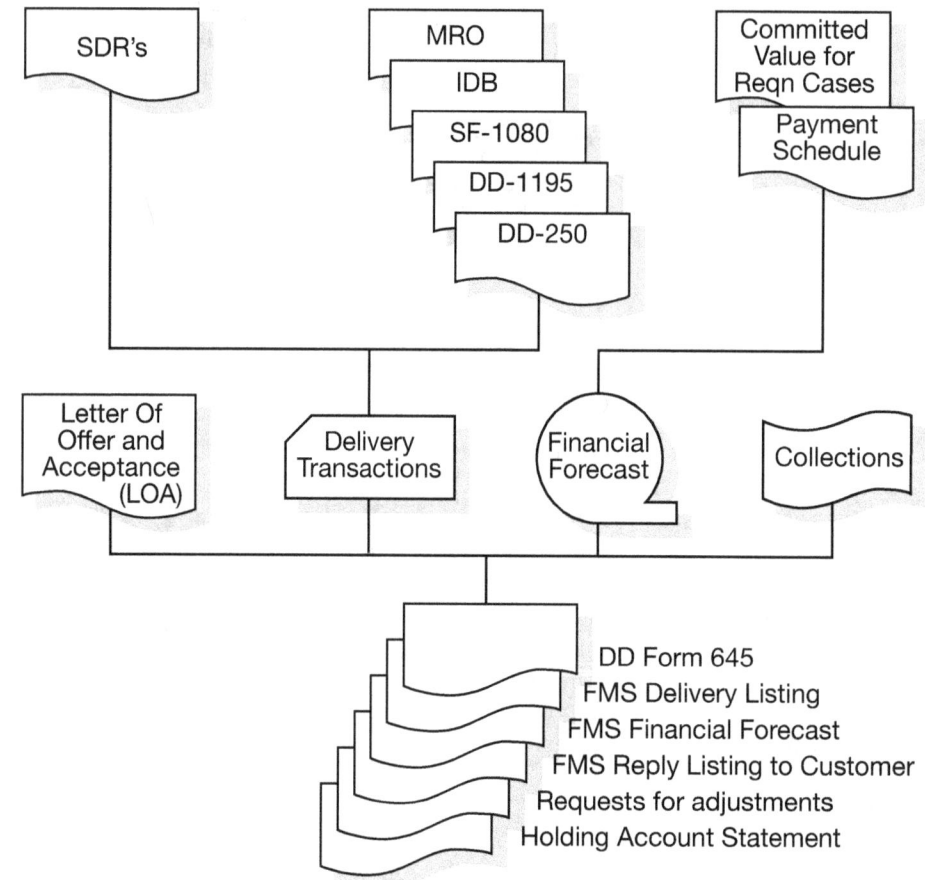

Chapter 3
Foreign Military Sales: Offer and Acceptance Documentation

Purpose

The purpose of this chapter is to highlight those aspects of the United States of America Letter of Offer and Acceptance (LOA) and Amendments/Modifications thereto which are fundamental to an understanding of the foreign military sales (FMS) billing process. The LOA is highly important inasmuch as it forms the basis for many data elements contained in the FMS Billing Statement (DD Form 645).

Letter of Offer and Acceptance

Foreign Military Sales Record Keys

FMS Case Identifier. An FMS case is a contractual sales agreement between the U.S. and an eligible foreign country or international organization documented by an LOA, see Figure 3-1. Each FMS case is identified by a six-character case identifier (e.g., BN-B-AAA), which is assigned by the DoD component having overall cognizance and responsibility for the FMS case. The case identifier consists of:

- A two-character country code (e.g., BN for the fictitious country of Bandaria).

- A one-character DoD component/implementing agency (IA) code (e.g., B for U.S. Army).

- A three-character case designator (e.g., AAA in this example). The first character of the case designator may identify the commodity or service furnished. The second and third characters are assigned in sequence as new cases for the country are prepared.

Item Number. Each FMS case consists of one or more item numbers which appear in column (1) of the LOA.

Document Identifier (Number). Each item number, in turn, may be further broken down into one or more "transactions"– each having a unique document number. Document numbers are assigned to requisitions for items to be delivered from DoD inventory, from contracts issued under *Federal Acquisition Regulation* (FAR) procedures, and so forth. The document number is the "lowest system level" record key used in transaction status and delivery reporting.

The relationship of the FMS case to the item numbers(s) to the document number(s) which is basic to the interpretation of FMS financial/billing reports and statements provided to the FMS customer is illustrated in Figure 3-2.

Based on:

Pursuant to the *Arms Export Control Act*, the Government of the United States (USG) offers to sell _____the defense articles or defense services (which may include defense design and construction services) collectively referred to as "items," set forth herein, subject to the provisions, terms, and conditions in this LOA.

This LOA is for _____

Estimated Cost: Initial Deposit:

Terms of Sale:

This offer expires on _____. Unless a request for extension is made by the Purchaser and granted by the USG, the offer will terminate on the expiration date.

This page through page ___ plus Letter of Offer and Acceptance Standard Terms and Conditions attached, are a part of this LOA.

The undersigned are authorized representatives of their Governments and hereby offer and accept, respectively, this LOA:

_____   _____   _____   _____
U.S. Signature   Date   Purchaser Signature   Date

_____   _____
Typed Name and Title   Typed Name and Title

_____   _____
Implementing Agency   Agency

_____   _____
DSCA   Date

Information to be provided by the Purchaser:

Mark for Code ____, Freight Forwarder Code ___, Purchaser Procuring Agency__, Name and Address of the Purchaser's Paying Office _____

_____

_____

Figure 3-1 (Page 2)

Explanations for acronyms and codes, and financial information, may be found in attached "Letter of Offer and Acceptance Information."

Items to be Supplied (costs and months for delivery are estimates):

(1) Itm Nbr	Qty, (2) Description/Condition	(3) Unit of Issue	(4) Costs (a) Unit	(b) Total	(5) SC/MOS/ TA Notes	(6) Ofr Rel Cde	(7) Del Trm Cde

Estimated Cost Summary

(8) Net Estimated Cost		$00.00
(9) Packing, Crating, and Handling (PC&H)		$00.00
(10)	Administrative Charge	$00.00
(11)	Transportation	$00.00
(12)	Other Asset Use	$00.00
(13)	Total Estimated Cost	

To assist in fiscal planning, the USG provides the following anticipated costs of this LOA:

Estimated Payment Schedule

Payment Date	Quarterly	Cumulative

Letter of Offer and Acceptance Standard Terms and Conditions

Section

1. Conditions – United States Government (USG) Obligations

1.1 Unless otherwise specified, items will be those which are standard to the U.S. Department of Defense (DoD), without regard to make or model.

1.2 The USG will furnish the items from its stocks and resources, or will procure them under terms and conditions consistent with DoD regulations and procedures. When procuring for the Purchaser, DoD will, in general, employ the same contract clauses, the same contract administration, and the same quality and audit inspection procedures as would be used in procuring for itself, except as otherwise requested by the Purchaser and as agreed to by DoD and set forth in this LOA. Unless the Purchaser has requested, in writing, that a sole source contractor be designated, and this LOA reflects acceptance of such designation by DoD, the Purchaser understands that selection of the contractor source to fill requirements is the responsibility of the USG, which will select the contractor on the same basis used to select contractors for USG requirements. Further, the Purchaser agrees that the U.S. DoD is solely responsible for negotiating the terms and conditions of contracts necessary to fulfill the requirements in this LOA.

1.3 The USG will use its best efforts to provide the items for the dollar amount and within the availability cited.

1.4 Under unusual and compelling circumstances, when the national interest of the U.S. requires, the USG reserves the right to cancel or suspend all or part of this LOA at any time prior to the delivery of defense articles or performance of defense services. The USG shall be responsible for termination costs of its suppliers resulting from cancellation or suspension under this section. Termination by the USG of its contracts with its suppliers, other actions pertaining to such contracts, or cessation of deliveries or performance of defense services is not to be construed as cancellation or suspension of this LOA itself under this section.

1.5 U.S. personnel performing defense services under this LOA will not perform duties of a combatant nature, including duties relating to training and advising that may engage U.S. personnel in combat activities outside the U.S., in connection with the performance of these defense services.

1.6 The assignment or employment of U.S. personnel for the performance of this LOA by the USG will not take into account race, religion, national origin, or sex.

1.7 Unless otherwise specified, this LOA may be made available for public inspection consistent with the national security of the United States.

2 Conditions – General Purchaser Agreements

2.1 The Purchaser may cancel this LOA or delete items at any time prior to delivery of defense articles or performance of defense services. The Purchaser is responsible for all costs resulting from cancellation under this section.

2.2 The Purchaser agrees, except as may otherwise be mutually agreed in writing, to use the defense articles sold hereunder only:

2.2.1   For purposes specified in any *Mutual Defense Assistance Agreement* between the USG and the Purchaser;

2.2.2   For purposes specified in any bilateral or regional defense treaty to which the USG and the Purchaser are both parties, if section 2.2.1 is inapplicable; or,

2.2.3   For internal security, individual self-defense, or civic action, if sections 2.2.1 and 2.2.2 are inapplicable.

2.3 The Purchaser will not transfer title to, or possession of, the defense articles, components and associated support material, related training or other defense services (including plans, specifications, or information), or technology furnished under this LOA to anyone who is not an officer, employee, or agent of the Purchaser (excluding transportation agencies), and shall not use or permit their use for purposes other than those authorized, unless the written consent of the USG has first been obtained. The Purchaser will ensure, by all means available to it, respect for proprietary rights in any items and any plans, specifications, or information furnished, whether patented or not. The Purchaser also agrees that the defense articles offered will not be transferred to Cyprus or otherwise used to further the severance or division of Cyprus, and recognizes that the U.S. Congress is required to be notified of any substantial evidence that the defense articles sold in this LOA have been used in a manner which is inconsistent with this provision.

2.4 To the extent that items, including plans, designs, specifications, technical data, or information, furnished in connection with this LOA may be classified by the USG for security purposes, the Purchaser certifies that it will maintain a similar classification and employ measures necessary to preserve such security, equivalent to those employed by the USG and commensurate with security agreements between the USG and the Purchaser. If such security agreements do not exist, the Purchaser certifies that classified items will be provided only to those individuals having an adequate security clearance and a specific need to know in order to carry out the LOA program and that it will promptly and fully inform the USG of any compromise, or possible compromise, of U.S. classified material or information furnished pursuant to this LOA. The Purchaser further certifies that if a U.S. classified item is to be furnished to its contractor pursuant to this LOA: (a) items will be exchanged through official government channels, (b) the specified contractor has been granted a facility security clearance by the Purchaser at a level at least equal to the classification level of the U.S. information involved, (c) all contractor personnel requiring access to such items have been cleared to the appropriate level by the Purchaser, and (d) the Purchaser will assume responsibility for administering security measures while in the contractor's possession. If a commercial transportation agent is to be used for shipment, the Purchaser certifies that such agent has been cleared at the appropriate level for handling classified items. These measures will be maintained throughout the period during which the USG may maintain such classification. The USG will use its best efforts to notify the Purchaser if the classification is changed.

3 Indemnification and Assumption of Risks

3.1 The Purchaser recognizes that the USG will procure and furnish the items described in this LOA on a non-profit basis for the benefit of the Purchaser. The Purchaser therefore undertakes to indemnify and hold the USG, its agents, officers, and employees harmless from any and all loss or liability (whether in tort or in contract) which might arise in connection with this LOA because of:

3.1.1   Injury to or death of personnel of Purchaser or third parties, or

3.1.2   Damage to or destruction of (a) property of DoD furnished to Purchaser or suppliers specifically to implement this LOA, (b) property of Purchaser (including the items ordered by Purchaser pursuant to this LOA, before or after passage of title to Purchaser), or (3) property of third parties, or

3.1.3   Infringement or other violations of intellectual property or technical data rights.

3.2 Subject to express, special contractual warranties obtained for the Purchaser, the Purchaser agrees to relieve the contractors and subcontractors of the USG from liability for, and will assume the risk of, loss or damage to:

3.2.1   Purchaser's property (including items procured pursuant to this LOA, before or after passage of title to Purchaser), and

3.2.2   Property of DoD furnished to suppliers to implement this LOA, to the same extent that the USG would assume for its property if it were procuring for itself the items being procured.

4 Financial Terms and Conditions

4.1 The prices of items to be procured will be billed at their total cost to the USG. Unless otherwise specified, the cost of items to be procured, availability determination, payment schedule, and delivery projections quoted are estimates based on the best available data. The USG will use its best efforts to advise the Purchaser or its authorized representatives of:

4.1.1   Identifiable cost increases that might result in an overall increase in the estimated costs in excess of ten percent of the total value of this LOA,

4.1.2   Changes in the payment schedule, and

4.1.3   Delays which might significantly affect estimated delivery dates. USG failure to advise of the above will not change the Purchaser's obligation under all subsections of section 4.4.

4.2 The USG will refund any payments received for this LOA which prove to be in excess of the final total cost of delivery and performance and which are not required to cover arrearages on other LOAs of the Purchaser.

4.3 Purchaser failure to make timely payments in the amounts due may result in delays in contract performance by DoD contractors, claims by contractors for increased costs, claims by contractors for termination liability for breach of contract, claims by USG or DoD contractors for storage costs, or termination of contracts by the USG under this or other open Letters of Offer and Acceptance of the Purchaser at the Purchaser's expense.

4.4 The Purchaser agrees:

4.4.1   To pay to the USG the total cost to the USG of the items even if costs exceed the amounts estimated in this LOA.

4.4.2   To make payment(s) by check or wire transfer payable in U.S. dollars to the Treasurer of the United States.

4.4.3   If Terms of Sale specify "Cash with acceptance", to forward with this LOA a check or wire transfer in the full amount shown as the estimated Total cost, and agrees to make additional payment(s) upon notification of cost increase(s) and request(s) for funds to cover such increase(s).

4.4.4   If Terms of Sale specify payment to be "Cash prior to delivery", to pay to the USG such amounts at such times as may be specified by the USG (including initial deposit) in order to meet payment requirements for items to be furnished from the resources of DoD. USG requests for funds may be based on estimated costs to cover forecasted deliveries of items. Payments are required 90 days in advance of the time DoD plans such deliveries or incurs such expenses on behalf of the Purchaser.

4.4.5   If Terms of Sale specify payment by "Dependable undertaking", to pay to the USG such amounts at such times as may be specified by the USG (including initial deposit) in order to meet payments required by contracts under which items are being procured, and any damages and costs that may accrue from termination of contracts by the USG because of Purchaser's cancellation of this LOA. USG requests for funds may be based upon estimated requirements for advance and progress payments to suppliers, estimated termination liability, delivery forecasts, or evidence of constructive delivery, as the case may be. Payments are required 90 days in advance of the time USG makes payments on behalf of the Purchaser.

4.4.6   If Terms of Sale specify "Payment on delivery", that bills may be dated as of the date(s) of delivery of the items, or upon forecasts of the date(s) thereof.

4.4.7   That requests for funds or billings are due and payable in full on presentation or, if a payment date is specified in the request for funds or bill, on the payment date so specified, even if such payment date is not in accord with the estimated payment schedule, if any, contained in this LOA. Without affecting Purchaser's obligation to make such payment(s) when due, documentation concerning advance and progress payments, estimated termination liability, or evidence of constructive delivery or shipment in support of requests for funds or bills will be made available to the Purchaser by DoD upon request. When appropriate, the Purchaser may request adjustment of any questioned billed items by subsequent submission of discrepancy reports, Standard Form 364.

4.4.8   To pay interest on any net amount by which it is in arrears on payments, determined by considering collectively all of the Purchaser's open LOAs with DoD. Interest will be calculated on a daily basis. The principal amount of the arrearage will be computed as the excess of cumulative financial requirements of the Purchaser over total cumulative payments after quarterly billing payment due dates. The rate of interest paid will be a rate not less than a rate determined by the Secretary of the Treasury taking into consideration the current average market yield on outstanding short-term obligations of the USG as of the last day of the month preceding the net arrearage and shall be computed from the date of net arrearage.

4.4.9   To designate the Procuring Agency and responsible Paying Office and address thereof to which the USG will submit requests for funds and bills under this LOA.

5   Transportation and Discrepancy Provisions

5.1 The USG agrees to deliver and pass title to the Purchaser at the initial point of shipment unless otherwise specified in this LOA. With respect to items procured for sale to the Purchaser, this will normally be at the manufacturer's loading facility; with respect to items furnished from USG stocks, this will normally be at the U.S. depot. Articles will be packed, crated, or otherwise prepared for shipment prior to the time title passes. If "Point of Delivery" is specified other than the initial point of shipment, the supplying U.S. Department or Agency will arrange movement of the articles to the authorized delivery point as a reimbursable service but will pass title at the initial point of shipment. The USG disclaims any liability for damage or loss to the items incurred after passage of title irrespective of whether transportation is by common carrier or by the U.S. Defense Transportation System.

5.2 The Purchaser agrees to furnish shipping instructions which include Mark For and Freight Forwarder Codes based on the Offer/Release Code.

5.3 The Purchaser is responsible for obtaining insurance coverage and customs clearances. Except for articles exported by the USG, the Purchaser is responsible for ensuring that export licenses are obtained prior to export of U.S. defense articles. The USG incurs no liability if export licenses are not granted or they are withdrawn before items are exported.

5.4 The Purchaser agrees to accept DD Forms 645 or other delivery documents as evidence that title has passed and items have been delivered. Title to defense articles transported by parcel post passes to the Purchaser at the time of parcel post shipment. Standard Form 364 will be used in submitting claims to the USG for overage, shortage, damage, duplicate billing, item deficiency, improper identification, improper documentation, or non-shipment of defense articles and non-performance of defense services and will be submitted promptly by the Purchaser. DoD will not accept claims related to items of $200. or less for overages, shortages, damages, non-shipment, or non-performance. Any claim, including a claim for shortage (but excluding a claim for nonshipment/ nonreceipt of an entire lot), received after one year from passage of title to the article or from scheduled performance of the service will be disallowed by the USG unless the USG determines that unusual and compelling circumstances involving latent defects justify consideration of the claim. Claims, received after one year from date of passage of title or initial billing, whichever is later, for nonshipment/nonreceipt of an entire lot will be disallowed by the USG. The Purchaser agrees to return discrepant articles to USG custody within 180 days from the date of USG approval of such return.

6   Warranties

6.1 The USG does not warrant or guarantee any of the items sold pursuant to this LOA except as provided in section 6.1.1. DoD contracts include warranty clauses only on an exception basis. If requested by the Purchaser, the USG will, with respect to items being procured, and upon timely notice, attempt to obtain contract provisions to provide the requested warranties. The USG further agrees to exercise, upon the Purchaser's request, rights (including those arising under any warranties) the USG may have under contracts connected with the procurement of these items. Additional costs resulting from obtaining special contract provisions or warranties, or the exercise of rights under such provisions or warranties, will be charged to the Purchaser.

6.1.1　The USG warrants the title of items sold to the Purchaser hereunder but makes no warranties other than those set forth herein. In particular the USG disclaims liability resulting from infringement or other violation of intellectual property or technical data rights occasioned by the use or manufacture outside the U.S. by or for the Purchaser of items supplied hereunder.

6.1.2　The USG agrees to exercise warranties on behalf of the Purchaser to assure, to the extent provided by the warranty, replacement or correction of such items found to be defective, when such materiel is procured for the Purchaser.

6.2 Unless the condition of defense articles is identified to be other than serviceable (for example, "As is"), DoD will repair or replace at no extra cost defense articles supplied from DoD stocks which are damaged or found to be defective in respect to material or workmanship when it is established that these deficiencies existed prior to passage of title, or found to be defective in design to such a degree that the items cannot be used for the purpose for which they were designed. Qualified representatives of the USG and of the Purchaser will agree on the liability hereunder and the corrective steps to be taken.

7　Dispute Resolution

7.1 This LOA is subject to U.S. Federal procurement law.

7.2 The USG and the Purchaser agree to resolve any disagreement regarding this LOA by consultations between the USG and the Purchaser and not to refer any such disagreement to any international tribunal or third party for settlement.

Letter of Offer and Acceptance Information

1. General

This provides basic information pertaining to the LOA for U.S. and Purchaser use. Additional information may be obtained from the *Security Assistance Management Manual*, DoD 5105.38-M, the in-country Security Assistance Office, the DSCA Country Director, or from the IA.

2. Information Entered By The USG

a. Terms of Sale. The Purchaser's responsibilities under those Terms, are described on the LOA. A list of all Terms of Sale, with explanations for each, are shown in DoD 5105.38-M.

b. Description/Condition. The item description consists of coding for use in U.S. management of the LOA (starting with Generic/MASL and MDE "(Y)" or non-MDE "(N)" data such as that in DoD 5105.38-M, Appendix D) plus a short description of what is to be provided. When items are serviceable, Code "A" (new, repaired, or reconditioned material which meets U.S. Armed Forces standards of serviceability) may be used; otherwise, Code "B" (unserviceable or mixed condition without repair, restoration, or rehabilitation which may be required) may be used. In some instances, reference to a note in the Terms and Conditions may complement or replace these codes.

c. Unit of Issue. Is normally "EA" (each, or one; for example, 40 EA) or blank (unit of issue not applicable; for example, services or several less significant items consolidated under one LOA Item Number). When blank, a quantity or Unit Cost is not shown.

d. The Source Code. (SC) in the Articles or Services to be Supplied Section is one or more of the following:

S - Shipment from DoD stocks or performance by DoD personnel

P - From new procurement

R - From rebuild, repair, or modification by the USG

X - Mixed source, such as stock and procurement, or undetermined

E - Excess items, as-is

F - Special Defense Acquisition Fund (SDAF) items

e. Availability lead time cited is the number of months (MOS) estimated for complete delivery of defense articles or performance of defense services. The lead time starts with Acceptance of this Offer, including the conclusion of appropriate financial arrangements, and ends when items are made available to transportation.

f. Type of Assistance (TA) Codes are as follows:

3 Source Code S, R, or E; based on *Arms Export Control Act* (AECA) Section 21(b).

4 Source Code X; AECA Sections 21(b), 22(a), 29, or source undetermined.

5 Source Code P; AECA Section 22(a).

6 Source Code S, R, or E, payment on delivery; AECA Section 21(d).

7 Source Code P, dependable undertaking with 120 days payment after delivery; AECA Section 22(b).

8 Source Code S, R, or E, stock sales with 120 days payment after delivery; AECA Section 21(d)

M MAP Merger; Foreign Assistance Act (FAA) Section 503(a)(3)

N FMS Credit (Nonrepayable); AECA Sections 23 or 24

U Source Code P; Cooperative Logistics Supply Support Arrangement (CLSSA) Foreign Military Sales Order (FMSO) I

V Source Code S; CLSSA FMSO II stocks acquired under FMSO I

Z FMS Credit; AECA Sections 23 or 24

g. Training notes: AP - Annual training program; SP - Special training designed to support purchases of U.S. equipment; NC - This offer does not constitute a commitment to provide U.S. training; SC - U.S. training concurrently being addressed in separate LOA; NR - No U.S. training is required in support of this purchase.

h. Offer Release Codes (Ofr Rel Cde) and Delivery Term Codes (Del Trm Cde) below may also be found in DoD 4500.9-R. Part III. The following Offer Release Codes also pertain to release of items for shipment back to Purchaser on repair LOAs:

A Freight and parcel post shipments will be released automatically by the shipping activity without advance notice of availability.

Y Advance notice is required before release of shipment, but shipment can be released automatically if release instructions are not received by shipping activity within 15 calendar days. Parcel post shipments will be automatically released.

Z Advance notice is required, before release of shipment. Shipping activity will follow-up on the notice of availability until release instructions are furnished. Parcel post shipments will be automatically released.

X The IA and country representative have agreed that the:

- The IA will sponsor the shipment to a country address. Under this agreement, the Freight Forwarder Code must also contain X and a Customer-within-Country (CC) Code must be entered in the Mark For Code on the front page of the LOA. The MAPAD must contain the CC Code and addresses for each type of shipment (parcel post or freight).

- Shipments are to be made to an assembly point or staging area as indicated by clear instructions on exception requisitions. Under this agreement, the Freight Forwarder Code must contain W. A Mark For Code may be entered in the Mark For Code space on the front page of the LOA and the MAPAD must contain the Mark For Code if the Mark For Address is to be used on the shipment to the assembly point or staging area.

i For the following Delivery Term Codes, DoD delivers:

2 - To a continental United States (CONUS) inland point (or overseas inland point when the origin and destination are both in the same geographic area)

3 - At the CONUS POE alongside the vessel or aircraft

4 - Not applicable (Purchaser has full responsibility at the point of origin. Often forwarded collect to country freight forwarder.)

5 - At the CONUS POE on the inland carrier's equipment

6 - At the overseas POD on board the vessel or aircraft

7 - At the overseas inland destination on board the inland carrier's equipment

8 - At the CONUS POE on board the vessel or aircraft

9 - At the overseas POD alongside the vessel or aircraft

Delivery Term Codes showing DoD transportation responsibility for repair LOAs are shown below. The LOA will provide a CONUS address for each item identified for repair. The customer must assure this address is shown on all containers and documentation when materiel is returned.

A - From overseas POE through CONUS destination to overseas POD on board the vessel or aircraft

B - From overseas POE through CONUS destination to CONUS POE on board the vessel or aircraft

C - From CONUS POD on board the vessel or aircraft through CONUS destination to CONUS POE on board the vessel or aircraft

D - From CONUS POD on board the vessel or aircraft through the CONUS destination to overseas POD on board the vessel or aircraft

E - Not applicable (Purchaser has complete responsibility.)

F - From overseas inland point through CONUS destination to overseas inland desination

G - From overseas POE through CONUS destination to overseas POD alongside vessel or aircraft

H - (For classified items) From CONUS inland point to CONUS POE alongside vessel or aircraft

J - (For classified cryptographic items) From CONUS inland point to overseas inland destination

3. Information to be Entered by the Purchaser.

Mark For and Freight Forwarder Codes are maintained in the Military Assistance Program Address Directory (MAPAD), DoD 4000.25-8. The purchaser procuring agency should show the code for the Purchaser's Army, Navy, Air Force, or other agency which is purchasing the item(s). The Name and Address of the Purchaser's Paying Office is also required.

a. Mark For Code. This Code should be entered for use in identifying the address of the organization in the Purchaser country which is to receive the items. This includes return of items repaired under an LOA.

- This address will be added by the U.S. DoD to the Ship To address on all freight containers. It will also appear on items forwarded by small parcel delivery service, including parcel post. The address should include the port of discharge name and designator (water or air); country name, country service name, street, city, state or province, and (if applicable) in-country zip or similar address code.

- Shippers are not authorized to apply shipment markings. If codes and addresses are not published, containers will be received at the freight forwarder or U.S. military representative in-country unmarked for onward shipment with resultant losses, delays, and added costs. The USG will sponsor shipment of this materiel to FOB U.S. point of origin.

b. Freight Forwarder Code. When Offer Release Code X applies, Code X or W, discussed under Offer Release Code X above, must be entered.

4. Financial

a. The method of financing is shown in the LOA, Amendment, or Modification. The initial deposit required with Purchaser signature of the LOA is an integral part of the acceptance.

b. LOA payment schedules are estimates, for planning purposes. DFAS-IN will request payment in accordance with the payment schedule unless DoD costs, including 90-day forecasted requirements, exceed amounts required by the payment schedule. When this occurs, the U.S. will use its best efforts to provide a new schedule via LOA Modification at least 45 days prior to the next payment due date. The Purchaser is required to make payments in accordance with quarterly DD Forms 645 issued by DFAS regardless of the existing payment schedule.

c. The DD Form 645 serves as the bill and statement of account. An FMS Delivery Listing, identifying items physically or constructively delivered and services performed during the billing period, will be attached to the DD Form 645. DFAS-IN forwards these forms to the Purchaser within 45 days before payments are due and Purchasers must forward payments in U.S. dollars to the USG in time to meet prescribed due dates. Costs in excess of amounts funded by FMF agreements must be paid by the Purchaser. Questions concerning the content of DD Forms 645 and requests for billing adjustments should be submitted to the Defense Finance and Accounting Service (DFAS-IN/JAXBC), 8899 East 56th Street, Indiannapolis, Indiana 46249. The preferred method for forwarding cash payments is by bank wire transfer to the Department of the Treasury account at the Federal Reserve Bank of New York using the standard federal reserve funds transfer format. Wire transfers will be accepted by the Federal Reserve System (FRS) only from banks that are members of the FRS, therefore, non-U.S. banks must go through a U.S. correspondent FRS member bank. The following information is applicable to cash payments:

Wire transfer	Check mailing address:
Federal Reserve Bank of New York Treasury NYC (3801), DFAS-JAX/IN ABA#021030004	DFAS, 3801 Center Collections DFAS-JAX/IN P.O. BOX 269490 Indianapolis, Indiana 46226-9490

e. To authorize payments from funds available under FMF loan or grant agreements, the Purchaser may be required to submit a letter of request to the Defense Finance and Accounting Service (DFAS-IN/JAXBC), 8899 East 56th Street, Indianapolis, Indiana 46249. Purchasers should consult applicable FMF agreements for explicit instructions. Questions pertaining to the status of FMF financing and balances should be directed to DSCA Comptroller.

f. Payments not received by DFAS-IN, by the due date may be subject to interest charges as outlined in paragraph 4.4.8 of the LOA Standard Terms and Conditions.

g. The values on the LOA are estimates. The final amount will be equal to the cost to the USG. When deliveries are made and known costs are billed and collected, DFAS-IN will provide a "Final Statement of Account" which will summarize final costs. Excess funds will be available to pay unpaid billings on other statements or distributed as agreed upon between the Purchaser and the Comptroller, DSCA.

h. The Purchaser may cancel this LOA upon request to the IA. An administrative charge that equals one-half of the applicable administrative charge rate times the ordered LOA value, which is earned on LOA acceptance, or the applicable administrative charge rate times the actual LOA value at closure, whichever is higher, may be assessed if this LOA is cancelled after implementation.

5. Changes to the Letter of Offer and Acceptance. Changes may be initiated by the USG or by requests from the Purchaser. After acceptance of the basic LOA, these changes will take the form of Amendments or Modifications.

a. Amendments encompass changes in scope, such as those which affect the type or number of significant items to be provided. Amendments require acceptance by the USG and the Purchaser in the same manner as the original LOA.

b. Modifications include changes which do not constitute a change in scope, such as increases or decreases in estimated costs or delivery schedule changes. Modifications require signature only to acknowledge receipt by the Purchaser.

c. When signed, and unless alternate instructions are provided, copies of Amendments and Modifications should be given the same U.S. distribution as the basic LOA.

d. Requests for changes required prior to acceptance by the Purchaser should be submitted to the IA for consideration. See DoD 5105.38-M, section 70105.M.2.

6. Correspondence. Questions or comments regarding this LOA should identify the Purchaser request reference and the identification assigned by the IA within DoD.

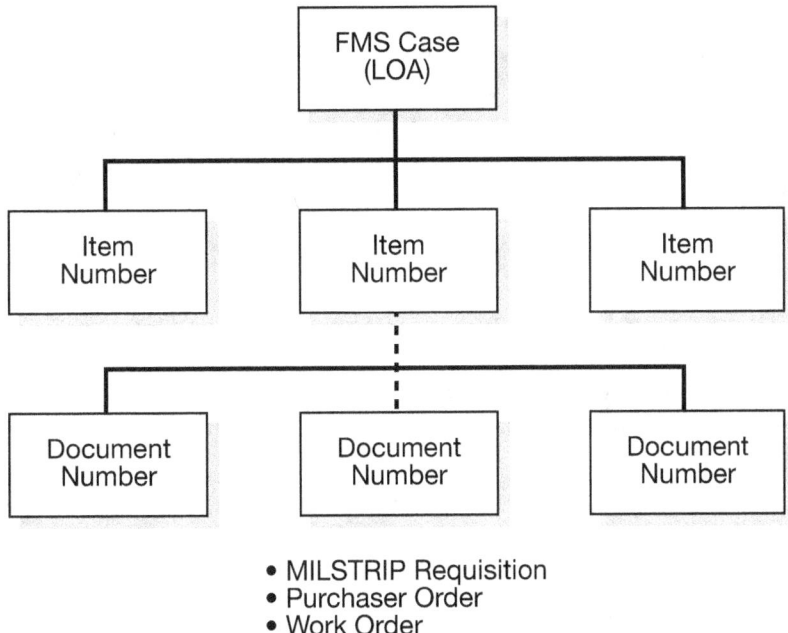

- MILSTRIP Requisition
- Purchaser Order
- Work Order

Notes, Standard Terms and Conditions, and Letter of Offer and Acceptance Information

Individual LOAs differ in scope, complexity, and length. Additional information pertinent to a given LOA may be incorporated by means of notes. For example, the assumptions that the DoD component used in computing PC&H estimated charges may sometimes be found in a note. Notes plus LOA Standard Terms and Conditions, and LOA Information are part of every LOA.

- LOA Standard Terms and Conditions is an instrumental part of every LOA. It defines the roles and responsibilities of both the USG and the FMS customer. In this regard:

- Section 1 describes the rights and responsibilities of the U.S. government.

- Section 2 describes the rights and responsibilities of the FMS purchaser.

- Section 3 addresses the subject of Indemnification and Assumption of Risk.

- Section 4 addresses the subject of Financial Terms and Conditions.

- Section 5 addresses the subject of Transportation and Discrepancy Provisions

- Section 6 addresses the subject of Warranties.

- Section 7 addresses the subject of Dispute Resolution.

- LOA Information provides basic information pertaining to the LOA for U.S. and Purchaser use. Additional information may be obtained from the *Security Assistance Management Manual*, DoD 5105.38-M, the in-country Security Cooperation Office, DSCA, or from the IA.

Foreign Military Sales Payment Schedule

The payment schedule is also an important part of the LOA. It is designed to provide budgetary planning information to the FMS customer. The *Arms Export Control Act* (AECA), as amended, and DoD policy require that payments be made in advance of delivery/performance. Unless the LOA indicates that the total estimated cost of the case should be paid as an initial deposit, a payment schedule (showing the estimate amount payable by quarter) will be provided.

Concept

The payment schedule, which is an integral part of the LOA, contains estimates based upon forecasted:

- Defense articles/services to be provided by the DoD.
- New procurement contractor "progress payments," "contractor holdback," and remaining "termination liability" as of each scheduled payment date. (The terms are defined below.)
- Associated administrative, accessorial, and other authorized charges, as appropriate.

Definitions

Progress Payments. Those payments made to contractors or DoD industrial fund activities as work progresses under a contract, on the basis of cost incurred or percentage of completion, or of a particular stage of completion, accomplished prior to actual delivery and acceptance of contract items.

Contractor Holdback. Amount earned by contractors or suppliers during the production period but not paid to the contractor/supplier to ensure future performance.

Termination Liability Reserve. That amount collected from a purchaser in anticipation of any liability that would accrue to the U.S. government should a particular case or program be terminated prior to the normal completion of the contract. The reserve is not always a constant amount but must be adjusted regularly as contracts are awarded, work progresses, payments are received, and deliveries are made.

A primary point to remember is that progress payments, contractor hold back, and termination liability reserve are included in the Payment Schedule and the FMS Billing Statement (DD Form 645). Within the DD Form 645, progress payments are identified at case level as work in progress (WIP) in Column 6. The aggregated WIP is shown in Column 10. Once deliveries of equipment are subsequently made and posted in Column 9 of the DD Form 645, an attendant amount of the WIP liability is liquidated.

Payment Schedule Development

As noted in the LOA Standard Terms and Conditions, it is USG policy to obtain funds 90 days in advance (e.g., a payment due 15 June covers requirements of the 1 July - 30 September period) of the time that the DoD plans such deliveries or incurs such expenses on the part of the FMS Purchaser. The payment schedule, along with the initial deposit, provides the mechanics for implementing this policy.

Every LOA, except for the Foreign Military Sales Order (FMSO I) case under a Cooperative Logistics Supply Support Arrangement, will have a payment schedule. For illustration purposes, an FMS case having a total estimated value of $500,000 might have a payment schedule as follows:

Payment Date	Amount
Initial Deposit	$200,000
15 March 200X	$100,000
15 June 200X	$100,000
15 September 200X	$100,000

The dates indicated above (e.g., 15 March 200X) relate to the dates the estimated payments are due at DFAS-IN, i.e., the date which would be reflected in Block 2 of the applicable DD Form 645, "Foreign Military Sales Billing Statement." Of course, since the payment schedule reflects "estimated" payments based on anticipated implementation dates, the amounts subsequently indicated as due on the DD Form 645 can and often do differ. For example, if the case is signed but the implementation is delayed, the payment schedule could be one quarter ahead of the DD Form 645 bill amount.

The FMS customer should pay the amounts indicated as due on the DD Form 645, rather than the amounts reflected on the payment schedule. The DD Form 645 - and not the payment schedule - is the "official" DFAS-IN billing notification.

Relationship of the Payment Schedule to the DD Form 645

In recognition of the importance of firm and meaningful budgetary estimates to the FMS customer, DoD policy - to the extent possible and feasible - is to use the amounts reflected in the payment schedule as the forecasting mechanism for the DD Form 645. In theory, as illustrated in Figure 3-3, Column 12 of the DD Form 645 (the header of which reads "Total Financial Requirements") should balance to the cumulative payment schedule through the applicable forecast quarter. Furthermore, assuming the FMS customer has made all required payments at the appropriate times, Column 14 of the DD Form 645 (the header of which reads "Amount Due and Payable") should equate to the corresponding incremental amount shown by the appropriate date in the payment schedule. This balancing formula will not materialize, however, if actual deliveries/expenses have exceeded forecasted estimates, if the FMS customer has paid an amount(s) different from that required (or payment is received late), or if amendments/modifications have just entered the billing system, just to name a few reasons. Still, the point is:

> Every effort is made by the DoD component and DFAS-IN to enhance the reliability of the budgetary estimates contained in the payment schedule.

One system exception to the above balancing formula needs to be briefly addressed. For Cooperation Logistics Supply Support Arrangement FMSO II and other repair part cases, experience has shown that variations in both requisitioning and supply actions render most payment schedules for these cases highly overstated. To preclude substantial over billing, each IA provides DFAS-IN with a quarterly "Committed Values for Requisition Cases" report. These up-to-date forecast amounts are subsequently incorporated into the DD Form 645 billing criteria if less than the payment schedule.

Figure 3-3
Relationship of Payment Schedule to DD Form 645

Goal: Balance

| Cumulative (to date) estimated payment schedule amounts in LOA payment schedule | Total financial requirements (column 12) of DD Form 645 |

Revisions to Financial Annex Payment Schedules

Whenever a substantive change in payment requirement is evident, an LOA modification shall be issued to provide a new payment schedule. Such action is required if the LOA total estimated cost vaires by more than $5000,000 or 10% (whichever is greater) during a 12 month perion.

Foreign Military Sales Pricing Elements

General

The elements of an FMS price can be combined into two major categories; base price and other authorized charges. The base price generally refers to the price of the item or service, i.e., contract price, inventory price, etc. The authorized charge, on the other hand, related to the application of a cost (often on a percentage or pro-rata basis) that is dependent to some degree on the value of a base price or other combinations. A description of base prices and other authorized charges follows.

It is DoD policy that, to the degree possible, only the single selling be shown on the LOA and associated DD Form 645 billing documentation. It is not normal FMS practice to provide a detailed description of the components of prices included for line items on the LOA. This means that prices relevant to unit costs [column (4)(a)], total cost [column (4)(b)], and Net Estimated Cost [line (8)] are "rolled-up" single selling prices. For instance, a military equipment item may reflect a $100,000 cost in column (4)(a) (Unit Cost) and included or rolled-up in this price would be the base materiel price, any nonrecurring costs, contract administration, etc.

The degree of detail on the LOA theoretically corresponds to and drives the level of detail on the DD Form 645. The $100,000 equipment item in the above example would initially show up in Column 7 (Total Value Ordered) of the DD Form 645, and as deliveries were made, such delivery information would be reflected in Column 9 (Current Period Delivery Costs), and other aggregated columns. The FMS Delivery Listing, which supports the current period entries in Column 9 of the DD Form 645, would reflect the estimated or actual price (as coded by the IA) under the subheading "Articles/Services Transactions . . . Unit Price." This Unit Price would include applicable authorized charges.

The authorized charge(s) computations would be reflected in the "Administrative/Accessorial Transactions" portion of the FMS Delivery Listing, where the costs would be broken down in terms of generic code descriptions–for example, L1A Inland Transportation CONUS, L1D Parcel Post, L6A Administrative Costs.

It is DoD policy that the percentages used in determining the estimated costs on the LOA will not be shown in the related line of the LOA. This is because, in part, these percentages are estimates and have been known to change. However, the percentages applied in administrative/accessorial cost calculations on the FMS Delivery Listing attachment to the DD Form 645 are available for the FMS customer's review.

Letter of Offer and Acceptance Materiel and Services Costs

This general category of prices refers to the primary item or service being sold (as well as the authorized surcharge costs which are above and beyond the accessorial surcharges/add-ons). Some of the more common items and services are discussed next, starting with the Defense Working Capital Fund (DWCF).

Defense Working Capital Fund

These fund items may be thought of as "consumable bits and pieces," such as repair parts, lubricants, hand tools, etc., and most reparable items. DWCF catalog prices are usually updated once a year. This catalog price includes the following cost elements:

- Materiel procurement cost
- Operating costs
- CONUS first destination transportation cost (i.e., manufacturer to depot), and second destination cost to the CONUS POE
- Surcharges to recover estimated net stock losses from pilferage, damage, obsolescence, and a price stabilization factor for inflation

Sample Price Computation of a DWCF Item:

Catalog price current at date of drop-from-inventory	XXX
(Column (4)(a), Unit Cost*	XXX)

[Also the "Unit Price" in the FMS delivery listing attachment to the DD Form 645; the "FMS Selling Price" in DoD pricing directives/instructions, hereafter referred to as the "Unit Cost."]

Principal and Major Items

This equates to the larger items such as a tank, a vehicle, an aircraft, or an aircraft engine. These items may be priced differently depending on whether the item is to be replaced or not replaced at all. Some special rules which pertain to principal/major items are:

- Reductions to the sale price may be made when there is an actual difference in utility or desirability among units due to age or condition. For example, if an item has a useful peacetime life of twenty years and ten years have expired, the sale price of the item may be reduced by 50 percent. However, overhaul costs may also be an additive.

- In no event will the sale price be lower than the scrap value plus the cost of any major overhaul or outfitting accomplished prior to the sale.

- A pro rata share of any nonrecurring RDT&E and nonrecurring production costs. These costs are in accordance with DoD Directive 2140.2, which indicates that pro rata shares shall be computed for major defense equipment (MDE) which is defined as significant military equipment (SME) having a nonrecurring RDT&E cost of more than $50 million or a total production cost of more than $200 million. The pro rata share is determined by dividing the total of the nonrecurring cost investment (nonrecurring RDT&E and nonrecurring production) by the total estimated number of units to be produced over the life of the system.

- When the price of the item is reduced as result of age, condition, or supply status (excess), the same percentage reduction shall be made to the pro rata share of nonrecurring costs.

Sample Price Computation of Principal/Major Item Not to be Replaced:

Acquisition cost of item sold from stock	XXX
Less adjustment for expired peacetime useful life	XXX
Plus nonrecurring RDT&E/production costs	XXX
Plus overhauls (Prorated)	XXX
Unit Cost	XXX
Sample Price Computation of Principal/Major Item to Be Replaced:	
Contract cost of new item serving as the replacement	XXX
Less adjustment for expired service life of item sold from stock	XXX
Plus nonrecurring costs	XXX
Unit Cost	XXX

Excess Materiel

Excess equipment will normally be sold in an "as-is" condition; any costs associated with repairing, rehabilitating, or modifying such materiel are additive. The selling price of excess equipment, exclusive of repair and modification costs, will be the higher of:

- Its market value as military hardware.

- Its fair value computed using the appropriate fair value table rate (times the acquisition value of the item) promulgated in the *DoD Financial Regulation Volume 15*, "Security Assistance Policy and Procedures" (DoD 7000.14-R).

- Its scrap value

Sample Price Computation of Excess Materiel:

Higher of market value/fair value/scrap value	XXX
Nonrecurring costs	XXX
Pro rata overhaul cost before sale date	XXX
Unit Cost	XXX

New Procurement

The basic rule with regard to the base price of articles or services from new procurement/production is that the FMS purchaser is required to pay the full amount of the contract. In addition, there are other additive costs which may be included in the base price:

- Contract administration costs, computed as a percent surcharge (currently 1.5 percent) on all disbursements which are reported to DFAS-IN as made to contractors for FMS new procurements on which applicable contract administration costs have not been waived.
- The costs of any government furnished materiel (GFM) or government furnished equipment (GFE, including applicable DTS rates and a 3.5/1.0 percent PC&H surcharge, if applicable.

Sample Price Computation of New Procurement Item:

Contract price	XXX
Plus:	
Nonrecurring costs	XXX
Contract administration	XXX
GFM/GFE	XXX
Unit Cost	XXX

Department of Defense Personal Services

This refers to services involving DoD civilian and/or military personnel, such as a technical assistance or site survey. The base price of these services include:

- For civilians, the General Schedule (GS), or other appropriate wage schedule, rates. To this is added:
  - •• The applicable acceleration rate (percentage) for the USG share of retirement costs, fringe benefit costs, and leave and holiday period costs.
  - •• Actual temporary duty (TDY) (i.e., travel and per diem) costs.
  - •• Actual permanent change of station (PCS) costs, if made to implement the FMS case.
- For U.S. military personnel, the appropriate amount (factored on an hourly rate, as necessary) from the DoD Annual Composite Standard Rates Table (comprised of basic pay, retirement, basic allowance for quarters, miscellaneous expense, pro rata share of normal PCS, incentive and special pay). To this is added:
  - •• Actual TDY costs
  - •• Actual PCS cost, if made to implement the FMS case
  - •• Fringe benefit and leave and holiday period costs

Sample Price Computation for DoD Personal Services:

Direct civilian labor or Military Composite Standard Rate	XXX
Plus:	
Acceleration (retirement, fringe benefits, leave and holiday)	XXX
PCS/TDY	XXX
Unit Cost	XXX

Administrative and Accessorial Costs

As was noted in the above discussion, several FMS authorized charges appear in the LOA Materiel/Services lines and as authorized charges in lines (9), (10), (11), and (12). The authorized charges in lines (9), (10), (11), and (12) are reflected by means of two basic generic categories on the DD form 645:

Administrative Fee (Generic Code L6A in Column 6 of the DD Form 645). As the title suggests, this cross-references to the Administrative Costs in Line (10) [or Line (12) for Supply Support Arrangements] of the LOA. A further breakdown of current period administrative costs can be found in the FMS delivery listing, under the subheading "Administrative/Accessorial Transactions." . . . [and Generic Description] L6A ADMIN COSTS."

Accessorial Costs (Generic Code LOO in Column 6 of the DD Form 645). These, too, show up on the FMS delivery listing under the subheading "Administrative/Accessorial Transactions." Included in this accessorial grouping are:

- PC&H Costs: "L2A PC&H." (Cross-references to Line (9) of the LOA). Applies to non-DWCF items only.

- Defense Transportation Service (DTS) Costs: "L1A CONUS TRANS, L1B OCEAN TRANS, L1C AIR TRANS, L1D PARCEL POST, L1E COMM PKG, L1F OS INLAND." (Cross-references to Line (11) of the LOA).

- Port Handling Costs: "L2B CONUS PORT, L2C OS PORT." (Cross-references to Line (11) of the LOA).

- Staging Costs: "L4O STAGING." (Cross-references to Line (11) of the LOA).

These administrative/accessorial costs are now defined and discussed in some detail.

PC&H (Line (9) of the LOA). Standard PC&H rates are applied to the selling price of certain materiel sold from DoD inventories. Prescribed PC&H rates are:

- 3.5 percent of material with a unit price of $50,000 or less.

- 1.0 percent of that portion of the selling price above $50,000.

Notes: (1) In accordance with DoD policy, the above PC&H percentage rates will not be shown in Line (9) of the LOA. Rather, only the whole dollar amounts computed will be shown. This guidance applies to the other authorized charges discussed below. (2) Standard PC&H rates of 3.5/1.0 percent apply unless RIC begins with "G," then the rate provided by GSA applies.

Administrative Costs (Line (10) of the LOA). The purpose of the general administrative cost element is to recover DoD expenses related to the functions of sales negotiations, case implementation, funds control of FMS, and related general costs of an administrative nature. The prescribed standard rates charged are as follows:

- Supply Support Arrangements: Shown in Line (12) of the LOA.
- Nonstandard Articles: 5%
- All Other FMS Orders:
  - 29 Jan 70 - 9 Mar 77 (i.e., Date of Offer): 2%, unless otherwise prescribed.
  - 10 Mar 77 - 30 Sep 77: 2% uniform rate.
  - 1 Oct 77 - 31 May 99: 3% uniform rate.
  - 1 June 99 - Present 2.5%

Defense Transportation System (DTS) Costs. Although normally the transportation of non-DBOF funded FMS materiel will be on collect commercial bills of lading from the U.S. depot to the freight forwarder agent of the FMS customer, there are occasions (e.g., shipment of hazardous material) where the DTS must be used. The DTS percentages are as shown in Figure 3-4 and apply to that portion of the unit price up to $10,000; for that portion of the unit price above $10,000, the appropriate percentage rate is multiplied by a 0.25 factor. Also, on occasion, actual transportation billings may be applicable.

Cooperative Logistics Supply Support Arrangement (CLSSA). Charges (Line (12) of the LOA). 5% uniform rate applicable to the FMSO I, Part A, portion; 2.5% uniform rate of FMSO II, Line (8), amount.

Attrition. The attrition charge may be applicable to training cases. The attrition cost factors, four percent for flying training and one percent for non-flying, will be included in tuition rates whenever the training or educational course includes the use of training equipment or operational equipment used as training aids.

Terms of Sale

The Security Assistance Management Manual (SAMM), Chapter 9, and the LOA Standard Terms and Conditions depict the various terms of sale which may appear on the LOA. There are several terms of sale which are available to accommodate the specific circumstances of the sale to include:

- The time that the payment(s) is needed based upon delivery and contractor financing requirements.
- The source of supply (DoD stocks or new procurement).
- The type of financing (cash or credit).

Cash financing is defined as payment(s) coming from FMS customer resources or through financing arrangements which do not involve the DoD FMS Financing (Credit) Program. Credit financing involves payments being made into the FMS trust fund, the source of which is the Foreign Military Financing Program. Further information about these programs can be found in the SAMM, Chapter 9.

There are seven general terms of sale, the first four of which appear in paragraph 4.4, LOA Standard Terms and Conditions. A listing of the terms and their general wording follows.

Cash with Acceptance. The Purchaser agrees to forward with the LOA a check or wire transfer in the full amount shown as the estimated total cost [Line (13)], and agrees to make such additional payment(s) as may be specified upon notification of cost increase(s) and request(s) for funds to cover such increases.

Cash Prior to Delivery. The Purchaser agrees to pay to the USG such amounts at such times as may be specified from time to time (including any initial deposit required) in order to meet payment requirements for articles or services to be furnished from the resources of the DoD. USG requests for funds may be based on estimated requirements to cover forecasted deliveries of articles or costs to provide defense services. It is USG policy to obtain funds 90 days in advance of the time DoD plans such deliveries or incurs such expenses on behalf of the Purchaser.

Dependable Undertaking. The Purchaser agrees to pay to the USG such amounts and a such times as may be specified from time to time by the USG (including any initial deposit required) in order to meet payments required by contracts under which items are being procured, and any damages and costs that may accrue, or have accrued, from termination of contracts by the USG because of the Purchaser's cancellation of the LOA. USG requests for funds may be based upon estimated requirements for advance and progress payments to suppliers, estimated termination liability, delivery forecasts or evidence of constructive delivery, as the case may be. It is the USG policy to obtain such funds 90 days in advance of the time that the USG makes payments on behalf of the Purchaser.

Payment on Delivery. The Purchaser agrees that bills may be dated as of the date(s) of delivery of the defense articles or rendering of the defense services, or upon forecasts of the date(s) thereof. (Consistent with Section 21(b) and (d) of the AECA, this term of sale is used only pursuant to a written determination delegated to the Director of DSCA, that it is in the national interest to do so. When used, billings to country are accomplished quarterly.)

FMS Credit. This term applies to payment in whole or in part with FMS credit funds. In accordance with LOA information, the purchaser may be required to submit a letter of request to the Defense Finance and Accounting Service (DFAS/IN/JAXBC) Indianapolis, Indiana to authorize payments from funds available under FMS loan or grant agreements.

Figure 3-4
Defense Transportation System (DTS) Percentage Rates

Rate Area	DoD Movement: Point of origin to destination	DTC **4** TBC **D,K,L**	DTC **5** CONUS port of exit TBC **A,B,E**	DTC **8** CONUS port aboard vessel TBC **H,U**	Port to port discharged TBC **J**	DTC **6** Overseas port TBC **F,X**	DTC **9** Overseas port discharged TBC **C,V**	DTC **7** Overseas inland destination TBC **G,Y**
1	Europe Central America Mediterranean	0	3.75 <u>0</u>	**6.25** <u>2.50</u>	7.5	**10.25** <u>6.50</u>	**11.25** <u>7.50</u>	**14.25** <u>10.50</u>
2	Newfoundand, Labrador, Thule, Iceland, South America, Far East, Africa, Near East			**6.25** <u>2.50</u>	9.5	**12.25** <u>8.50</u>	**13.25** <u>9.50</u>	**16.25** <u>12.50</u>

Note 1:   In most instances, the Transportation Bill Code (TBC), e.g., A, B, contained in the IA's delivery transaction determines the surcharge rate. The TBC reflects the actual level of transportation effort, whereas the Delivery Term Code (DTC), e.g., 5, indicates the planned transportation effort. However, in the absence of a TBC in the delivery transaction, the DTC will determine the surcharge rate. The DTC and TBC descriptions are contained in Appendices G and N of this handbook, respectively.

Note 2:   Above rates are applied in full up to a unit price of $10,000. For that portion of the unit price in excess of $10,000, 25 percent of the rate is applied.

Other Terms and Conditions Having Financial Implications

The following terms and conditions are also contained in the LOA or the LOA Standard Terms and Conditions:

Payment of Total Cost. The Purchaser shall pay to the USG the total cost to the USG of the items, even if the final total cost exceeds the amounts estimated in the LOA.

Payment Method. The Purchaser shall make payment(s) for the items by check(s) or by wire transfer payable in U.S. dollars to the Treasurer of the United States. Requests for funds or billings are due and payable in full on presentation, even if such payment date is not in accord with the estimated payment schedule.

Requests for Adjustments. The Purchaser will request adjustments of any questioned billed items by subsequent submission of required deficiency reports in accordance with paragraph 5, LOA Standard Terms and Conditions, which indicates:

• The Purchaser shall accept title to the defense articles at the initial point of shipment.

• The Purchaser shall be responsible for in-transit accounting and settlement of claims against common carriers.

- Standard Form 364 shall be used in submitting claims to the USG for overage, shortage, damage, duplicate billing, item deficiency, improper identification or improper documentation and shall be submitted by the Purchaser promptly.

- Claims of $200 or less will not be reported for overages, shortages, or damages (except for older cases reflecting a $25 or $100 limitation).

- Claims (excluding a claim for nonshipment/nonreceipt of an entire lot) received one year after date of passage of title or initial billing, whichever is later, will be disallowed by the USG, unless the USG determines that unusual and compelling circumstances involving latent defects justify consideration of the claim. [Initial billing is interpreted as applicable either to estimated (price code E), incremental (price code N) or actual (price code A) costs reported on the first quarterly billing for the item.]

Interest on Net Arrearages. The Purchaser is required to pay interest on any net amount by which it is in arrears on payments, determined by considering collectively all of the Purchaser's open LOAs with the DoD.

Designation of Procuring Agency and Paying Office. The purchaser shall designate the Procuring Agency and responsible Paying Office and address thereof to which the USG shall submit requests for funds and bills under the LOA. (Note: This information goes on page 1 of the LOA).

Acceptance of the LOA. The purchaser shall, in the process of accepting an LOA, return three copies properly signed to DFAS-IN, accompanied by the initial deposit or other payment arrangement as may be required. These actions must be done not later than the expiration date as shown on the LOA (except when the expiration date is extended). In addition, the Purchaser will concurrently return three (or more, if so specified) copies properly signed to the U.S. Military Department or Defense Agency making the offer. When properly accepted and returned, the provisions of the LOA shall be binding upon the USG and the Purchaser. It is emphasized that implementation of the LOA cannot proceed without a proper acceptance. A delay in submission of any required initial deposit or payment of full estimated cost, may require revision or reissue of the LOA.

Refunds. DFAS-IN shall refund to the Purchaser any payments which prove to be in excess of the final total cost of delivery and performance of a given LOA, provided arrearages do not exist. Refund agreements between the FMS customer and DFAS-IN will specify either blanket (automatic) or case-by-case processing. Case-by-case processing must be confirmed in writing from the FMS customer.

Cancellation. Either the USG or the Purchaser may cancel the LOA with respect to any or all items listed therein at any time prior to delivery of defense articles or performance of defense services (including training). The party initiating the cancellation shall be responsible for any termination or other cancellation costs as provided in the LOA and/or DSCA case policy decisions.

Type of Assistance Codes

The type of assistance (TA) Code distinguishes the various types of FMS agreements for *Military Standard Requisitioning and Issue Procedures* (MILSTRIP) requisitioning purposes, i.e., code is entered in data position 35 of the MILSTRIP DD-1348. The IA generally enters the TA code on the LOA or in the internal IA implementing directives for an FMS case for subsequent transcription to the DD-1348. These codes are found in Appendix H of this Handbook and paragraph 2.F of the LOA Information.

Amendments and Modifications To The Letter of Offer and Acceptance

Amendment

The United States of America Amendment to Letter of Offer and Acceptance, is used for changes in "scope" to the LOA and requires FMS customer's signature (acceptance).

Modification

The United States of America Modification to Letter of Offer and Acceptance, is used to record modifications to an existing LOA, not affecting the LOA "scope," and does not require the FMS customer's acceptance. It is often used to notify the FMS customer of estimated price increases and/or revised schedule of payments (Payment Schedule).

Impact of Amendments and Modifications

The impact and significance of the Amendments and Modifications, as they relate to the FMS billing system, are as follows:

- Payment schedules may have to be revised which, in turn, impact on the amounts "forecasted" in the DD Form 645.
- Unit prices which may have processed through the FMS billing system (and appeared on the FMS Delivery Listing) may have to be revised (i.e., the old price "credited out" and the new price "debited in"). The authorized charges, in this event, would also have to be revised accordingly.

Summary

In this chapter, the role of the LOA and amendments/modifications thereto were discussed in the context of their importance to the FMS billing process. Some of the key points were:

- The DFAS-IN inventory of implemented LOAs serves as the initial basis for preparation of the DD Form 645. However, the prices shown on the LOA and the payments contained in the Payment Schedule are estimates only; actual costs and possibly updated payment forecasts will be reflected in the DD Form 645.
- There are three primary record keys associated with the LOA (or the FMS case):
  - •• The FMS Case Identifier
  - •• The Item Numbers
  - •• **Document Numbers.** The first two record keys are found in the LOA; the latter (i.e., Document Numbers) are compiled during the case implementation process and may be verified by comparison to the shipping document (DD Form 250 or DD Form 1348-1, as applicable).

[This page intentionally left blank.]

Chapter 4
The Foreign Military Sales Billing System

Purpose

The *Arms Export Control Act* (AECA), as amended, (Sections 21 through 24) provides the legal basis for foreign military sales (FMS) billing policies and procedures. These policies and procedures are further defined and expressed, in part, in the DoD *Financial Management Regulation*, "Security Assistance Policy and Procedures" (DoD 7000.14R, Vol. 15), in the *Security Assistance Management Manual* (SAMM) (DoD 5105.38-M), and in the United States of America Letter of Offer and Acceptance (LOA) Standard Terms and Conditions. The purpose of this Chapter is to describe the Defense Finance and Accounting Service-Indianapolis, Indiana (DFAS-IN) function in the billing cycle, responsibilities of the implementing agencies (IAs), DFAS-IN cash management and reports/ products provided by DFAS-IN to the FMS customer.

The Billing Cycle

DFAS-IN issues quarterly billing statements (DD Form 645) to FMS customers based upon payment schedules in the LOA by the applicable IA. DFAS-IN bills for costs related to defense articles, services, and training that have been sold pursuant to the AECA, as amended. Implementing agencies report FMS deliveries of materiel, services, training, accrued expenditures (work in process), and other related costs to DFAS-IN for the purpose of obtaining reimbursement or reporting performance under an allotment of trust fund budget authority.

Inputs to DFAS-IN

To prepare a proper bill (DD Form 645) for a given FMS case, DFAS-IN must have certain information from implementing agencies (IAs). When an LOA is sent to the FMS customer, a copy is also provided to DFAS-IN with its Payment Schedule loaded into the Defense Integrated Financial System (DIFS). After the FMS customer accepts the LOA and provides DFAS-IN with signed copies of the LOA and the applicable initial deposit, DFAS-IN updates DIFS and prepares for case implementation and IA delivery reports. The initial deposit accompanying most FMS cases provides sufficient cash advance to cover disbursements from the time the case is accepted until the first billing payment due date.

Payment Schedules

It is DoD policy that FMS customers be requested to pay amounts reflected in the Payment Schedule to the LOA. The purpose of the Payment Schedule is to supplement and amplify terms in Section 4 of the LOA Standard Terms and Conditions, and to provide a clear understanding between the United States Government (USG) and the purchaser as to the estimated rate and timing of the payments to be made. The Payment Schedule is prepared by IAs. DoD policy essentially fulfills dual objectives:

- The FMS purchaser is assured of having sound budgetary information at his immediate disposal
- The USG is assured of receiving monies in advance of anticipated expenditures

Payment schedules are a consolidated formal presentation to the FMS customer of the estimates of cash requirements and potentially consist of two financial categories:

- An initial deposit
- Estimated quarterly billing amounts. If initial deposits are required upon acceptance of a sales agreement, the amount of the initial deposit should be sufficient

to cover all costs and contingencies (e.g., contract holdback, potential termination liability) anticipated to be incurred until the first billing statement can be rendered and monies collected

IAs are expected to closely monitor the accuracy of payment schedules on all cases to insure that cash is available when the necessity for disbursements arises.

Foreign Military Sales Detail Delivery Transaction

IAs must report the performance and execution (e.g., deliveries from DoD stock, progress payments, etc.) of the FMS program to DFAS-IN by use of the Delivery Transactions. The Delivery Transaction formats are explained in the DoD *Financial Management Regulation*, "Security Assistance Policy and Procedures" (DoD 7000.14R, Vol. 15). Among other things, the Delivery Transactions reflects the *Military Standard Requisitioning and Issue Procedures* (MILSTRIP) document number, the stock or part number, quantity, mode of shipment, delivery source code, transportation bill code, and dollar value. For several FMS cases (e.g., FMSO II), thousands of delivery transactions are received by DFAS-IN on a monthly basis. The delivery data transmissions are due to arrive at DFAS-IN by the 16th calendar day of the month following the end of the month being reported. The Delivery Transactions provides the basis for the detailed entries which appear in the FMS Delivery Listing, and further prompts reimbursement/liquidation of transactions reported by the IAs.

Cash Accounting

Foreign Military Sales Trust Fund

The FMS country trust fund is a fund credited with receipts which are earmarked by law and held in trust or in a fiduciary capacity by the USG for use in carrying out specific purposes and programs. The FMS trust fund (accounting classification 97-8242) represents the aggregation (corpus) of cash received from purchaser countries and international organizations credited to open FMS cases, funds that are excess to closed FMS case financial requirements, and/or funds held pending implementation of new cases or other agreed financial arrangements.

DFAS-IN is responsible for recording transactions that impact the FMS trust fund. FMS customer cash deposits for defense articles and services sold under Sections 21 and 22 of the AECA are to be made in advance of delivery, performance or progress payments to contractors. The DD Form 645 ("FMS Billing Statement") and LOA direct that foreign customer payments (initial deposits or in response to billing statements) be forwarded by wire transfer or check to DFAS-IN. If your country has a Federal Reserve Bank of New York (FRBNY) account agreement your remittances should be sent to:

> Federal Reserve Bank of New York (Foreign Accounts Department)
> Treasury NYC (3801)
> DFAX-JAX/IN
> ABA#021030004

If you do not have a Federal Reserve Bank of New York account, wire transfers are preferred and should be sent to the Federal Reserve Bank of New York, following the Fedwire System procedures with the following identifications: U.S. Treasury NYC (3801) Agency Location Code (ALC), DFAS-IN, ABA #021030004.

If wire transfer is not utilized, make checks payable to U.S. Treasury, payable in U.S. dollars and forwarded to:

> DFAS, 3801 Center Collections DFAS-JAX/JA
> P.O. Box 269490
> Indianapolis, Indiana 46226-9490

All payments should properly identify the customer country making the payment, FMS case designator, amounts being paid on each case, and the U.S. service responsible for managing the case(s).

DFAS-IN exercises stringent controls over the FMS trust fund to insure proper visibility and accountability are maintained for all payments made by a customer for every FMS case. There are certain principles of trust fund management to include:

- One FMS customer's trust fund balance cannot be used to finance another customer's programs. In other words, DoD does not view the overall FMS trust fund balance as "one big account" from which any customer-related bills or reimbursements can be paid. The integrity of customer country monies is strictly observed.

- Cash disbursements are controlled on a country basis, although accounting for FMS transactions are maintained on an FMS case basis. In other words, cash deposits of a given country are used to pay U.S. military departments or contractors for costs associated with any of that country's cases, but the accounting will be maintained and reported on individual cases. All cash disbursements for a purchaser shall not exceed the customer's cash deposits.

- Dollars received into the FMS trust fund are subject to United States Treasury accounting system controls from date of receipt to date of expenditure or refund. DFAS-IN, as the accountable agency, renders periodic reports to the United States Treasury and performs a monthly reconciliation of balances.

Foreign Military Sales Customer Funds

The FMS customer is billed for USG requests for payments (initial deposits, quarterly billing statements, or supplemental billing arrangements) and (if applicable) direct commercial contract progress payments. The customer may make payments in the form of United States dollars directly to DFAS-IN or, when authorized, utilize foreign military financing (FMF) funds through the USG. There are presently two types of FMS financing programs authorized by the AECA, as described below.

- DoD Guaranteed Loans. (Section 24, AECA). This kind of financing constituted the major portion of the FMF program prior to fiscal year (FY) 1985. Under the guaranteed loan concept, DoD (DSCA) submitted a guaranty (against all political and credit risks of nonpayment) for principal and interest installments defaulted by the borrower to the Federal Financing Bank (FFB - an agency of the Treasury Department). The FFB was responsible for signing the loan agreement with the borrowing country and for disbursing loan funds upon receipt of drawdown requests from the borrower. This form of financing was terminated at the end of FY 1984.

  •• The FMS customer will normally be required to make semi-annual payments of interest and (once the grace period expires) principal. Current loan repayments should be sent directly to the FFB; however, repayments of arrearages on FFB loan installments should be sent to DFAS-IN (since the FFB has already been paid by DFAS-IN under provisions of the guaranty noted above).

- DoD Direct Credit. (Section 23, AECA). With the exception of a few direct credits in the early 1970s, this form of financing commenced in FY 1985. The source of funding to finance this program is appropriated by Congress through annual Foreign Operations legislation. Direct Credit can be provided either in the form of grants (non-repayable) or loans (repayable). A discussion of these funding categories is provided below.

•• FMF Grants. FMS grant funds are availed upon apportionment of country-level funds. If a country is authorized to use FMF funds to finance direct commercial purchase, a grant agreement certifying compliance with various requirements must be implemented prior to the utilization of funds for commercial contacts. If countries cannot use FMS for direct commercial purchases, no agreement is required. In this latter instance, DFAS-IN can unilaterally disburse funds for LOAs financed with FMF in accordance with billing procedures for that country.

•• FMF Loans. FMF loan funds are availed upon implementation of a bilateral loan agreement, signed by the USG and the borrower. Generally, loan repayment terms are a total of 12 years (7 of which are principal); interest rates are determined by the Department of the Treasury. The FMS customer will normally be required to make semi-annual payments of interest and (once the grace period expires) principal. FMF loan repayments should be sent directly to DFAS-IN.

•• Once an FMF loan has been established, all requests for disbursement of those funds must be submitted by the borrower to DFAS-IN for processing/approval. For commercial contract disbursements, the requests must be accompanied by relevant invoices, bills of lading, various certificates, and other documentation as prescribed in the Annexes and Attachments to the loan agreement. Regarding FMS cases, the customer also issues a disbursement request for LOA initial deposits or DD Form 645 billing requirements.

Whenever an FMS case has multiple financing, FMF funds are considered to be applied first and cash funds second. If the case is closed and excess funds exist, the excess cash funds would be considered available to the FMS customer absent arrearages or funding shortfalls on other cash cases. Excess FMF funds, however, cannot be refunded to the FMS customer. The FMF funds can be used to pay down arrearages on FMF loan installments, DFAS-IN will normally not initiate this action and must have DSCA authorization prior to doing so.

Cross-leveling

Cross-leveling is an accounting technique by which DFAS-IN transfers excess funds (i.e., cash receipts) from one FMS case to another FMS case. This transfer permits the FMS purchaser to minimize payments due on a billing by fully utilizing all funds previously paid on FMS cases. For example, if DFAS-IN has collected excess funds on a case or a case has been closed and there are excess funds, these funds may be transferred to other open cases thereby reducing the amount due on the bill.

There are two methods through which cross-leveling of excess funds may be accomplished. In the first method, the customer conducts a cash analysis and, in a letter (usually with a payment), requests DFAS-IN make specific cash transfers among designated FMS cases. The second method authorizes DFAS-IN to automatically cross-level based on case needs.

In order for DFAS-IN to perform cross-leveling, a written agreement must be accomplished between DFAS-IN and the FMS customer. In order to initiate this action, the customer should advise DFAS-IN of an interest in entering into a cross-leveling arrangement and specify the name and office of the individual to sign a Memorandum of Agreement (MOA) on behalf of the FMS customer. DFAS-IN will prepare the agreement in duplicate, sign and forward it for the customer's signature. Upon receipt of the signed agreement, DFAS-IN will begin cross-leveling on the next succeeding billing statement.

In order to provide the FMS customer with a complete record of cross-leveling transactions, the transfer of excess cash is processed to the country holding account and then withdrawn from the holding account to be applied to a case requiring payment. For example, consider the situation where FMS case ABC is in a $10,000.00 over-payment surplus status but case ABD is underpaid by $10,000.00. Under cross-leveling, DFAS-IN could transfer, via the Holding Account, $10,000.00 from case ABC to ABD. The basic procedure is to record such transfers (as the $10,000.00 amount above) as a withdrawal (credit) transaction to the cash position of the FMS case with a surplus (case ABC) and as a deposit (debit) to the Holding Account. Simultaneously, $10,000.00 is recorded as a deposit (debit) to the underpaid case (ABD) and a withdrawal (credit) is recorded against the Holding Account. In other words, the $10,000.00 is "washed through" the Holding Account for control and reporting purposes. See Figure 4-1 for a sample cross-leveling agreement. DFAS-IN will also honor individual FMS cross-leveling in lieu of blanket authorizations based on letter or message requests from the FMS customer.

DFAS-IN Reports

The basic FMS billing document is the DD Form 645, which is prepared at the end of each calendar quarter. The DD Form 645 serves as both a billing document and a statement of account. Numerous attachments, as applicable, accompany the DD Form 645, to include the "FMS Delivery Listing," the "FMS Reply Listing to Customer Requests for Adjustments," the "FMS Financial Forecast," the "ULO Report," and the "Holding Account Statement."

Figure 4-1
Sample Memorandum of Agreement

Memorandum of Agreement
Between

The Government of _____

and

Defense Finance and Accounting Service (DFAS-JAX/IN

3801 Center Collections
P.O. Box 269490
Indianapolis, Indiana 46226-9490

(Date)

The Government of _____ requests the Defense Finance and Accounting Service to use its best efforts to lessen cash requirements related to _____ foreign military sales (FMS) cases by cross-leveling monies on deposit in FMS Trust Fund Account. Cross-leveling shall include the identification of over-payments (cash surpluses) and under-payments (amounts due and payable) and the transfer of such surplus monies to liquidate current amounts due and payable. DFAS-IN is requested to implement the following specific procedures:

1. Transfer surplus monies among FMS cases and provide a full accounting of such transfers to _____ at least quarterly.

2. Record such transfers as a withdrawal (credit) transaction to cash position of FMS cases with surplus funds and as a deposit (debit) to the cash position of the Holding Account. Simultaneously, record a deposit (debit) to the gaining case and a withdrawal (credit) to the Holding Account.

3. Transfers other than those made by DFAS-IN, or a reversal of transfers made by DFAS-IN, will be made if requested by _____.

Foreign Military Sales Billing Statement (DD Form 645)

DoD billings to FMS customers are issued by DFAS-IN. A computer-produced DD Form 645 or supplementary billing arrangements (official claim for payment by the USG) is used in billing the FMS customer. In addition, it furnishes an accounting to the FMS purchaser for all costs incurred under each LOA agreement.

Detail on the face of the billing statement segregates the cost elements in a manner parallel to the presentation of line item detail on the LOA. Physical performance of services or delivery of materiel is shown against the item number of the LOA. Administrative charges, accessorial costs, and work in process are separately listed.

Billing statements are prepared and forwarded to the FMS purchaser on a quarterly basis (i.e., for quarters ending March, June, September, and December). The billing cycle is essentially as follows:

Period Ending	DD 645 Mailed	Payment Due at DFAS-IN	Forecast Quarter
31 MAR	15 APR	15 JUN	JUL-SEP
30 JUN	15 JUL	15 SEP	OCT-DEC
30 SEP	15 OCT	15 DEC	JAN-MAR
31 DEC	15 JAN	15 MAR	APR-JUN

For example, the 31 December (period ending) bill reflects physical deliveries and cash collections recorded for the FMS case through the December cut-off for entries into the FMS accounting system. It also contains a forecast of estimated advance cash requirements through the month of June. This period's bill is mailed on or about January 15, with a due date for payment of March 15. The March, June, and September statements follow the same basic time frames. (Please note that the FMS Delivery Listing will only include delivery data received in DFAS-IN by the end of each quarter, thus military department reporting for March, June, September, and December will appear in the next quarterly billing statements.)

In addition to identifying deliveries (or performance of services) made on the FMS purchaser's behalf, the DD Form 645 also reflects the forecasted costs which relate to a given FMS case. These forecasted costs equate to a number of factors, to include: anticipated progress pay¬ments/advances, contractor holdbacks, termination liability reserve, accrued and future deliveries, pro rata share of non-recurring charges, contract administration costs, and administrative/ accessorial costs, as applicable. Previous schedule of payment amounts on requisition-type cases may be replaced by military department reporting of open requisition values on hand or anticipated.

Essentially, the DD Form 645 provides current period (the calendar quarter preceding the period ending date) delivery costs as well as cumulative delivery costs for all prior periods and work in process costs for the period subsequent to the period ending date. The bill normally requests monies to cover the planned deliveries for the forecast quarter (the calendar quarter subsequent to DFAS-IN payment due date). This concept is illustrated in Figure 4-2.

Figure 4-2
The "Four Periods" of the DD 645

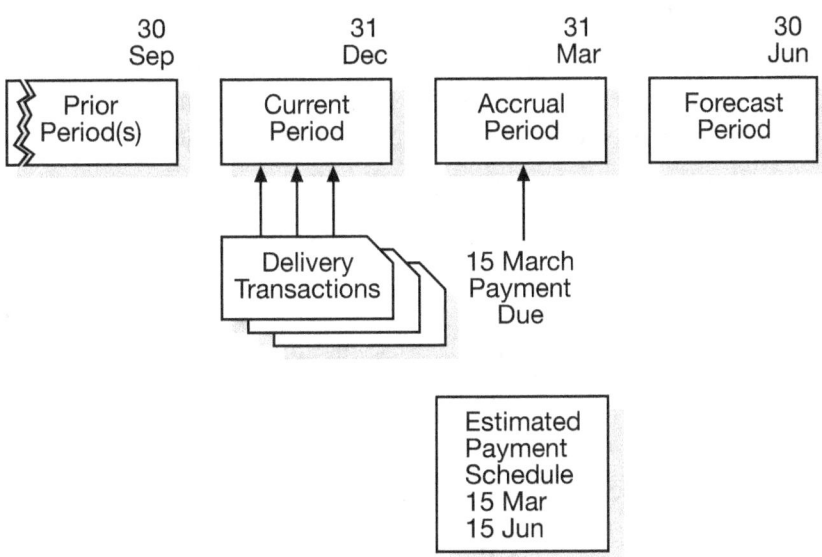

Foreign Military Sales Delivery Listing

This is a computer printout of the performance reporting of articles/services/Supply Discrepancy Reports (SDRs)/ notice of action taken which have been reported to DFAS-IN by the Military Departments or DoD agencies. An FMS Delivery Listing will be provided if deliveries have been received in DFAS-IN during the Current Quarter Period (column 9) of the DD Form 645.

The FMS Delivery Listing provides delivery information by case and by item number. Detailed information regarding articles/services transactions, administrative/accessorial transactions and a summary of delivery costs for each item number is provided.

Foreign Military Sales Reply Listing to Customer Requests for Adjustments

This is a computer printout which reflects all transactions relating to the final disposition/action taken with respect to any SDRs and may contain other internal USG billing transactions which also require an Adjustment Reply Code (ARC) and which are being billed the FMS customer. Close review should be made to ascertain that the adjustment does or will satisfy a SDR requirement in the event the SDR number is not present.

In the event customer review of the DD Form 645 and/or the supporting FMS Delivery Lists identifies the necessity for an adjustment, the FMS customer should submit a formal request for adjustment. Requests for billing and supply adjustments for materiel and service performance should be submitted to the IA. Requests for adjustments pertaining exclusively to administrative and accessorial charges should be submitted to DFAS-IN. FMS customers should submit all requests for billing and supply adjustments on a Standard Form (SF) 364, clearly indicating the specific adjustment or billing action requested. The form, instructions for completion and definitions are prescribed in *Joint Regulation DLAI* 4140.55, AR 735-11-2, SECNAVINST 4355.18A, and AFJMAN 23-215. After resolution of SDRs applicable to materiel and services, IAs report the action which is being taken to DFAS-IN. DFAS-IN will prepare a consolidated listing of the actions taken in response to the SDRs, and this listing will be mailed with the DD Form 645 to the country involved. All responses to SDRs are listed separately for each country, service, sase, and item number. The Reply Listing is prepared in the same basic sequence as the billing statement and FMS Delivery Listing. All SDRs appearing on the FMS Delivery Listing are included in the Reply Listing.

Foreign Military Sales Financial Forecast

This is a computer printout which reflects future forecast amounts of payments due, by quarter, for the FMS case. It essentially portrays the same information as the LOA payment schedule. The FMS Financial Forecast is provided only at the FMS customer's request.

Foreign Military Sales Accelerated Case Closure Suspense Account

This is a computer printout which shows FMS cases of participating countries where all ordered goods and services have been provided and only final financial reporting is necessary. It depicts the country, IA, case and closure date with the previous quarters unliquidated obligations (ULO) and current quarters activity. The balance column represents those outstanding financial obligations yet to be reported by the military department.

Holding Account Statement

As a convenience to the FMS purchaser, procedures are available for the establishment of a purchaser holding account. The holding account is a subaccount of monies not identified to a specific FMS case, reserved for identified cases, and/or funds not required when a case is closed. The FMS customer may request DFAS-IN to "draw upon" their holding account for transfers to specific cases as the need arises. The holding account balances are not included in the totals of the DD Form 645. A separate statement is provided to the country showing deposits and withdrawals to the holding account and is considered an off-line billing statement. The following information may appear on the holding account statement:

- Debit or credit transactions affecting FMS closed cases for Calendar year 1992 and prior. This may consist of deliveries not previously reported, and/or adjustments due to approved SDRs. [Effective with the March 1993 billing statement all cases with post closure activity will be reopened for those customers not participating in the DoD accelerated closure program.]
- Recording of funds received prior to implementation of a case.
- Transfer of funds to a newly implemented case that were held in the holding account until the case was implemented.
- Authorized transfers of collections between open cases or refunds requested by the FMS customer.

For those FMS customers receiving holding account statements, the combination of the DD Form 645 and holding account statement will reflect the total activity for the accounting period.

The FMS customer needs to advise DFAS-IN of its desires relative to the controls over holding account transactions. For example, DFAS-IN needs to know if the customer will allow automatic use of the funds for other open FMS cases, if the customer desires automatic refunds, or if the customer wants to request refunds on a case-by-case basis. Please note that funds temporarily held for new case implementation are not available for cross-leveling or refund. DFAS-IN will state the total reserved balance for each account.

Foreign Military Sales Case Closure

A logical follow-on event to a case that has been completely delivered and billed is case closure. FMS customers are encouraged to request status from the IA on undelivered/unbilled items prior to case closure. An FMS case is considered closed when all material has been delivered and/or all services have been performed, the IA has certified the final delivered cost, all financial transactions (including all collections) have been completed, and the customer has received a Final Statement of Account (i.e., a "Final" DD Form 645). DFAS-IN is the final determining organization for case closures; however, an IA may consider their records as logistically closed at the time a closure certificate is released to DFAS-IN. After processing, DFAS-IN confirms closure data to the IAs to ensure that records are logistically and financially complete. FMS cases are either closed using standard closure procedures or accelerated closure procedures.

Standard Case Closure Procedures

Before a case can be considered to be in a candidate status for closure, several actions are required.

- For Blanket Order and Cooperative Logistics Supply Support Arrangement (CLSSA) cases, the purchaser's requisitioning action must have been completed. (Defined Order case requisitions would, of course, be controlled by the CONUS case manager.)

- Appropriate management follow-up action should be initiated to validate any and all outstanding requisitions/purchase orders. This may require discussions (during country program reviews, etc.) with the purchaser's representatives. Cancellation action should be attempted on invalid (i.e., no longer needed) requisitions. The IA must then take action to insure final delivery and reporting to DFAS-IN for billing purposes.

- For reconciliation purposes, an initial objective is that each MILSTRIP requisition will have its own audit trail from "cradle to grave." Ideally, each requisition can be traced back to a given item number on the LOA, to the Case Directive (if applicable), to the assignment of the MILSTRIP document number itself, to the issue/procurement document, to completion of delivery or performance of service, to the reporting of the delivery/performance to DFAS-IN via the Delivery Transaction, to the billing statement (with the FMS Delivery Listing) provided by DFAS-IN to the country. Throughout this process, efforts must be taken to reconcile the International Logistics Control Office (ILCO) records with those of the stock point, accounting office, and DFAS-IN. The case manager must process Supply Discrepancy Reports (SDRs) and record any adjustments to the case financial records.

- To allow an FMS case to be closed, the following actions are required:
  - IAs will:
    - Ensure that all known SDRs have been resolved.
    - Ensure that all articles/services have been fully delivered to the FMS customer and reported to DFAS-IN.
    - Formally advise DFAS-IN that the cost of applicable articles and services have been fully reimbursed to financing U.S. Treasury Accounts.
    - Once all of the above conditions are met, will provide DFAS-IN with the certified closure certificate indicating total costs incurred including disbursements.

- •• DFAS-IN responsibilities.
  - ••• Affirm the values (from IAs) have been billed to the FMS customer.
  - ••• Ensure that all funds due have been collected and that delivered values and disbursements are equal.
  - ••• Ensure that no inhibitors exist to preclude issuance of final billing statement and/or excess funds have been transferred to the applicable holding account.
  - ••• If all of the above are met, DFAS-IN issues "Final Statement of Account" as part of the next quarterly DD Form 645 Billing cycle.
- • Effective FY 1993 (October 1992) cases not utilizing accelerated case closure procedures will be reopened if new activity (disbursements or deliveries) are reported after closure.

Accelerated Case Closure Procedures

Effective May 1, 1992, each FMS customer may elect to participate in an accelerated case closure (ACC) process. This process is intended primarily for FMS cases supported by long-running contracts, but can also be used to close other cases with uncleared activity.

Once selected by a country, accelerated procedures apply to all cases for that country. Participation is optional for customers with programs financed entirely by cash. The ACC procedures are mandatory for credit funded programs/cases.

In addition to the case closure reconciliation action defined for standard case closure, the following actions are also required:

- • The IAs will:
  - •• Identify and report delivery transactions to include any remaining unliquidated obligations (ULO) recorded against the case. This amount should include all remaining costs/contingent liabilities for contracts or other obligating documents that support the case.
  - •• Within 12-24 months after the case is supply complete, certify the case for "interim" closure to DFAS-IN. The certified cost should include actual disbursements recorded against the case and the ULO amount.
  - •• When actual contract or other financial activity costs for the case are known, certify the case for final closure to DFAS-IN. Return any unused ULO obligational authority to DFAS-IN.
- • DFAS-IN will:
  - •• Bill the amount reported by the IAs to the customer using normal billing procedures.
  - •• When the case is reconciled for closure, refund any cash collection in excess of actual case disbursements plus the ULO amount to the customer. Standard rules apply regarding the disposition of excess repayable/nonrepayable credit collections.
  - •• Record the recorded (and subsequently collected) ULO amounts in a summary liability account, "case closure suspense account," when the case is "interim" closed.
  - •• Provide a final statement of account to the customer at "interim" case closure.

- •• Record post-closure charges and credits by country and case against the country's suspense account.
- •• Bill the customer if that customer's case closure suspense account balance reflects a deficit of $100,000 or more for a period of six months.
- •• When case is certified for final closure, move the case to "final" closure status. Any remaining ULO funds on the case are made available at that point to support ULO cash shortages on other closed cases for that country.
- •• Cases utilizing accelerated case closure procedures may be reopened only if a major pricing error by the USG or contractor, in the amount of $100,000 or greater is discovered after case closure. DSCA approval is required before reopening an accelerated closed case.

Summary

The FMS Billing System provides a mechanism of complying with the AECA, as amended. Through the LOA and its included Payment Schedule, the FMS customer is able to determine the required initial deposit and programmed quarterly financial requirements.

DFAS-IN through its FMS Trust Fund management and related cash accounting procedures, is able to collect and track country monies by case. The basic FMS billing document is the DD Form 645, which is prepared at the end of each calendar quarter. The DD Form 645 serves as both a billing document and a statement of account. The "FMS Delivery Listing," the "FMS Reply Listing to Customer Requests for Adjustment," and the "Holding Account Statement" are all documents that are included with the DD Form 645 when applicable.

Case closure is accomplished once all necessary logistical and financial actions have been completed on the part of both the USG and the foreign purchaser. Closed cases are identified by an asterisk on the DD Form 645 (Billing Statement) and a separate case level DD Form 645 (Final Statement) is printed for distribution to appropriate parties. Once a case appears with the closed case asterisk, it will be dropped from future DD Forms 645 unless the IA or DFAS-IN has cause to reopen the case.

Effective fiscal year 1993 (October 1, 1992), cases not utilizing ACC procedures will be reopened if new activity (disbursements or deliveries) are reported after closure. Cases utilizing ACC procedures will be reopened only if a major pricing error by the USG or contractor, in the amount of $100,000 or greater is discovered after case closure. DSCA approval is required before reopening an accelerated closed case.

[This page left intentionally blank.]

Chapter 5
Defense Finance and Accounting Service, Indianapolis Indiana
Customer Assistance

Purpose

There are certain initiatives foreign military sales (FMS) customers may take which can facilitate their understanding of the financial documents received from DFAS-IN. These initiatives consist of writing or calling DFAS-IN points of contact and visiting the Center. Also provided is the information necessary to arrange for a visit to the Center.

Visits to DFAS-IN

Policy

FMS customers are encouraged to visit DFAS-IN from time to time. A visit may be warranted for any number of reasons, to include:

- To resolve problems or misunderstandings

- To discuss the realignment/redistribution of billing products which are sent to country addresses

- To meet with your country manager and other DFAS-IN officials for orientation purposes

Visits, of course, are most productive when DFAS-IN is afforded sufficient advance notification and time for preparation. Please attempt to furnish advance agenda items on specific problem/subject areas to DFAS-IN for research.

Visit Requests

In order for DFAS-IN to make the proper preparations for a visit, to include building/parking clearances, etc., the following information should be provided to DFAS-IN 30 days in advance of the intended visit:

- Name, Rank, and Position of Visitor(s). Equivalent rank should be furnished if military rank does not apply

- Desired Visit Dates.

- Lodging and Protocol Requirements.

- Topics to be Discussed.

The visit authorization must be approved by the Defense Intelligence Agency (DIA), Foreign Liaison Branch, CO8-4, Washington, D.C.

DFAS-IN Visits to Customer Site

Based on resource availability, DFAS-IN is available to send a representative to your country, embassy/mission in Washington, D.C. In circumstances where extensive/extraordinary services or assistance are needed, it may be necessary to have the associated costs directly funded through a "services line" on an FMS case. All in-country visits will be reviewed on a case-by-case basis.

Summary

Good communications are essential to any endeavor of importance, and such communications are vital to positive DFAS-IN customer relations. The policies regarding customer visits to DFAS-IN and, conversely, DFAS-IN visits to the customer site are also outlined.

Chapter 6
The Foreign Military Sales Billing Statement
(DD Form 645)

Purpose

The purpose of this chapter is to introduce the reader to the format of, and the types of information contained in, the Foreign Military Sales Billing Statement, DD Form 645.

Introduction

The final Foreign Military Sales (FMS) Bill (DD 645) and attachments are produced by the DFAS-IN billing subsystem.

Attachments are produced in conjunction with the FMS billing, and are listed below:

- Delivery Listing
- Financial Forecast Report
- Reply Listing to Customer Requeste for Adjustments
- Holding Accounts Statement
- Accelerated Case Closure Suspense Account tatement

Utilizing the Country Address/Distribution file, customized print packets are generated for each addressee. Their packets contain only the reports or portions of the reports in the number and sort sequence required by a specific country addressee. The select and variable sort sequence parameters used are Bill Code, implementing agency, in-country service, and report type. The proper mailing label is also printed for each packet. All report copies printed are originals and the special form required for the DD Form 645 is formatted within the computer system. The unliquidated obligation (ULO) report is prepared separately and included is the DD Form 645 and attachments.

General Information Regarding DD Form 645

Function and Content

The DD Form 645, prepared by DFAS-IN, represents the official claim for payment by the United States (U.S.) government referred to in the United States of America Letter of Offer and Acceptance (LOA) Information (attached to the original LOA). In addition, it furnishes an accounting to the FMS purchaser for all costs incurred under each agreement. Detail on the face of the billing statement segregates the cost elements in a manner parallel to the presentation of item number detail on the LOA. Physical performance of services or delivery of materiel is shown against the item number of the LOA. Administrative surcharges, accessorial costs, progress payments, and a forecast of future performance/deliveries are provided at case, as opposed to item number level.

Cycle

The DD Form 645 is prepared and forwarded to the FMS purchaser on a quarterly basis in accordance with the following cycle:

Period/Quarter Ending	Projected Mailing Date	Payment Due to DFAS-IN	Forecast Quarter
31 MAR	15 APR	15 JUN	JUL-SEP
30 JUN	15 JUL	15 SEP	OCT-DEC
30 SEP	15 OCT	15 DEC	JAN-MAR
31 DEC	15 JAN	15 MAR	APR-JUN

Types of Statements

The DD Form 645 has two basic variations:

- Billing Statement. Block 2, in the first instance, states "This is a Billing Statement based on cash (financial) requirements. Payment is due by: _____." The Billing Statement variation serves as a bill and statement of account for all open FMS cases and those cases which are closed during that quarterly period.

- Final Statement of Account. Block 2, in the second instance, states: "This is a Final Statement of Account." Each FMS case reflecting a closed status on the quarterly Billing Statement will be accompanied by a Final Statement, the latter of which may be conveniently detached by the FMS Purchaser and filed in any locally maintained case files. A closed case is depicted by an asterisk (*) at the beginning of the case designator in Column 6 of the Billing Statement and Final Statement.

Once a Final Statement has been submitted for an FMS case, no subsequent adjustment of such billings (upward or downward) is authorized, except under the following instances (Note: This information appears in the "Explanatory Notes" at the bottom of a Final Statement):

- Discovery of latent errors, such as obvious errors in addition or multiplication, unauthorized deviations from DoD policy, or computer errors in establishing unit prices.

- To provide charges/credits for Supply Discrepancy Reports (SDR) submitted by the purchaser in accordance with terms and conditions of the LOA.

- Discovery by the United States that it has shipped an item or rendered a service for a case but has failed to submit a bill.

- Discovery by the United States that the final price paid to a U.S. contractor for an item provided in accordance with Section 22 of the *Arms Export Control Act* (AECA) is different from the final amount billed for that item.

Explanation of Entries on the DD Form 645

Sample Documents

For ease of reference and illustration, the following documents (with sample information entries) are provided:

- Figure 6-1: The LOA for FMS case identifier BN-B-URK (for the fictitious country of Bandaria, country code BN), together with Payment Schedule information.

- Figure 6-2: DD Form 645 "Billing Statement," Statement Number 00-12NA, which is comprised of case designators CXY, URA, and URK.

- Figure 6-3: DD Form 645 "Final Statement," Statement Number 00-12NA, for case designator URA.

These sample documents are referred to in the following explanation of entries on the DD Form 645.

Figure 6-1

United States of America
Letter of Offer and Acceptance

BN-B-URK

Based on Bandaria Letter, 25 Sep 200X

Pursuant to the *Arms Export Control Act*, the Government of the United States (USG) offers to sell to the Government of Bandaria (GOB), Embassy of Bandaria, 6000 Massachusetts Avenue, Washington DC, 20036 the defense articles or defense services (which may include defense design and construction services) collectively referred to as "items," set forth herein, subject to the provisions, terms, and conditions in this LOA

This LOA is for Armament Systems and Support Equipment.

Estimated Cost: $72,725.00   Initial Deposit: $12, 150.00

Terms of Sale: Dependable Undertaking/Cash Prior to Delivery;

This offer expires on 3 January 200X. Unless a request for extension is made by the Purchaser and granted by the USG, the offer will terminate on the expiration date.

This LOA consists of page 1 through page XX

The undersigned are authorized representatives of their governments and hereby offer and accept, respectively, this LOA:

_____	_____	_____	_____
U.S. Signature	Date	Purchaser Signature	Date
_____		_____	
Typed Name and Title		Typed Name and Title	
_____		_____	
Implementing Agency		Agency	

_____ _____
DSCA   Date

Information to be provided by the Purchaser:

Mark For Code_X_, Freight Forwarder Code_2_, Purchaser Procuring Agency Code_B_, Name and Address of the Purchaser's Paying Office: Bandarian Embassy, 6000 Massachusetts Avenue, Washington, D.C. 20036 _____

Figure 6-1 (Continued)

Explanations for acronyms codes, and financial information, may be found in attached "Letter of Offer and Acceptance Information."

Items to be Supplied (costs and months for delivery am estimates):

(1) Itm Nbr	(2) Description/Condition	(3) Qty, Unit of Issue	(4) Costs (a) Unit	(b) Total	(5) SC/MOS/ TA Notes	(6) Ofr Rel Cde	(7) Del Trm Cde
001	F4Z 9F4ZOOM1SCWPN(Y) Armament System	4 Ea	$15,000	$60,000	P(30) TAS	Z	8
002	J6Z 9J6Z00SUPTEQP(N) Support Equipment	XX		$10,000	X(1-30) TA4	A	4

(8)	Net Estimated Cost	$70,000
(9)	Packing, Crating, and Handling	0
(10)	Administrative Charge	$2,100
(11)	Transportation	625
(12)	Other	0
(13)	Total Estimate Cost	$72,725

To assist in fiscal planning, the USG provides the following anticipated costs of this LOA:

Estimated Payment Schedule

Payment Date	Quarterly	Cumulative
Initial Deposit	$12,150	$12,150
15 June 200X	15,300	27,450
15 Sep 200X	12,000	39,450
15 Dec 200X	11,000	50,450
15 Mar 200X	8,550	59,000
15 Jun 200X	7,000	66,000
15 Sep 200X	5,000	71,000
15 Dec 200X	1,725	72,725

Figure 6-2
(page 1 of 3 pages)

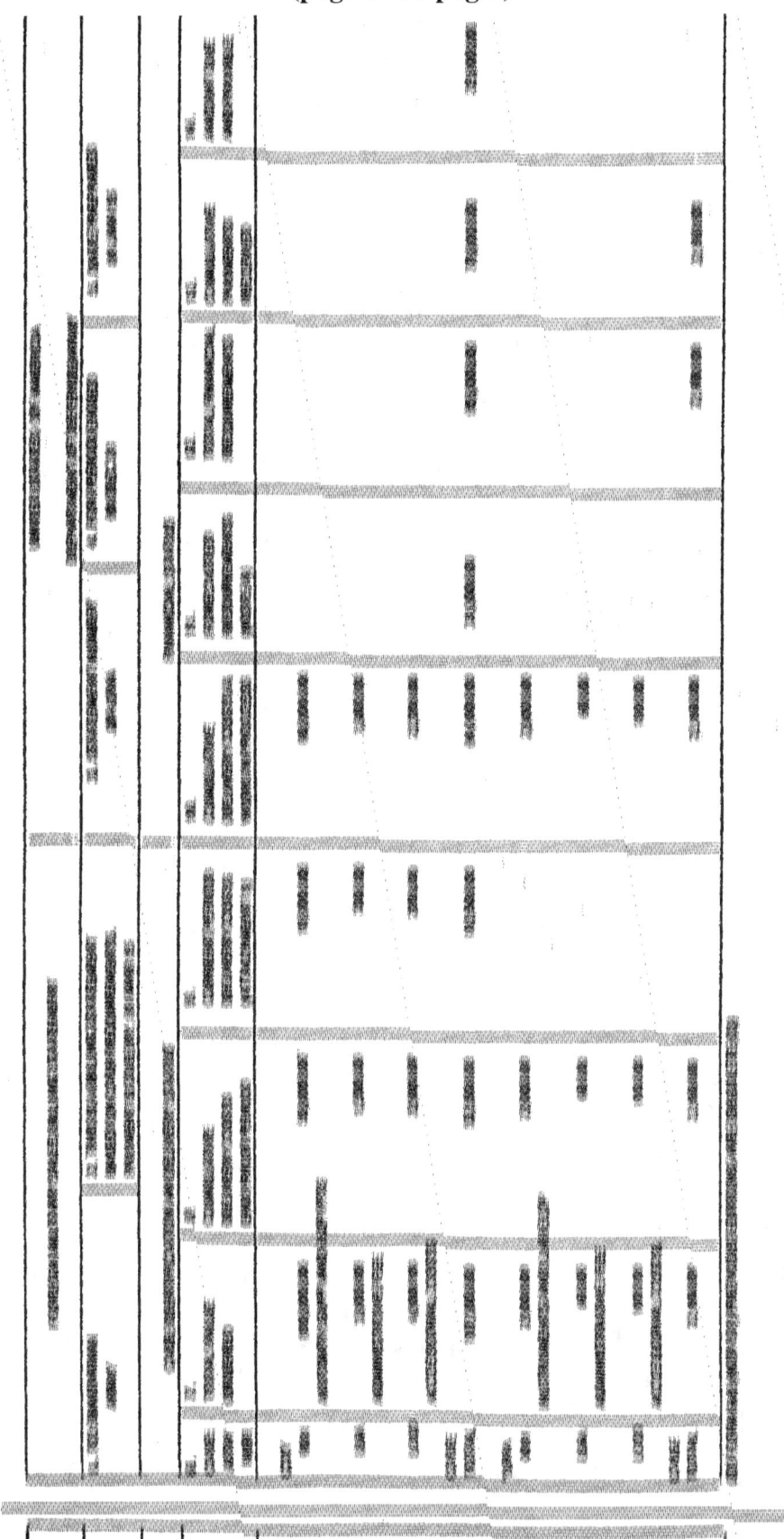

Figure 6-2
(page 2 of 3 pages)

Figure 6-2
(page 3 of 3 pages)

Figure 6-3
(page 1 of 3 pages)
Final Statement

UNITED STATES OF AMERICA
DEPARTMENT OF DEFENSE/ARMY

FOREIGN MILITARY SALES BILLING STATEMENT

1. TO: BANDARIAN ARMY
2. THIS IS A FINAL STATEMENT OF ACCOUNT.
3. STATEMENT NUMBER 00-12NA
4. FOR PERIOD ENDED 00 DEC 31
5. DATE PREPARED 01 JAN 15

CASE IDENTIFICATION AN DELIVERY STATUS / FINANCIAL STATUS

6. CASE & ITM NBR	7. TOTAL VALUE ORDERED	8. CUMULATIVE DELIVERY COSTS END PRIOR PERIOD	9. CURRENT PERIOD DELIVERY COSTS (ATTACHMENT 1)	10. CUMULATIVE DELIVERY COSTS & WORK IN PROCESS	11. FORECASTED REQUIREMENTS (NOTE A)	12. TOTAL FINANCIAL REQUIREMENTS	13. CUMULATIVE PAYMENTS RECEIVED	14. AMOUNT DUE AND PAYABLE
URA 001 INSTRUMENTS AND LAB EQP	2,000.00	2,000.00		2,000.00				
L6A ADMINISTRATIVE FEE	60.00	60.00		60.00				
L00 ACCESSORIAL COSTS	100.00	100.00		100.00				
CASE TOTAL	2,160.00	2,160.00		2,160.00		2,160.00	2,160.00	

DD FORM 645 (NOV 87) PREVIOUS EDITIONS ARE OBSOLETE (Q)

6-8

FOREIGN MILITARY SALES BILLING STATEMENT

UNITED STATES OF AMERICA

DEPARTMENT OF DEFENSE/ARMY

1. TO BANDARIAN ARMY

2. THIS IS A FINAL STATEMENT OF ACCOUNT

3. STATEMENT NUMBER 00-12NA

4. FOR PERIOD ENDED 00 DEC 31

5. DATE PREPARED 01 JAN 15

CASE IDENTIFICATION AND DELIVERY STATUS

6. CASE & ITM NBR	7. TOTAL VALUE ORDERED	8. CUMULATIVE DELIVERY COSTS END PRIOR PERIOD	9. CURRENT PERIOD DELIVERY COSTS (ATTACHMENT 1)
BILL TOTAL	2,160.00	2,160.00	

FINANCIAL STATUS

10. CUMULATIVE DELIVERY COSTS & WORK IN PROCESS	11. FORECASTED REQUIREMENTS (NOTE A)	12. TOTAL FINANCIAL REQUIREMENTS	13. CUMULATIVE PAYMENTS RECEIVED	14. AMOUNT DUE AND PAYABLE
2,160.00		2,160.00	2,160.00	

REVIEW PROCESS

SIGNATURE

ANALYST: _____
BRANCH CHIEF: _____
QUALITY ASSURANCE: _____

AUTHENTICATION

SIGNATURE

EXPLANATORY NOTES

ONCE FINAL STATEMENT/BILLINGS HAVE BEEN SENT FOR AN FMS CASE, NO SUBSEQUENT ADJUSTMENT OF SUCH BILLING, UPWARD OR DOWNWARD, IS AUTHORIZED EXCEPT UNDER THE FOLLOWING INSTANCES:

A. DISCOVERY OF PATENT ERRORS SUCH AS OBVIOUS ERRORS IN ADDITION OR MULTIPLICATION, UNAUTHORIZED DEVIATIONS FROM DOD FINANCIAL POLICY, OR COMPUTER ERRORS IN ESTABLISHING UNIT PRICES

B. TO PROVIDE CREDITS AND FOR DISCREPANCY REPORTS SUBMITTED BY THE PURCHASER IN ACCORDANCE WITH STANDARD TERMS AND CONDITIONS OF THE UNITED STATES OF AMERICA LETTER OF OFFER AND ACCEPTANCE.

C. DISCOVERY BY THE UNITED STATES THAT IT HAS SHIPPED AN ITEM OR RENDERED A SERVICE FOR A CASE BUT HAS FAILED TO SUBMIT A BILL

D. DISCOVERY BY THE UNITED STATES THAT THE FINAL PRICE PAID TO A U.S. CONTRACTOR FOR AN ITEM PROVIDED IN ACCORDANCE WITH SECTION 22 OF THE ARMS EXPORT CONTROL ACT IS DIFFERENT FROM THE FINAL AMOUNT BILLED FOR THAT ITEM.

OFFICE OF THE DEPUTY DIRECTOR FOR SECURITY ASSISTANCE
DEFENSE FINANCE AND ACCOUNTING SERVICE-DENVER CENTER
DD FORM 645 (NOV. 87) PREVIOUS EDITIONS ARE OBSOLETE (Q)

Figure 6-3
(page 3 of 3 pages)
Final Bill for Accelerated Case Closure

FOREIGN MILITARY SALES BILLING STATEMENT

UNITED STATES OF AMERICA

DEPARTMENT OF DEFENSE/ARMY

| 1. TO BANDARIAN ARMY | 2. THIS IS A FINAL STATEMENT OF ACCOUNT. | 3. STATEMENT NUMBER 00-12NA | 4. FOR PERIOD ENDED 00 DEC 31 | 5. DATE PREPARED 01 JAN 15 |

CASE IDENTIFICATION AND DELIVERY STATUS

6. CASE & ITM NBR	7. TOTAL VALUE ORDERED	8. CUMULATIVE DELIVERY COSTS END PRIOR PERIOD	9. CURRENT PERIOD DELIVERY COSTS (ATTACHMENT 1)
BILL TOTAL	2,160.00	2,160.00	

FINANCIAL STATUS

10. CUMULATIVE DELIVERY COSTS & WORK IN PROCESS	11. FORECASTED REQUIREMENTS (NOTE A)	12. TOTAL FINANCIAL REQUIREMENTS	13. CUMULATIVE PAYMENTS RECEIVED	14. AMOUNT DUE AND PAYABLE
2,160.00		2,160.00	2,160.00	

REVIEW PROCESS

SIGNATURE

ANALYST: _____

BRANCH CHIEF: _____

QUALITY ASSURANCE: _____

AUTHENTICATION

SIGNATURE

EXPLANATORY NOTES

ONCE FINAL STATEMENT/BILLINGS HAVE BEEN SENT FOR AN FMS CASE, NO SUBSEQUENT ADJUSTMENT OF SUCH BILLING, UPWARD OR DOWNWARD, IS AUTHORIZED EXCEPT ON THE DISCOVERY BY THE UNITED STATES THAT A FINAL PRICE PAID TO A U.S. CONTRACT FOR AN ITEM PROVIDED IN ACCORDANCE WITH SECTION 22 OF THE ARMS EXPORT CONTROL ACT IS SIGNIFICANTLY DIFFERENT FROM THE FINAL AMOUNT BILLED FOR THAT ITEM

OFFICE OF THE DEPUTY DIRECTOR FOR SECURITY ASSISTANCE
DEFENSE FINANCE AND ACCOUNTING SERVICE-DENVER CENTER
DO FORM 645 (NOV. 87) PREVIOUS EDITIONS ARE OBSOLETE (Q)

Entries on DD Form 645

Foreign Military Sales Billing Statement

Upper Left-Hand Corner. Title of DD Form 645.

United States of America Department of Defense/Army

Upper Right-Hand Corner. Identifies the U.S. Department of Defense Component acting as the implementing agency (IA) for the cases shown on the statement. In this example, the U.S. Army is the IA.

1. To Bandarian Army

Block 1. Identifies the FMS Purchaser Service who is the recipient of the statement. Reflects full country/activity name followed by Military Service within country or special paying office. In this example, we show the Bandaria Army.

2. This is a Billing Statement Based on Cash Requirements. Payment is Due By: 01 Mar 15

Block 2. Identifies the statement as a "Billing Statement based on cash requirements" or a "Final Statement of Account," whichever is applicable. If the statement is a Billing Statement, this block also indicates the date payment is due. The due date is about 60 days after the preparation date in Block 5, but in any event will be the 15th day of the last month of the quarter, e.g., 15 March 2001 in this example.

3. Statement Number 00-12NA

Block 3. Statement number is assigned mechanically and is composed of the numeric year and month representing the period ended followed by an alphabetic management code assigned by DFAS-IN. The management code (also referred to as the "bill code") is used to sort cases for distribution, and normally identifies the paying office. The foreign customer can request and obtain billing sorted in some other manner. In this example, the statement number is "00-12NA," with "00" standing for calendar year 2000; "12" standing for the 12th month or December; and "NA" standing for the applicable management and/or paying office bill code. Those cases not identifiable or reflected on a specific Paying Office alpha code will be included on the standard statement number: i.e., "00-01--" and require FMS customer advice to DFAS-IN as to the proper billing code layout for future billings.

4. For Period Ended 00 Dec 31

Block 4. Contains the last calendar day of the month for which the statement is prepared. It is normally the last day of the month at the end of each calendar quarter, e.g., 31 December 2000 in this example.

5. Date Prepared 01 Jan 15

Block 5. Reflects the actual date on which the statement was prepared/mailed, e.g., 15 January 2001 in this example.

Case identification and delivery status

Middle-Left Portion. Descriptor for Columns 6 through 9.

6. Case and item nmber URK 002, 002, L6A, L00, WIP Case Total

a.   Identifies the FMS case designator (URK in this illustration), and the item number identification (e.g., 001, 002) from the LOA. Immediately below and slightly to the right of each item number(and spilling over into Columns 7 and 8) is the abbreviated/short title of articles/services taken from the Military Articles and Services List (MASL) (Reference: SAMM, Appendix D); an abbreviated title in this illustration would be "ARMAMENT SYS" which relates to item number 001 or the major element of the LOA.

b.   Additionally, this column contains identification of administrative surcharges (Generic Code L6A), accessorial costs (LOO), and work in process (WIP) related to the case, as well as the Case Total.

c.   As noted earlier, an asterisk (*) preceding the case designator indicates a completed case (closed). A case which has been closed since the previous Billing Statement was issued will appear on the current Billing Statement with an asterisk. Concurrently, a Final Statement of Account is prepared mechanically for the case and presented following the billing statement. Figure 6-2 reflects case designator URA (shown as *URA) as being a closed case. This case will not appear on a subsequent DD Form 645 unless the case is re-opened.

7. Total Value Ordered	
	60,000.00
Armament System	
	10,000.00
Support Equipment	
	2,100.00
Administrative Fee	
	625.00
Accessorial Cost Work in Process	
	72,725.00

Column 7. Contains the dollar value of articles/services associated with each item number /generic descriptor and the value of the entire case. These dollar values come from the LOA and amendments/ modifications thereto. Note that the abbreviated/short titles of the articles/ services (e.g., ARMAMENT SYS) carry over into Column 7 from Column 6.

8. Cumulative Delivery Cost End Prior Period
14,900.00
3,844.50
562.33
270.47
19,577.30

Block 8. Dollar value of cumulative delivery costs as of the end of the prior statement period (e.g., deliveries cumulative through 30 September 2000 in this example). No value is shown in this column for progress payments applicable to undelivered items.

9. Current Period Delivery Cost (Attachment)
15,100.00
1,155.00
487.67
150.70
16,893.87

Block 9. Dollar value of delivery costs reported since the end of the prior statement period, i.e., those delivery transactions received in and accepted by DFAS-IN during the current period (October through December in this example). Values shown in this column are supported in (transaction) detail by the FMS Delivery Listing (identified in the Column 9 heading as Attachment 1). In Chapter 7, the FMS Delivery Listing for item number 002 which relates to the $1,155.50 figure in Column 9, is illustrated. No value is shown in this column for work in process applicable to undelivered items.

Financial Status

Middle-Right Portion. Descriptor for Columns 10 through 14.

10. Cumulative Delivery Cost and Work in Process
30,000.00
5,000.00
1,050.00
421.17
13,978.83
50,450.00

Column 10. This column contains the totals of values shown in Columns 8 and 9, plus work in process applicable to undelivered items. The value in Column 10 for work in process represents accrued costs incurred on behalf of the FMS Purchaser which are not yet supported by physical or constructive deliveries. These costs include contractor holdbacks on work in process made to contractors, potential termination liabilities, and any other applicable authorized charges.

11. Forecasted Requirements Note:
8,550.00

Column 11. Contains the forecasted requirements for the case, i.e., the value of potential costs to be incurred during the calendar quarter following the payment due date of the current statement. This value appears on the "Case Total" line only and may be derived from one of two different sources.

a.   The quarterly deposit identified in the payment schedule for the case which has a due date that coincides with the payment due date of the current statement. In this illustration, the $8,550.00 figure comes from the payment schedule (see Figure 6-1).

b.   For all requisition type cases (i.e., Supply Support Arrangement - FMSO 2, and other repair part cases), the Defense Component may provide DFAS-IN with a "Committed Values for Requisition Cases" report. This report reflects the current value of on-hand, unfilled requisitions for each case.

This report will be submitted to DFAS-IN by automated means. These inputs will be submitted to DFAS-IN by the 15th day of the last month of each calendar quarter (i.e., by 15 March, 15 June, 15 September, and 15 December) reflecting the most recent status for each case. The committed value will be used as the forecasted requirements in Column 11 for the case in lieu of the quarterly deposit in the payment schedule when the committed value is less than the payment schedule quarterly deposit. Forecasted amounts may be adjusted by DFAS-IN based on documented information.

The Column 11 heading makes reference to "Note A," which is one of the "Explanatory Notes" at the bottom of the certification page of the Billing Statement (see Figure 6-2). Note A reads as follows: "The terms of the U.S. public law, the *Arms Export Control Act*, require the Department of Defense to collect payments from foreign purchasers in advance of the time that DoD incurs costs on the purchaser's behalf. Therefore, this Billing Statement requests payment of monies that are anticipated to be expended between the time this Billing Statement is paid and the following Billing Statement is paid."

12. Total Financial Requirements
59,000.00

Column 12. A value appears in this column on the "Case Total" line only. It represents the total of the Column 10 and Column 11 values for the case. Note also that for those cases where the forecasted requirements are derived from the payment schedule, the figure in Column 12 equates to cumulative payment schedule amounts up through the current forecast period.

13. Cumulative Payments Received
50,450.00

Column 13. A value appears in this column on the "Case Total" line only. It represents the total amount of payments received by DFAS-IN in behalf of the FMS customer through the official date of billing in Block 5.

14. Amount Due and Payable
8,550.00

Block 14. A value appears in this column on the "Case Total" line only. It represents a calculation, Column 12 value minus Column 13 value, and is the additional payment which is due from the customer. In the event the calculation shows a negative amount due, the negative amount will not normally be shown. [Excess payments on one case does not reduce or eliminate the requirement to pay on another case, since billing is required on a case-by-case basis.] This is of particular significance for those cases subject to case closure actions.

Additional Information

- The last page of Figure 6-2 reflects the Bill Total for case designators CXY, URA, and URK -- which collectively comprise Statement Number 00-12NA for U.S. Army implemented cases to Bandaria. The Bill Total figure is the summation of all entries in Columns 8 through 13 for applicable cases. It should be noted that the Bill Total amount will not be equal to Column 12 minus Column 13, if one or more of the cases have excess payments, which are computer suppressed.

- The bottom left-hand portion of the last page of the DD Form 645 (Figure 6-3) is titled Review Process and contains space for DFAS-IN signatures. However, as of the 96-12 Billing Statement a validation and signature letter took the place of individually signed bills. Exceptions to this procedure are made only at customers request.

- The bottom right-hand portion of the last page of the DD Form 645 is titled Explanatory Notes. Note A was addressed as part of the discussion for Column 11. There is another note which reads: "*Denotes cases closed during the current period."

- Directly below the Explanatory Notes portion are the Payment Instructions, which read: "Your payments may be made using either checks or wire transfer procedures. Wire transfers are preferred and should be sent to the Federal Reserve Bank of New York, with the following identifications: U.S. Treasury of New York, Treasury NYC (3801), DFAS/JAX/IN, ABA#021030004."

If wire transfer is not utilized, make checks payable to U.S. Treasury, in U.S. dollars and forwarded to:

DFAS-3801 Center Collections DFAS-JAX/IN
P.O. Box 269490
Indianapolis, Indiana 46226-9490

For those FMS Customer Countries who have entered either a tripartite, or quadripartite agreement authorizing the establishment of a Federal Reserve Bank account New York (FRBNY), the following applies:

- Initial deposits required on newly accepted FMS cases are to be made to your respective account as part of the LOA acceptance terms.

- Payments due based on the DD Form 645 billings are also to be deposited to your FRBNY account.

Federal Reserve Bank of New York
Treasury NYC (3801)
DFAS/JAX/IN
ABA#021030004

- It is imperative that confirmation of all deposits made to the FRBNY account be furnished direct to DFAS-IN by the FMS customer office making such deposits. These advances must contain country code, implementing agency of the USG and case designator, i.e., BN-B-XYZ. This action will help ensure that DFAS-IN records are properly updated and credit will appear on subsequent DD Form 645s. Failure to advise DFAS-IN will result in an imbalance between the payment records of the FMS customer and DFAS-IN billing cumulative payments received (column 13) on DD Form 645s.

Summary

The DD Form 645 is prepared and distributed to the FMS Purchaser on a quarterly basis. This document consists of two parts: a "Billing Statement," and a "Final Statement of Account" for each closed case.

The DFAS-IN data base relative to LOA provides the basis for the degree of information detail provided on the DD Form 645. Specifically, those item numbers on the LOA are transferred to the DD Form 645, and detailed delivery costs are shown accordingly. For most FMS cases (with the exception being requisition type cases to include Supply Support Arrangement - FMSO 2 and other repair part cases), the Payment Schedule is the source of the forecasted requirements which appear in Column 11 of the DD Form 645.

This page intentionally left blank.

Chapter 7
Foreign Military Sales Delivery Listing

Purpose

In this chapter, the Foreign Military Sales (FMS) Delivery Listing - which is an attachment to the DD Form 645 - is addressed. The discussion centers on how to read the FMS Delivery Listing and how such Listing relates to the DD Form 645.

General Information

Function and Format

The FMS Delivery Listing (see Figure 7-1) is prepared in support of entries in Column 9, "Current Period Delivery Costs," of the DD Form 645. The Listing identifies items physically or constructively delivered and services performed that are received and accepted by DFAS-IN during the reporting period. It is cross referenced to specific document numbers and allows FMS customers to validate receipt of the materiel or services. This Delivery Listing also includes DFAS/IN's computations of authorized charges applied by that organization in accordance with established pricing policy. Those performance reporting items rejected back to an implementing agency (IA) must be researched by them for determination of errors, correction and/or re-input in subsequent reporting. The FMS delivery list is in item number sequence and delivery source code sequence within item number and subtotaled by delivery source code.

Cycle

The FMS Delivery Listing, being an attachment to the DD Form 645, is prepared and distributed on a quarterly basis.

Explanation of Entries on the Foreign Military Sales Delivery Listing

The FMS Delivery Listing essentially consists of four sections or groupings of information:

- Header Information, e.g., identification of country, service, statement number, case, item number, etc.
- Articles/Services Transactions, which support the Column 9, DD Form 645, entry for the given item number, e.g., Item Number 001, 002, etc.
- Administrative/Accessorial Transactions, which provide a breakout of administrative and accessorial costs by generic code and the accounting date/month.
- Summary of Delivery Costs, reflecting the net total of articles/services costs, the net total of administrative and accessorial costs, and total delivery costs.

Figure 7-1
Foreign Military Sales Delivery Listing
(page 1 of 3 pages)

Figure 7-1
Foreign Military Sales Delivery Listing
(page 2 of 3 pages)

Figure 7-1
Foreign Military Sales Delivery Listing
(page 3 of 3 pages)

			PAGE 3
SUMMARY OF DELIVERY COSTS			TOTAL COSTS
PLA ARTICLES/SERVICES COSTS			[illegible]
PSB ARTICLES/SERVICES COST ADJUSTMENTS			[illegible]
NET TOTAL OF ARTICLES/SERVICES COSTS			[illegible]
	ACTUAL COSTS	COMPUTED COSTS	
PSC ADMINISTRATIVE COSTS	.00	[illegible]	[illegible]
PSD ADMINISTRATIVE COSTS ADJUSTMENTS	.00	[illegible]	[illegible]
NET TOTAL ADMINISTRATIVE COSTS	.00	[illegible]	[illegible]
PSE ACCESSORIAL COSTS			
L1C AIR TRANSPORTATION	.00	[illegible]	[illegible]
L1F INLAND TRANSPORT OVERSEAS	.00	[illegible]	[illegible]
L2B CONUS PORT HANDLING	.00	[illegible]	[illegible]
L2C OVERSEAS PORT HANDLING	.00	[illegible]	[illegible]
NET TOTAL ACCESSORIAL COSTS			[illegible]
TOTAL DELIVERY COSTS			[illegible]

The sections of the FMS Delivery List and associated data fields are discussed below.

Header Information

[Reference: Figure 7-1, Page 1 of 3]

```
FMS Delivery Listing
Statement Number: 00-12NA
Case: URK ITM NBR: 002
```

Top Center Portion. Identifies the type of listing, the statement number, the case and item number.

```
                                    Page

For Period Ended: 00 Dec 31
Date Prepared: 01 Jan 15

   U.S. Department/Agency Army
```

Top Right-Hand Portion. Identifies the period ended date, the actual date prepared, the U.S. IA (e.g., U.S. Army), and the page number of the listing.

```
Country: Bandaria
Service: Army
```

Top Left-Hand Portion. Identifies the FMS recipient country and Service within that country.

Articles and Services Transactions

[Reference: Figure 7-1, Page 1 of 3]

```
Document Identifier (DOC ID)

FKB
FKA
FKA
FKA
FKA
```

Document Identifier (DOC ID). The DOC ID identifies the type of transaction. In the "Articles/Services Transactions" section, there are two possibilities:

- FKA: Materiel/Service Transaction (Debit).

- FKB: Materiel/Service Transaction (Credit). In the event of an FKB, the abbreviation for credit (CR) follows the quantity in the QUAN SHIP column and the dollar amount in the Extended Value column.

```
Routing Identifier Code (RIC)

B14
B14
S9J
B14
B14
```

Routing Identifier Code (RIC). Three position (alpha/numeric) code which identifies the shipping depot or activity performing services as established in MILSTRIP procedures. S9C, for example, equates to the Defense Supply Center, Columbus, OH.

```
Price Code (PRC CD)

A
E
E
A
A
```

Price Code (PRC CD). An alpha code which identifies the price as being:

- A = An actual price. A blank in the PRC CD field is also treated as an actual price.

- E = An estimated price. Used to report physical deliveries at an estimated price. This transaction will eventually be reversed when an actual price (PRC CD "A") is submitted by the IA.

```
Stock Number

C0001BNURK
493000926123400
473000016267800
Contract Administration
493000928111100
```

Stock Number. Shows stock or part number, training course number, film number, publication number, phrase "SERVICE," etc. In reporting cost of DoD Services, the following cost codes or similar information will be used in the last two positions of the stock number field;

> 11 - Civilian Personnel Services and Benefits
> 17 - Military Personnel Services and Benefits
> 21 - Travel and Transportation of Personnel
> 22 - Transportation of things
> 23 - Rent, Communications, and utilities
> 24 - Printing and Reproduction
> 25 - Other Services
> 26 - Supplies and Materials
> 31 - Equipment

```
Unit Issue

EA
EA
EA
XX
EA
```

Unit of Issue. Abbreviation for unit of issue, e.g., EA equates to Each.

```
Quantity Shipped (QUAN SHIP)

5CR
10
 2
 1
 1
```

Quantity Shipped (QUAN SHIP). Self-explanatory. For FKB transactions, the quantity is followed by the abbreviation "CR" standing for Credit.

```
Document Number

BBNC4481009004
BBNC4481009001
BBNC4481009009
BBN00000005330
BBNC4481009010
```

Document Number. Composed of 14 alpha/numeric characters identifying the transaction.

- Position 1: Implementing agency code, as shown in Part III, Appendix F. For example, "B" equates to U.S. Army.

- Position 2-3: Country code, e.g., BN equates to fictitious country of Bandaria.

- Position 4: Customer in-country code (or mark for code). Comes from the LOA, e.g., code "C" in the above example.

- Position 5: Delivery Term Code as shown in Appendix G, of this Handbook. This is the negotiated/anticipated method of movement of the material.

- Position 6: Type of Assistance Code as shown in Appendix H, of this Handbook.

- Position 7-10: Four numeric characters representing calendar year and Julian date. For the date 8100: 8 = calendar year 1998; and 100 = the 100th calendar day of 1998, or 9 April.

- Position 11-14: Serial number of the transaction/requisition. In the illustration above, the serial numbers are 5330, 9001, 9004, 9009, and 9010.

Document SFX (DOC SFX)
A

Document Suffix Code (DOC SFX). If this field contains an alpha/ numeric entry, it indicates a partial supplying action on the part of the supplier. Block assignment of the suffix codes is accomplished essentially as follows:

Processing Source	Assigned Suffix Codes
Initial Source	A through E
First Secondary Source	F through H, J, and K
Second Secondary Source	L, M, Q, T, and U
Third Secondary Source	V through X
Fourth Secondary Source	Z through 9

Supplementary Address (SUPL ADRS)
BZ2URK
BZ2URK
BZ2URK
URK
BZ2URK

Supplementary Address (SUPL ADRS).

- Position 1: In-country Service Code, e.g., "B" = Bandaria Army

- Position 2: Offer/release code from column (6), LOA, e.g., "Z" in this illustration, which advises that a Notice of Availability (NOA) is required prior to item release.

- Position 3: Freight Forwarder Code from the LOA, e.g., "2" in this illustration.

- Position 4-6: Case designator, e.g., "URK" in this example.

Mode of Shipment (MS)
G
F
G
B

Mode of Shipment (MS) Code. Codes listed in Appendix L. Code "F," for example, indicates transportation was accomplished by the Air Mobility Command (AMC).

Adjustment Reply Code j(ARC)
CB

Adjustment Reply Code (ARC). May be used to explain material cost or quantity adjustment, either as the result of a SDR or some other billing adjustment input to DFAS-INDFAS-IN by the shipper. A list of ARCs is contained in Appendix M. Code "CB" indicates that a credit adjustment will be made. Some MILSTRIP adjustments may also be coded that do not directly relate to a SDR; therefore further comparison to the stock number field is recommended to determine the validity.

ACTG Date
0010
0010
0011
0011
0011

Accounting Date (ACTG DATE). Calendar year (e.g., "00" = 2000) and month (e.g., 10 = October) that a transaction is processed by DFAS-INDFAS-IN.

TDC
A
G
A
DD
D

Transportation Bill Code (TBC). An alpha character used by DFAS-INDFAS-IN to recognize the necessity to charge for the transportation of materiel. TBCs are listed in Appendix N. Code "G," for example, indicates that the materiel was moved to the FMS consignee at an overseas inland destination.

DSC
AB
AB
AB
BD
DC

Delivery Source Code (DSC). Comprised of two alpha characters. Codes in this field provide an audit trail between delivery transactions and FMS pricing policies. Code is also used by DFAS-INDFAS-IN to recognize the necessity to charge for packing, crating and handling (PC&H) and contract administration on new procurement contract disbursements. DSCs are listed in Appendix O. Code "AB," for example, relates to a non-excess stock fund Defense Working Capital Fund (DWCF) (other than matured FMSO) item from inventory.

SHIP DATE
9140
9250
9280
9330
9281

Date Shipped (DATE SHIP). Four numeric characters with the first being the last digit of the calendar year (e.g., "0" = 2000) followed by the three position Julian Date (e.g., 250).

UNIT PRICE
70.00
120.00
50.00
2.96
197.04

Unit Price. Derived in DFAS-INDFAS-IN by dividing quantity shipped into extended value reported by IA. An asterisk (*) in this Column means that the extended value is "not divisible" (in whole dollars and cents by quantity shipped).

Extended Value. Quantity times Unit Price.

Administrative and Accessorial Transactions
   [Reference: Figure 7-1, Page 2 of 3]

DOC ID
FKC
FKC
FKD
FKE
FKE
FKE
FKE

Document Identifier (DOC ID).

- FKC - Administrative Costs (Debit).
- FKD - Administrative Cost Adjustments (Credit).
- FKE - Accessorial Costs (Debit)
- FKF - Accessorial Cost Adjustments (Credit)

   Generic Code. Selected Administrative and Accessorial cost related generic codes (reference: SAMM, Appendix D, for a list of all generic codes). The following generic codes, together with their long and short titles, may be shown in this portion of the DD Form 645:

Generic Code	Generic Long Title	Generic Short Title
L1A*	INLAND TRANSPORT CONUS	CONUS TRANS
L1B*	OCEAN TRANSPORTATION	OCEAN TRANS
L1C	AIR TRANSPORTATION	AIR TRANS
L1D**	PARCEL POST	PARCEL POST
L1E**	COMMERCIAL PKG CARRIERS	COMM PKG
L1F	INLAND TRANSPORT OVERSEAS	OS INLAND
L1O	TRANSPORTATION COSTS	TRANS COSTS
L2A*	PACK CRATE & HANDLE	PCH
L2B	CONUS PORT HANDLING	CONUS PORT
L2C	OVERSEAS PORT HANDLING	OS PORT
L4A	STORAGE#	STORAGE
L4B	STORAGE#	STORAGE
L4O	STAGING	STAGING
L6A	ADMINISTRATIVE COSTS	ADMIN COSTS
N7E	MEDICAL#	MEDICAL
N7F	QUARTERS#	QUARTERS
R9D	TDP ROYALTY FEE#	TDP ROYALTY
R9H***	ASSET USE CHARGE#	ASSET USE
U10	NORMAL INVENTORY LOSS#	INV LOSS

\# LIST CONTAINS SOME GENERIC CODES WHICH MAY BE INCLUDED WITHIN THE LOA

*   Effective October 1990, these charges are not applied if the DSC is AA, AB, AC, AD, AH, AJ, AK, CA, EF, or EG, and the ship date is greater than 1 October 1990.

**   Effective October 1991, these charges are not applied if the DSC is AA, AB, AC, AD, AH, AJ, AK, CA, EF, or EG and the ship date is greater than 1 October 1991.

*** Asset use charges are not applicable after November 1989 per Public Law. 101-167.

COST
DESCRIPTION

ADMIN COSTS
ADMIN COSTS
ADMIN COSTS

AIR TRANS
OS INLAND

CONUS PORT
OS PORT

Cost Description. Generic short title of cost. See discussion immediately preceding this block.

Document Number. Comprised of three positions:

- Position 1: U.S. IA, e.g., B = U.S. Army.

- Position 2-3: Country code of recipient, e.g., BN.

Adjustment Reply Code (ARC). Same meaning as in "Articles/Services Transactions" discussion. Normally, no entries are shown here because this is a summation of many entries in the "ARTICLES/ SERVICES TRANSACTIONS" portion of the Delivery Listing. See Appendix M for listing of ARCs.

ACTG DATE
0010
0010
0010
0011
0010
0010
0010

Accounting Date (SDR DATE). Same meaning as in "Articles/Services Transactions" discussion. Note that all administrative/accessorial costs are summarized in terms of document identifier, generic code(s) relevant to that document identifier, and accounting date/month.

TYPE OF COST
COMPUTED
COMPUTED
COMPUTED
COMPUTED
COMPUTED
COMPUTED
COMPUTED

Type of Cost. Can be of two types:

- Computed - Meaning that the routine percentage charge is used, e.g., 3.00% for general administrative costs. The type of computation is denoted by the word "COMPUTED."

- Actual - Meaning that actual, in lieu of percentage derived, charges are applicable. This type of computation is denoted by the word "ACTUAL."

PERCENT FACTOR
3.00
3.00
3.00
6.00
3.00
2.50
1.00

Percent Factor. Denotes the percentage used on "COMPUTED" costs described above. When "ACTUAL" charges are used, the words "FLAT CHARGE" appear in lieu of the percentage rate.

TOTAL VALUE APPLIED
1205.50
300.00
350.00 CR
1205.00
1205.00
1205.00
1205.00

Total Value Applied. Relates to the total value (from the "Articles/Services Transactions" section) to which the percentage or flat charge, in the previous column, is applied. This total value figure is sorted/summarized by document identifier, generic code, and accounting date.

ADMIN/ACSRL COST
36.17
9.00
10.50CR
72.33
36.17
30.14

Administrative/Accessorial Cost (ADMIN/ ACSRL COST). Equates to the end results following the application of percentage or flat charges.

Summary of Delivery Costs
[Reference: Figure 7-1, Page 3 of 3]

```
SUMMARY OF DELIVERY COSTS

FKA     ARTICLES/SERVICES COSTS
FKB     ARTICLES/SERVICES COST ADJUSTMENTS

NET TOTAL OF ARTICLES/SERVICES COSTS

FKC     ADMINISTRATIVE COSTS
FKD     ADMINISTRATIVE COST ADJUSTMENTS

NET TOTAL OF ADMINISTRATIVE COSTS

FKE     ACCESSORIAL COSTS

        L1C  AIR TRANSPORTATION
        L1F  INLAND TRANSPORTATION OVERSEAS

        L2B  CONUS PORT HANDLING
        L2C  OVERSEAS PORT HANDLING

NET TOTAL OF ACCESSORIAL COSTS

TOTAL DELIVERY COSTS
```

Cost Descriptions Summary. In this portion of the FMS Delivery Listing, the aggregated costs (irrespective of accounting date/month) are identified to their document identifier (e.g., FKA, FKB) and the Net Total is shown. Accessorial costs are further displayed by generic code. "Total Delivery Costs" equal to the net totals of articles/services costs, administrative costs, and accessorial costs.

ACTUAL COSTS	COMPUTED COSTS
.00	45.17
.00	10.50 CR
.00	34.67
.00	72.33
.00	36.17
.00	30.14
.00	12.06

TOTAL COSTS
1505.50
350.00 CR
1155.50
45.17
10.50 CR
34.67
72.33
36.17
30.14
12.06
150.70
1340.87

Cost Information Summary. Displays the costs in terms of "ACTUAL COST," "COMPUTED COSTS," and "TOTAL COSTS."

Note that the "Net Total of Articles/Services Costs" ($1155.50 in this illustration) equates to the amount for that FMS case/item number in Column 9 of the DD Form 645. The "Net Total of Administrative Costs" ($34.67 in this illustration) represents a portion the L6A ADMINISTRATIVE FEE figure (i.e., $487.67 in Column 9 of the DD Form 645 - see Figure 6-2, page 2 of 3). The L00 line on the DD Form 645 is the total of all assessed accessorial charges.

Automated Products

The customer may request that DFAS-IN provide data to support the FMS Delivery Listings. Specific data formats prepared by DFAS-IN based upon Delivery Transactions are shown in Figures 7-2 through 7-7 for the following transactions.

- Articles/Service Transaction (Data Tape)- Figure 7-2.
- Training Transaction (Data Tape) - Figure 7-3.
- Administrative Transaction (Data Tape) - Figure 7-4.
- Accessorial/Additional Cost Transaction (Data Tape) - Figure 7-5

- Articles/ Services Transaction (Diskette) – Figure 7-6
- Administrative/Accessorial Cost Transactions (Diskette) – Figure 7-7

Summary

The FMS Delivery Listing is a key attachment to the DD Form 645. Essentially, it contains detailed transaction data to support the entries in Column 9 of the DD Form 645. The FMS Purchaser may request data tapes to support the FMS Delivery Listings.

Figure 7-2
Data Tape Format for Articles/Service Transaction[1]

Transaction Position	Field Contents
1-3	Document Identifier Code[2]
4-6	Routing Identifier Code
7	Price Code
8-22	Stock or Part Number/SDR Response
23-24	Unit of Issue
25-29	Quantity Shipped[3]
30-43	Document Number
44	Suffix Code
45-50	Supplemental Address
51	Mode of Shipment
52-53	Adjustment Reply Code
54-57	Accounting Date (numeric year and month in which processed at DFAS-IN
58	Transportation Bill Code (second position of original code)
59-60	Delivery Source Code
61-64	Date Shipped
65-73	Extended Value[3, 4]
74-80	Unit Price[4]
81-83	Item Number
84	Cost Identification Code
85	In-Country Service

1   The majority of data in this transaction is perpetuated from the Delivery Transaction report.

2   Document identifier code will be FKA for debits, FKB for credits, and FKG for reply to customer requests for adjustments. FKG cards may contain either debit or credit values and are financial information relating to the original FKA/FKB transaction.

3   A credit value is indicated by a CR or - after the value.

4   For items which exceed $99,999.99 in unit price, the extended value and unit price fields contain dollars only.

Figure 7 3
Data Tape Format for Training Transaction

Transaction Position	Field Contents
1-3	Document Identifier Code (FKA, FKB)
4-6	Routing Identifier Code
7	Price Code (normally "A")
8-22	Course Number or Brief Description
23-24	Unit of Issue (normally "XX")
25-29	Quantity
30-43	Document Number (normally contains zeros in cc 33-35 and ITO date and/or number in cc 36-43)
44	Suffix Code or Blank
45-50	Supplemental Address (normally contains zeros in cc 46-47)
51-53	Blank or Zero
54-57	Accounting Date
58	Normally Blank
59-60	Delivery Source Code
61-64	Course Commencement Date or Blank
65-73	Extended Value (cost involved with training)
74-80	Unit Price (normally same as extended value)
81-83	Item Number
84	Cost Identification Code
85	In-Country Service

FIGURE 7-4
Data Tape Format for Administrative Transaction

Transaction Position	Field Contents
1-3	Document Identifier Code (FKC for debits, FKD for credits)
4-6	Routing Identifier Code of activity which reported materiel/services to which administrative costs apply
7	Blank
8-19	Contains constant "ADM COST," left-justified
20-29	Value to which cost applies, if applicable
30	U.S. Implementing Agency Code
31-32	FMS Country Code
33-44	Blank
45	FMS Country Service
46-47	Blank
48-50	FMS Case Designator
51	Blank
52-53	Adjustment Reply Code, if applicable
54-57	Accounting Date
58-60	Generic Code (L6A)
61-64	Blank
65-73	Value of Administrative Cost
74-80	Percentage rate used, if applicable
81-83	Item Number
84	Cost Identification Code
85	In-Country Service

Figure 7-5
Data Tape Format for Accessorial/Additional Cost Transaction

Transaction Position	Field Contents
1-3	Document Identifier Code (FKE for debits, FKF for credits)
4-6	Routing Identifier Code of activity which reported materiel/services to which accessorial costs apply
7	Blank
8-19	Phrase identifying type of cost, e.g., "CONUS T," "OSEAS T," "P POST," "PCH," "STAGING," "MEDICAL," etc.
20-29	Value to which cost applies, if applicable
30	U.S. Implementing Agency Code
31-32	FMS Country Code
33-44	Blank
45	FMS Country Service
46-47	Blank
48-50	FMS Case Designator
51	Blank
52-53	Adjustment Reply Code, if applicable
54-57	Accounting Date
58-60	Generic Code for type of cost as prescribed by the Security Assistance Management Manual (SAMM)
61-64	Blank
65-73	Value of Accessorial Cost
74-80	Percentage rate used, if applicable
81-83	Item Number
84	Cost Identification Code
85	In-Country Service

Figure 7-6
Data Diskette Format for Articles/Service Transaction[1]

Transaction Position	Field Contents
1-3	Document Identifier Code
4-6	Routing Identifier Code
7	Price Code
8-22	Stock or Part Number/SDR Response
23-24	Unit of Issue
25-30	Quantity Shipped2
31	Blank
32-45	Document Number
46	Suffix Code
47-52	Supplemental Address
53	Mode of Shipment
54-55	Adjustment Reply Code
56-59	Accounting Date (numeric year and month in which processed at DFAS-IN
60	Transportation Bill Code (second position of original code)
61-62	Delivery Source Code
63-66	Date Shipped
67-79	Extended Value [2,3]
80-88	Unit Price [2,3,4]
89-91	Item Number
92	Cost Identification Code[5]
93	In-Country Service

1 The majority of data in this transaction is perpetuated from the Delivery Transaction report.

2 The sign positions are '0' for positive and '-' for negative quantities.

3 For items that exceed $9,999,999.99 in the extended value field, the extended value is expressed as rounded whole dollars only (no cents).

4 For items that exceed $99,999.99 in the unit price field, the extended value and unit price fields contain dollars only.

5 This field always contains an 'A' (above the line costs, articles and services).

Figure 7-7

Data Diskette Format for Administrative and Accessorial Transactions

Transaction Position	Field Contents
1-3	Document Identifier Code (DIC)
4-6	Routing Identifier Code of activity which reported materiel/services to which administrative/accessorial costs apply
7	Blank
8-19	Cost Description [1]
20-31	Extended Value Total [2,3,4]
32	U.S. Implementing Agency Code
33-34	FMS Country Code
35	Type Cost [5]
36-46	Blank
47	FMS Country Service
48-49	Blank
50-52	FMS Case Designator
53	Blank
54-55	Adjustment Reply Code, if applicable
56-59	Accounting Date
60-62	Generic Code (L6A) [6]
63-66	Blank
67-77	Value of Administrative/Accessorial Cost [3,4]
78-85	Percentage rate used, if applicable4
86-88	Blank
89-91	Item Number
92	Cost Identification Code [7]
93	In-Country Service

1 If the DIC is FKC or FKD, 'ADMIN-COSTS' should appear this space. If DIC is FKE or FKF, the generic description of the accessorial charges (i.e., CONUS TRANS, PCH, P Post, etc) should appear in this space.

2 If the actual cost is used (see Note 5), this field will be spaced out. If the computed cost is used, the extended value total is placed here.

3 The sign position is designated by a '0' for positive and '-' for negative.

4 An actual decimal point is used.

5 If the input is actual cost, this field will contain an 'A'. Otherwise, this field will contain a 'C' (computed cost).

6 If DIC is FKC or FKD, the generic code is L6A. If DIC is FKE or FKF, the generic code is the code to the accessorial charge, i.e., LIA, L2B, L2C, etc.

7 This field always contains a 'B' (below-the-line costs, i.e., accessorial and admin).

Chapter 8
The Foreign Military Sales Financial Forecast

Purpose

The purpose of this chapter is to provide information on how to read and understand the Foreign Military Sales (FMS) Financial Forecast, an attachment to the DD Form 645.

General Information

Function and Format

An FMS Financial Forecast (Figure 8-1) is prepared to show the anticipated forecast amounts which will eventually be posted to Column 11 (Forecasted Requirements) of the DD Form 645. In theory and most actual practice, the amounts contained in the FMS Financial Forecast are extracted from the most recent amended/modified Payment Schedule. The FMS Financial Forecast, in this instance, is valuable inasmuch as it reflects the latest payment schedule information as received by DFAS-IN. In other instances, such as requisition type, repair part, and FMSO II cases, where a quarterly "Committed Values for Requisition Cases" report is submitted the FMS Financial Forecast reflects the latest outlying forecasts. Also refer to the Payment Schedule for further clarity and understanding.

Cycle

This report is produced quarterly, along with the DD Form 645.

Figure 8-1
Foreign Military Sales Financial Forecast

US DEPT/AGENCY: ARMY			FMS FINANCIAL FORECAST		DATE PREPARED: 01 JAN 15			PAGE: 1
COUNTRY: DANDARIA			STATEMENT NR: 00-12WA		FOR PERIOD ENDED: 00 DEC 31			
SERVICE: ARMY								
CASE	FORECAST BY QUARTER	1ST	2ND	3RD	4TH	5TH	6TH	7TH
		8TH	9TH	10TH	11TH	12TH	13TH	14TH
		15TH	16TH	17TH	18TH	19TH		
CXY		12000	0	0	0	0	0	0
		0	0	0	0	0	0	0
		0	0	0	0	0		
URK		7000	5000	1725	0	0	0	0
		0	0	0	0	0	0	0
		0	0	0	0	0		
TOTAL STATEMENT		19000	5000	1725	0	0	0	0
		0	0	0	0	0	0	0
		0	0	0	0	0		

Explanation of Entries on the Foreign Military Sales Financial Forecast

The following segmented illustrations are taken from Figure 8-1, which is a hypothetical FMS Financial Forecast for Statement Number 96-12NA and relates to FMS case designators CXY and URK each of which reflect future forecast amounts.

Header Information

U.S. Department/Agency: Army
Country: Bandaria
Service: Army

Upper Left-Hand Portion. Self-explanatory.

FMS Financial Forecast Statement NR: 0012NA

Upper Center Portion. Self-explanatory.

Date Prepared: 01 Jan 15
For Period Ended: 00 Dec 31

Upper Right-Hand Portion. Self-explanatory.

The Header Information, illustrated above, follows essentially the same pattern as the FMS Delivery Listing and no further discussion is needed.

Case
CXY
URK
Total Statement

Left-Hand Side. Reflects the heading "CASE" (and the cases CXY and URK in this illustration). The "Total Statement" heading relates to the Statement Number (00-12NA in this illustration).

Forecast By Quarter:	1st
	8th
	15
	12000
	0
	0
	7000
	0
	0
	19000
	0
	0

Forecast by Quarter. There is space on this report for 19 future quarterly forecasts - normally enough for most cases. The 1st quarterly forecast case entry (i.e., the $12,000 boxed figure in the illustration) cross-references to the 15 JUN XX payment date and amount on the Payment Schedule (Figure 8-2) for FMS Case BN-B-CXY. The $7,000 boxed entry for FMS case URK also cross references to the Figure 8-2.

Rule

The 1st quarterly forecast entry equates to the DD Form 645. Block 2 (Payment Due Date), plus 90 days, e.g., if the DD Form 645, Block 2, date is 15 MAR 00, then the 1st quarterly forecast entry on the FMS Financial Forecast will equate to the 15 JUN 00 amount from the payment schedule. The 2nd quarterly forecast entry will be 15 SEP 00 in this example, and so on.

Figure 8-2
Payment Schedule Information

For FMS Case BN-B-CXY

Payment Date	Amount	Cumulative
Initial Deposit[1]	$35,000	$35,000
15 SEP 99	15,000	50,000
15 DEC 99	20,000	70,000
15 MAR 00	25,000	95,000
15 JUN 00	12,000	107,000
Total	**$107,000**	

For FMS Case BN-B-URK

Payment Date	Amount	Cumulative
Initial Deposit[1]	$12,150	$12,150
15 JUN 00	15,300	27,450
15 SEP 00	12,000	39,450
15 DEC 00	11,000	50,450
15 MAR 01	8,550	59,000
15 JUN 01	7,000	66,000
15 SEP 01	5,000	71,000
15 DEC 01	1,725	72,725
TOTAL	**$72,725**	

1 The initial deposit normally consists of one half of the total administrative cost (ADM Cost) for the FMS case (unless otherwise waived) plus the initial three months of anticipated costs (by the Implementing Agency).

The Total Statement entry (i.e., $19,000 in this illustration) is the sum of the $12,000 and $7,000 individual case entries.

Remaining Quarterly Amounts

2ND 9TH 16TH	3RD 10TH 17TH	4TH 11TH 18TH	5TH 12TH 19TH	6TH 13TH	7TH 14TH
0	0	0	0	0	0
0	0	0	0	0	0
0	0	0	0		
5000	1725	0	0	0	0
0	0	0	0	0	0
0	0	0	0		
5000	1725	0	0	0	0
0	0	0	0	0	0
0	0	0	0		

The remaining quarterly amounts also cross-reference to the payment schedule in the manner described above. Note that case BN-B-CXY reflects zeros inasmuch as its final estimated payment ($12,000 for payment date 15 JUN 00) was reflected in the 1st quarterly payment entry. However, case BN-B-URK reflects 2nd and 3rd quarter forecasted payment entries corresponding to the Payment Schedule for payment dates 15 SEP 01 and 15 DEC 01, respectively.

Summary

The FMS Financial Forecast is a rather straightforward report. It reflects anticipated, future payments starting with a payment due date 90 days beyond the date reflected in Block 2 of the DD Form 645. The FMS Financial Forecast has space for 19 quarterly forecasts, any forecasted payments beyond that period are "rolled up" into the 19th quarter entry.

Chapter 9
Foreign Military Sales Reply Listing to Customer Requests for Adjustments
Purpose

The purpose of this chapter is to provide information on how to read and understand the Foreign Military Sales (FMS) Reply Listing to Customer Requests for Adjustments, hereafter referred to as the Reply Listing. The Reply Listing - like the FMS Delivery Listing (Chapter 7) and the FMS Financial Forecast (Chapter 8) - is an attachment to the DD Form 645.

General Information

Function and Format

The Reply Listing is a consolidated listing of the actions/dispositions taken in response to Supply Discrepancy Reports (SDRs) Standard Form 364. SDR dispositions are commonly referred to as "FKG transactions" inasmuch as the Document Identifier on the Reply Listing is FKG. Each FKG transaction contains many of the same data elements as the FKA/FKB transaction shown on the FMS Delivery Listing. The FKG is a management/non-financial transaction generated from an original FKA/FKB transaction. The Reply Listing is prepared in the same basic sequence as the Billing Statement and the FMS Delivery Listing. If the FMS Purchaser uses mechanized procedures, the FKG data (tape/disc) (upon request) may be mailed with the Reply Listing.

The Reply Listing is illustrated in Figure 9-1, which contains a credit transaction to FMS case BN-B-URK, Item Number 002.

Cycle

The Reply Listing is prepared quarterly along with the DD Form 645.

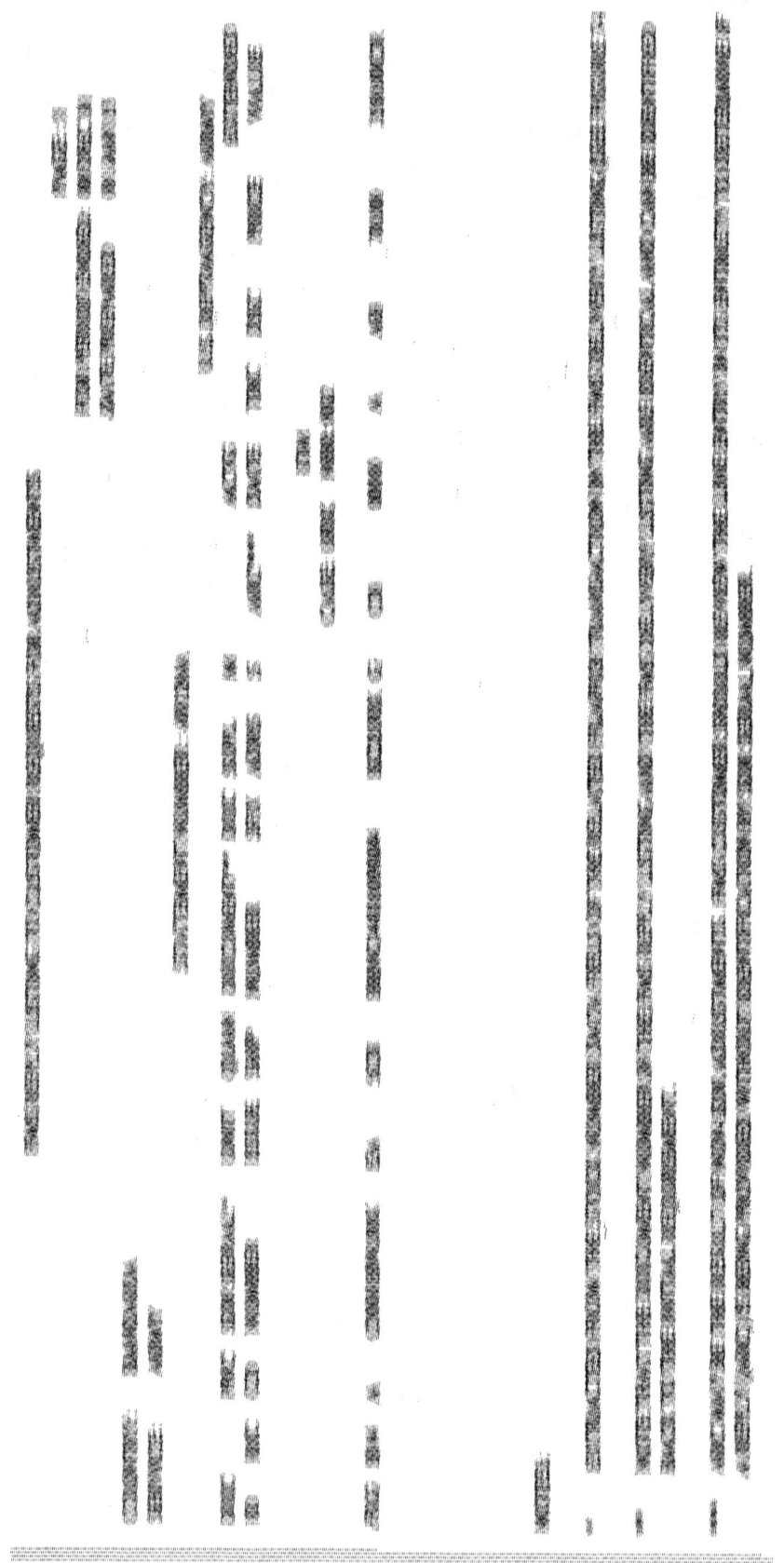

Explanation of Entries on the Reply Listing
[Reference: Figure 9-1]

Country: Bandaria Service: Army

Upper Left-Hand Portion. Self-explanatory.

Statement Number: 0012NA

Self-explanatory. Upper Center Portion

For Period Ended: 00 Dec 31 Date Prepared: 01 Jan 15   U.S. Department/agency   Army

Upper Right-Hand Portion. Self-explanatory

The header information (illustrated above) follows essentially the same pattern as the FMS Delivery Listing and no further discussion is needed.

Lower Portion

Case: URK   ITM NBR: 002

Case/Item Number. Self-explanatory. Located just above the transaction(s) data fields.

DOC		PRC
ID	RIC	CD
FKG	B14	A

The data fields at left are addressed in Chapter 7.

SDR Serial* Number C0001 BNURK

Supply Discrepancy Report (SDR). In accordance with the standard numbering system for SDRs, the 10 position SDR Serial Number consists of:

- Position 1: Alpha character to identify the preparing office in-country, e.g., "C" in this illustration.

- Positions 2-5: Four numeric characters for each FMS case for each in-country office, beginning with 0001.

- Positions 6-7: Country code, e.g., BN = Bandaria.

- Positions 8-10: Case Designator, e.g., URK.

UNIT ISSUE	QUAN SHIP	DOCUMENT** NUMBER	DOC SFX	SUPL ADRS	M S
EA	SCR	BBNC4481009004		BZ2URK	G

ARC	ACTG DATE	TBC	DSC	UNIT PRICE	EXTENDED VALUE
CB	0010	A	AB	70.00	350.00 CR

The above data fields are addressed in Chapter 7.

Summary

The FMS Reply Listing to Customer Requests for Adjustments (commonly referred to as the Reply Listing) is a consolidated listing of the actions taken in response to SDRs. SDR debit/credit transactions will appear both on the FMS Delivery Listing (as an FKA/FKB transaction) and the Reply Listing (as an FKG information transaction).

Chapter 10
Holding Accounts Statement

Purpose

The purpose of this chapter is to provide information on how to read and understand the Holding Account Statement.

General Information

Function

Cash payments are often received, for an individual foreign military sales (FMS) case, which are determined to be in excess of the final value of that particular case at time of closure. Also, there are instances where Purchaser funds are received prior to receipt of an accepted letter of offer and acceptance (LO)A or other identifying documentation; since these funds must be promptly deposited/recorded to the U.S. Treasury account for control purposes, they are deposited to the country's holding account pending identification. Unreserved funds in this account may be retained, applied to other FMS cases, or refunded at the purchaser's request, provided there are no collection delinquencies for other FMS cases.

Cycle

Transactions which effect a purchaser's holding account will be recorded on a holding account statement and forwarded with the DD Form 645, during the period in which the charge/credit occurred.

Explanation of Entries on the Holding Accounts Statement

Referring to Figure 10-1, the following comments are applicable:

If no transactions are processed during a given quarter, a holding accounts statement is prepared stating: "No activity during billing cycle."

- There is at least one, perhaps more, separate holding accounts for each Military Service of the Purchaser country. The Holding Account numbering system is explained below.

- Holding account transactions are recorded by date, detail, and amount of deposit/withdrawal. A holding accounts statement is required on a calendar quarter basis and also reflects the opening and closing balances. (Funds reserved for specific purposes/cases are not available for redistribution by the FMS customer.)

- A pseudo designator is assigned by DFAS-IN for each holding account. This three-position designator is structured as follows:

  •• The first position (numeric) describes the type of funds in the holding account.

Numeric	Type of Funds
0	Interest bearing account
1	Regular FMS payments by purchaser
2	Military Assistance Program (MAP) funds (MAP is non-refundable to FMS Customer)
3	Third country recoupments
4	Buybacks
5	Credit FMS funds (non-refundable to FMS Customer)

6	World-Wide Warehouse
7	ULO (Participating Countries) refundable to customer
8	Supply Discrepancy Report (SDR) Transportation Reimbursement

•• The second position (alpha) identifies the applicable U.S. implementing agency (IA). In some instances DFAS-IN may code the second position "Q" (or some other alpha) to either reduce the number of accounts or to satisfy some other customer country request. For a complete understanding of the coding of a specific holding account, the customer should contact DFAS-IN country manager.

•• The third position (alpha) identifies the applicable purchaser's in-country service.

Example: Holding account "1BD," illustrated in Figure 10-1, indicates regular FMS payments by Purchaser (numeric "1") applicable to a U.S. Army program/case (Alpha "B") and the purchaser's Air Force (Alpha "D").

Figure 10-1
Holding Account Bandaria Air Force 1BD for Calendar Quarter Ended 31 Dec 99

Date	Detail	Deposits	Withdrawls	Balance
30 Sep 99	Balance brought forward			$3,000.00
25 Oct 99	Funds transferred to 1 BB Holding Account		$200.00	
13 Nov 99	Credit delivery to closed Cases BN-B-CAX	$90.00		
30 Dec 99	Balance			$2,890.00

Summary

The holding accounts statement(s) is rendered on a quarterly basis. The holding account concept provides a simplified method for accounting for funds awaiting further disposition instructions. Each military service within a Purchaser country has at least one, maybe more, holding accounts.

Chapter 11
Accelerated Case Closure Suspense Account Statement
General Information

The Accelerated Case Closure Suspense Account statement depicts closed foreign military sales (FMS) cases of participating countries. These cases are "supply complete" (all ordered goods and services have been delivered or provided) and only final financial reporting is necessary.

Entries and information of the statement is basically self explanatory indicating the FMS Country, U.S. implementing agency (IA), case designator, and date the case was closed. Financial information by case is indicated in the last three columns. Reported financial obligations in the Current Quarter Activity column will adjust the Current Quarter Balance. The Current Quarter Balance then represents those outstanding financial obligations that are yet to be reported by the IA.

Defense Finance and Accounting Service-Indianapolis (DFAS-IN)
Accelerated Case Closure Suspense Account

CC CC	IA IA	CASE CASE	STATUS CHANGE	DT-CLSR	PREV QTR BAL (9909)	CURR QTR ACTIVITY	CURR QR BAL (9912)
BN	B	BGG		94150	1,480.00	0.00	1,480.00
BN	B	ZPK		98211	14,862.48	0.00	14,862.48
Subtotal By IA				**16,342.48**	**0.00**	**16,342.48**	
BN	D	GEX		98181	163,356.13	0.00	163,356.13
BN	D	GFU	*	99340	0.00	312.56	312.56
BN	D	NCO		98138	2,135.26-	0.00	2,135.26-
Subtotal By IA					**161,220.87**	**312.56**	**161,533.43**
BN	P	AQA		95263	7,771.27	7,463.57-	307.70
BN	P	BBK		98090	219,887.44	216,900.44	436,787.88
BN	P	GCC		95181	73,981.06	75,583.36-	1,602.30-
Subtotal By IA					**301,639.77**	**133,853.51**	**435,493.28**

Note: An asterisk (*) in Status Change column means the case was closed in the current quarter.
An R in the Status Change column means the case was reopened in the current quarter.

The 9909 under the PREV QTR BAL indicates the year and month of the previous quarter. (In this example, the previous quarter was September 1999). The next column indicates the net balance of all activity in the current quarter. The last column then indicates the balance, again by case, as of the end of the current quarter (December, 1999 in this example).

This page left intentionally blank

Appendix A
Foreign Military Sales Delivery Listing Document Identifiers and Headings Document Identifier Codes

General Description

Document Identifier Codes are assigned to the Delivery Listing transactions as follows:

FKA	Articles/Service Transactions (Debit)
FKB	Articles/Service Transactions Adjustments (Credit)
FKC	Administrative Costs (Debit)
FKD	Administrative Cost Adjustments (Credit)
FKE	Accessorial Costs (Debit)
FKF	Accessorial Cost Adjustments (Credit)
FKG	Reply to Customer Request for Adjustments (Debit or Credit).

This is a non-financial or management information only transaction. The actual adjustment is in the FKA/FKB transaction

Specific Explanation

Specific explanation of FMS Delivery Listing summary amounts follows:

- FKA and FKB Entries
  - •• FKA Articles/SErvice Transactions represent charges. Total of detail FKA (Debit) transactions.
  - •• FKB Articles/SErvice Transactions represent charge reversals (of FKAs). Total of detail FKB (Credit) adjustment transactions.
  - •• Net Total For Above Transactions. Total FKB (Credits) subtracted from total FKA (Debits) equals net Articles/Services extended values.
- FKC Administrative Costs and FKD Administrative Costs Administrative

If the cost is computed by DFAS-IN, the value against which the percentage (%) factor is applied, the percentage factor used, and the applied charge (under Total) are shown. The charge is shown as a debit (FKC) or credit (FKD) amount.

If actual costs have been applied, the words "Flat/Actual Charge" are shown as type of cost. FKC (Administrative Costs) transactions are applied against FKA (Articles/Services debit) transactions. FKD (Administrative Cost Adjustments) transactions are applied against FKB (credit Articles/ Service).

- FKE Accessorial Costs and FKF Accessorial Costs and KFK Accessorial Cost Adjustment

- FKE transactions are applied against FKA (Articles/Services debit) transactions, FKF transactions are applied against FKB (Articles/Services credit) transactions.

- Each accessorial cost applied is identified by Generic Code and description of cost below the FKE and FKF headings. For example:

- L1A Inland Transport CONUS L1B Ocean Transportation

- Net Total of Administrative Costs. All FKC (debit) and FKD (credit) transactions equal the net total of administrative costs.

- Net Total of Accessorial Costs. All FKE (debit) and FKF (credit) transactions equal the net total of accessorial costs.

- Total Delivery Costs. All summary costs are summed to provide the total delivery costs.

APPENDIX B

AUTHORIZED CHARGES TABLE

Generic Code (Notes 1,2,4&5)	Generic Long Title	Generic Short Title	Generic Percent
L1A	INLAND TRANSPORT CONUS	CONUS TRANS	3.75
L1B	OCEAN TRANSPORTATION	OCEAN TRANS	4.00/6.00 (Note 3)
L1C	AIR TRANSPORTATION	AIR TRANS	4.00/6.00 (Note 3)
L1D	PARCEL POST	PARCEL POST	3.75
L1E	COMMERCIAL PKG CARRIERS	COMM PKG	3.75
L1F	INLAND TRANSPORT OVERSEAS	OS INLAND	3.00
L1O	TRANSPORTATION COSTS	TRANS COSTS	0.00
L2A	PACK CRATE & HANDLE	PCH	3.50 of unit cost (Note 4) up to $50,000; 1.00 of unit cost over $50,000
L2B	CONUS PORT HANDLING	CONUS PORT	2.50
L2C	OVERSEAS PORT HANDLING	OS PORT	1.00
L4A	STORAGE (FMSO II ONLY)	STORAGE	1.50 Actual Cost
L4B	STORAGE (ALL OTHER STORAGE)	STORAGE	Actual Cost
L4O	STAGING	STAGING	3.00
L6A	ADMINISTRATIVE COSTS	ADMIN COSTS	2.5 current rate, standard items 3.00 1 Oct 77 to 1 June 99 2.00 rate prior to 1 Oct 77 5.00 nonstandard rate
N7E	MEDICAL	MEDICAL	0.00
N7F	QUARTERS	QUARTERS	Actual Cost
R9D	TDP ROYALTY FEE	TDP ROYALTY	0.00
R9H	ASSET USE CHARGE	ASSET USE	1.00 (on inventory issues)
U1O	NORMAL INVENTORY LOSS	INV LOSS	Actual Cost

NOTES:

(1) The above authorized charges appear in the FMS Delivery Listing.

(2) Generic Code LOO, which appears on the face of the DD Form 645 (in column 6), represents the summation (or roll-up) of the above L1_, L2_, and L4_ authorized charges for a given FMS Case. Generic Code L6A appears on both the face of the DD Form 645 and the FMS Delivery Listing.

(3) When two percents are shown, the first percent relates to Delivery Rate Area 1 and the second percent to Delivery Rate Area 2. Each FMS country is designated as either Delivery Rate Area 1 or 2; considering such factors as the distance/accessibility from the U.S. for shipment purposes.

(4) Standard PCH rates of 3.5/1.0 percent apply unless RIC begins with "G," then rate provided by GSA applies.

(5) DWCF Pricing Policy changed the computation of generic code L1A for CONUS transportation and generic code L2A for Packaging Creating and Handling. The following logic is now in place: Effective October 1, 1990, if Delivery Source Code equals AA, AB, AC, AD, AH, AJ, AK, CA, EF, or EG and the ship date is greater than or equal to October 1, 1990, bypass generic code L1A and generic code L2A.
Effective October 1, 1991, if Delivery Source Code equals AA, AB, AC, AD, AH, AJ, AK, CA, EF, or EG and the ship date is greater than or equal to October 1, 1991, bypass generic code L1D and generic code L1E.

[This page left intentionally blank.]

[This page left intentionally blank.]

APPENDIX C

ROUTING IDENTIFIER CODES (RIC)

[Following list represents only a few of the total. For a complete list see DoD 4000.25-1-S1]

RIC	RIC ADDRESS	RIC	RIC ADDRESS
AKZ	USA Tank Automotive and Armaments Command (TACOM) Warren MI 48397-5000	FHZ	Oklahoma City Air Logistics Center Tinker AFB OK 73145-3055
A12	USA Soldiers & Biological Chemical Command Aberdeen Proving Ground, MD.	FLZ	Warner Robins Air Logistics Center Robins AFB Warner Robins GA 31098-1640
BY7	U.S. Army Security Assistance Command New Cumberland PA 17070-5096	FPZ	San Antonio Air Logistics Center Kelly AFB San Antonio TX 78241-6425
BKZ	USA Tank Automotive and Armaments Command-Rock Island (Formerly ACALA) Rock Island IL. 61299	N21	Navy Materiel Naval Air Systems Command Washington DC 20360
B16	USA Communication & Electronics Command (CECOM) Fort Monmouth NJ 07703-5000	N23	Navy Materiel Naval Sea Systems Command Washington DC 20362
B46	USA Electronics Materiel Readiness Activity (ERMA) Warrenton VA 22186-5141	N24	Navy Materiel Naval Sea Systems Command Washington DC 20362
B56	U.S. Army Communication Security Logistics Activity (CSLA) Ft. Huachuca AZ 85613-7090	N32	Navy Material Aviation Supply Office Philadelphia PA 19111
B64	USA Aviation and Missile Command (AMCOM) Redstone Arsenal AL 35898-5239	N35	Navy Material Navy Ships Parts Control Center Mechanicsburg PA 17055
B69	USA Medical Materiel Agency (USAMMA) Frederick MD 21701-5001	N65	Navy Material Navy Inventory Control Point, Code OF Philadelphia PA 19111
CKT	Commander, TRADOC Fort Monroe VA 23651-5375	N77	Space and Warfare Systems Command Washington DC 20360
FFZ	Sacramento Air Logistics Center McClellan AFB Sacramento CA 95652-1062		
FGZ	Ogden Air Logistics Center Hill AFB Ogden UT 84056-5713		

RIC   RIC ADDRESS

RIC	RIC ADDRESS
S9F	Defense Energy Support Center Fort Belvoir VA 22060-6222
S9G	Defense Supply Center Richmond Richmond VA 23297-5000
S9I	Defense Industrial Supply Center 700 Robbins Avenue Philadelphia PA 19111
S9L	Defense Logistics Information Services Battle Creek MI 49017-3084
S9M	Defense Supply Center Philadelphia Directorate of Medical Materiel Philadelphia PA 19101
S9P	Defense Supply Center Philaeelphia Directorate of Subsistance, Philadelphia PA 19101
S9T	Defense Supply Center, Philadelphia Directorate of Clothing and Textiles Philadelphia, PA 19145

APPENDIX D
PRICE CODE (PRC CD)

CODE	MEANING
A	Actual price.
E	Estimated price. Used to report physical deliveries at an estimated price. This transaction will eventually be reversed when an actual price (PRC CD "A") is submitted by the implementing agency.
N	Used to determine if contract administration services (CAS) is to be computed on progress payments (FKP/Q) and on non-liquidating deliveries (FKA/B).

[This page intentionally left blank.]

[This page intentionally left blank.]

APPENDIX E

FOREIGN MILITARY SALES MILSTRIP DOCUMENT NUMBER
(CONSTRUCTION OF)

PURPOSE: To provide a document record under which order, performance, and billing can be traced (by means of a standard 15-digit number). The document number should be traceable from the country's requirement to the billing transaction on the Delivery Listing attached to the DD Form 645.

Position	Description of Data	Number of Digits	MILSTRIP C/C
1	Implementing Agency	1	30
2 and 3	Country Code	2	31-32
4	Customer in country (in MAPAD)	1	33
5	Delivery Term Code	1	34
6	Type of Assistance	1	35
7 thru 10	Date of Requisition (year, day, day, day)	4	36-39
11 thru 14	Serial Number of Requisition A. Numbered 0001 through 4999 if country prepared requisition. B. Numbered 5000 thru 9999 if DoD activity initiated action. C. Alphas in first position for unique identifier.	4	40-43
15	Document number suffix. Used to identify partial/split shipments (alphas/numerics).	1	44

[This page intentionally left blank.]

[This page intentionally left blank.]

APPENDIX F

IMPLEMENTING AGENCY CODES

CODE	IMPLEMENTING AGENCY
B	U.S. ARMY
C	DEFENSE INFORMATION SYSTEMS AGENCY
D	U.S. AIR FORCE
E	U.S. ARMY CORPS OF ENGINEERS
F	DEFENSE CONTRACT MANAGEMENT AGENCY
L	DEFENSE AUDIO VISUAL AGENCY (Transactions prior to 1 October 1985)
M	ARMY-G (SELPO)
P/K	U.S. NAVY/U.S. MARINE CORPS
Q	DEFENSE SECURITY COOPERATION AGENCY
R	DEFENSE LOGISTICS AGENCY
U	NATIONAL GEOPSPATIAL-INTELLIGENCE AGENCY
V	DEFENSE CONTRACT AUDIT AGENCY
W	DEFENSE ADVANCED RESEARCH PROJECTS AGENCY
X	DEFENSE FINANCE AND ACCOUNTING SERVICE DENVER ENTER, DFAS-IN
Z	DEFENSE SPECIAL WEAPONS AGENCY

[This page intentionally left blank.]

[This page intentionally left blank.]

APPENDIX G

DELIVERY TERM CODES AND RELATED CHARGES

DTC DESCRIPTIONS

DTC	APPLICABLE GENERIC CODE(S)	DESCRIPTION
A		U.S. DOD IS RESPONSIBLE FOR TRANSPORTATION FROM A DESIGNATED OVERSEAS PORT OF EMBARKATION (POE) TO A CONUS DESTINATION, AND RETURN TO A DESIGNATED OVERSEAS PORT OF DEBARKATION (POD). CUSTOMER COUNTRY IS RESPONSIBLE FOR OVERSEAS INLAND TRANSPORTATION OF MATERIAL TO OR FROM THE OVERSEAS POE/POD AND OVERSEAS PORT HANDLING.
B		U.S. DOD IS RESPONSIBLE FOR TRANSPORTATION FROM A DESIGNATED OVERSEAS PORT OF EMBARKATION (POE) TO A CONUS DESTINATION, RETURN TO A CONUS POE, AND CONUS PORT HANDLING. CUSTOMER COUNTRY IS RESPONSIBLE FOR OVERSEAS INLAND TRANSPORTATION TO THE OVERSEAS POE, OVERSEAS PORT LOADING, AND OVER-OCEAN TRANSPORTATION FROM THE CONUS POE TO ULTIMATE DESTINATION.
C		U.S. DOD IS RESPONSIBLE FOR CONUS PORT UNLOADING OF COUNTRY-ARRANGED CARRIER, TRANSPORTATION TO AND FROM A DESIGNATED CONUS DESTINATION, AND CONUS PORT LOADING OF COUNTRY ARRANGED CARRIER. CUSTOMER COUNTRY IS RESPONSIBLE FOR MOVEMENT OF MATERIEL TO AND FROM THE CONUS POD OR POE.
D		U.S. DOD IS RESPONSIBLE FOR CONUS PORT UNLOADING OF COUNTRY-ARRANGED CARRIER, TRANSPORTATION TO A CONUS DESTINATION, AND RETURN TO AN OVERSEAS DESIGNATED POD. CUSTOMER COUNTRY IS RESPONSIBLE FOR OVER-OCEAN TRANSPORTATION TO A CONUS POD, OVERSEAS PORT UNLOADING, AND OVERSEAS INLAND TRANSPORTATION TO ULTIMATE DESTINATION OF RETURNED MATERIEL.
E		CUSTOMER COUNTRY IS RESPONSIBLE FOR ALL TRANSPORTATION FROM OVERSEAS POINT OF ORIGIN TO CONUS ACTIVITY AND RETURN TO AN OVERSEAS DESTINATION.

DTC	APPLICABLE GENERIC CODE(S)	DESCRIPTION
F		U.S. DOD IS RESPONSIBLE FOR TRANSPORTATION FROM AN OVERSEAS INLAND LOCATION TO AN OVERSEAS PORT OF EMBARKATION (POE), OVERSEAS PORT HANDLING, OVERSEAS TRANSPORTATION TO A CONUS PORT OF DEBARKATION (POD), CONUS PORT HANDLING, INLAND TRANSPORTATION TO A DESIGNATED CONUS DESTINATION, AND RETURN TO AN OVERSEAS DESTINATION.
G		U.S. DOD IS RESPONSIBLE FOR OVERSEAS PORT HANDLING THROUGH AN OVERSEAS PORT OF EMBARKATION (POE), OVERSEAS TRANSPORTATION TO A CONUS PORT OF DEBARKATION (POD), CONUS PORT HANDLING, INLAND TRANSPORTATION TO A CONUS DESTINATION, RETURN TO AN OVERSEAS PORT OF DEBARKATION, AND OVERSEAS PORT HANDLING. CUSTOMER COUNTRY IS RESPONSIBLE FOR OVERSEAS INLAND TRANSPORTATION TO AND FROM THE OVERSEAS PORT.
H		CUSTOMER COUNTRY IS RESPONSIBLE FOR ALL TRANSPORTATION FROM OVERSEAS POINT OF ORIGIN TO CONUS ACTIVITY. U.S. DOD IS RESPONSIBLE FOR RETURN TRANSPORTATION FROM CONUS ACTIVITY TO CONUS POE. CUSTOMER COUNTRY IS RESPONSIBLE FOR RETURN ARRANGEMENTS, CONUS PORT HANDLING, AND ALL TRANSPORTATION TO OVERSEAS DESTINATION.
J		CUSTOMER COUNTRY IS RESPONSIBLE FOR ALL TRANSPORTATION FROM OVERSEAS POINT OF ORIGIN TO CONUS ACTIVITY. U.S. DOD IS RESPONSIBLE FOR ALL TRANSPORTATION FROM CONUS ACTIVITY TO OVERSEAS DESTINATION.
2	L1A[1]	FREE ON BOARD (FOB) DESTINATION — INLAND ORIGIN TO INLAND DESTINATION WITHIN CONUS/CANADA OR INLAND ORIGIN TO INLAND DESTINATION WITHIN THE SAME OVERSEAS GEOGRAPHICAL AREA. U.S. DOD IS RESPONSIBLE FOR INLAND TRANSPORTATION TO NAMED INLAND POINT. RECIPIENT COUNTRY IS RESPONSIBLE FOR UNLOADING AT NAMED POINT AND SUBSEQUENT ARRANGEMENTS AND COSTS.
3	L1A[1]	FAS (FREE ALONG SIDE) VESSEL CONUS/CANADA PORT OF EXIT. U.S. DOD IS RESPONSIBLE FOR TRANSPORTATION TO A POINT ALONGSIDE VESSEL. RECIPIENT COUNTRY IS RESPONSIBLE FOR LOADING ABOARD VESSEL AND SUBSEQUENT ARRANGEMENTS AND COSTS.

DTC	APPLICABLE GENERIC CODE(S)	DESCRIPTION
4		FOB ORIGIN. RECIPIENT COUNTRY IS RESPONSIBLE FOR COSTS OF CONUS INLAND TRANSPORTATION AND SUBSEQUENT ARRANGEMENTS FOR ONWARD MOVEMENT.
5	L1A[1]	FOB PORT OF EXIT. U.S. DOD IS RESPONSIBLE FOR INLAND TRANSPORTATION TO THE CONUS/CANADA PORT OF EXIT. RECIPIENT COUNTRY IS RESPONSIBLE FOR UNLOADING FROM INLAND CARRIER AT PORT OF EXIT AND SUBSEQUENT ARRANGEMENTS AND COSTS.
6	L1A[1],L2B,L1B	FOB OVERSEAS PORT OF DISCHARGE. U.S. DOD IS RESPONSIBLE FOR TRANSPORTATION FROM CONUS POINT OF ORIGIN TO AND INCLUDING OCEAN TRANSPORTATION TO THE OVERSEAS PORT OF DISCHARGE. RECIPIENT COUNTRY IS RESPONSIBLE FOR VESSEL DISCHARGE, PORT HANDING, AND SUBSEQUENT ARRANGEMENTS AND COSTS.
7	L1A[1],L2B,L1B L2C,L1F	FOB DESTINATION (NAMED INLAND POINT IN RECIPIENT COUNTY). U.S. DOD IS RESPONSIBLE FOR TRANSPOR-TATION FROM CONUS POINT OF ORIGIN TO AND INCLUDING OVER-SEAS INLAND CARRIER DELIVERY TO NAMED INLAND POINT. RECIPIENT COUNTRY IS RESPONSIBLE FOR UNLOADING AT NAMED POINT AND SUBSEQUENT ARRANGEMENTS AND COSTS.
8	L1A[1],L2B	FOB VESSEL — CONUS PORT OF EXIT. U.S. DOD IS RESPONSIBLE FOR TRANSPORTATION FROM CONUS POINT OF ORIGIN TO AND INCLUDING CARRIER UNLOADING, PORT HANDLING, AND STORAGE ABOARD VESSEL AT PORT OF EXIT. RECIPIENT COUNTRY IS RESPONSIBLE FOR OCEAN TRANSPORTATION AND SUBSEQUENT ARRANGEMENTS AND COSTS.
9	L1A[1],L2B,L1B,L2C	FOB PORT OF DISCHARGE (LANDED). U.S. DOD IS RESPONSIBLE FOR TRANSPORTATION FROM CONUS POINT OF ORIGIN TO AND INCLUDING VESSEL DISCHARGE AND PORT HANDLING AT OVERSEAS PORT OF DISCHARGE. RECIPIENT COUNTRY IS RESPONSIBLE FOR LOADING ON INLAND OVERSEAS CARRIER EQUIPMENT AND FOR SUBSEQUENT ARRANGEMENTS AND COSTS.

[1] THE CHARGE FOR L1A ON NON-DWCF ITEMS IS 3.75 PERCENT. DWCF ITEMS ARE IDENTIFIED BY DELIVERY SOURCE CODES

COMPUTING TRANSPORTATION CHARGES USING DELIVERY TERM CODE

IF THE REPORT DOES NOT CONTAIN A TRANSPORTATION BILL CODE (TBC), DFAS-DE WILL COMPUTE TRANSPORTATION AS FOLLOWS:[5]

IF DELIVERY TERM CODE (5TH POSITION OF DOCUMENT NO.) IS EQUAL TO:	APPLICABLE GENERIC CODE	PERCENTAGE BY GENERIC CODE	TOTAL
2	L1A[5] INLAND TRANSPORT CONUS	3.75	3.75
3	L1A[5] INLAND TRANSPORT CONUS	3.75	3.75
4	NOT APPLICABLE	- -	- -
5	L1A[5] INLAND TRANSPORT CONUS	3.75	3.75
6	L1A[5] INLAND TRANSPORT CONUS	3.75	
	L2B CONUS PORT HANDLING	2.5	
	L1B OCEAN TRANSPORT	4.0/6.0[4]	10.25/12.25
7	L1A[5] INLAND TRANSPORT CONUS	3.75	
	L1F INLAND TRANSPORT OVERSEAS	3.0	
	L2B CONUS PORT HANDLING	2.5	
	L1B OCEAN TRANSPORT	4.0/6.0[4]	
	L2C OVERSEAS PORT HANDLING	1.0	14.25/16.25
8	L1A[5] INLAND TRANSPORT CONUS	3.75	
	L2B CONUS PORT HANDLING	2.5	6.25
9	L1A[5] INLAND TRANSPORT CONUS	3.75	
	L2B CONUS PORT HANDLING	2.5	
	L1B OCEAN TRANSPORT	4.0/6.0[4]	
	L2C OVERSEAS PORT HANDLING	1.0	11.25/13.25
0	NO COMPUTATIONS PERFORMED		
A,B,C,D,E,F,G,H,J	NO COMPUTATIONS PERFORMED (SEE NOTE 3)		

NOTES:
1. GENERIC CODES (e.g., L1A) ARE DESCRIBED IN APPENDIX B.
2. ABOVE PERCENTAGE RATES ARE APPLIED IN FULL UP TO A UNIT PRICE OF $10,000. FOR THAT PORTION OF THE UNIT PRICE IN EXCESS OF $10,000 25% OF THE RATE IS APPLIED.
3. ACTUAL TRANSPORTATION COSTS FOR ALPHA DTCs ARE BILLED TO THE FMS CUSTOMER.
4. OCEAN TRANSPORTATION IS COMPUTED AT 4.0% or 6.0% DEPENDING ON AREA (1 or 2).
5. GENERIC CODES L1A, L1D, AND L1E WHEN USED IN CONJUNCTION WITH DELIVERY SOURCE CODES AA, AB, AC, AD, AH, AJ, AK, CA, EF, OR EG ARE NO LONGER APPLICABLE TO DWCF ASSETS.

APPENDIX H

TYPES OF ASSISTANCE CODES

T/A CODES	MEANING
3	Cash Sale for stock with Payment in Advance
4	Source of Supply not Predetermined, Payment in Advance
5	Cash Sale from procurement with Payment in Advance
6	Cash Sale from Stock with Payment on Delivery
7	Cash Sale from Procurement with 120 Day Payment
8	Cash Sale from Stock with 120 Day Payment
N	FMS Credit (Non-Repayable)
U	Foreign Military Sales Order No. I, Equity in DoD Inventory
V	FMSO No. II, Requisition from Equity with automatic replenishment action
Z	FMS Credit

APPENDIX I

JULIAN DATE CALENDAR

Day	Jan	Feb	Mar	Apr	May	Jun	July	Aug	Sept	Oct	Nov	Dec	Day
1	001	032	060	091	121	152	182	213	244	274	305	335	1
2	002	033	061	092	122	153	183	214	245	275	306	336	2
3	003	034	062	093	123	154	184	215	246	276	307	337	3
4	004	035	063	094	124	155	185	216	247	277	308	338	4
5	005	036	064	095	125	156	186	217	248	278	309	339	5
6	006	037	065	096	126	157	187	218	249	279	310	340	6
7	007	038	066	097	127	158	188	219	250	280	311	341	7
8	008	039	067	098	128	159	189	220	251	281	312	342	8
9	009	040	068	099	129	160	190	221	252	282	313	343	9
10	010	041	069	100	130	161	191	222	253	283	314	344	10
11	011	042	070	101	131	162	192	223	254	284	315	345	11
12	012	043	071	102	132	163	193	224	255	285	316	346	12
13	013	044	072	103	133	164	194	225	256	286	317	347	13
14	014	045	073	104	134	165	195	226	257	287	318	348	14
15	015	046	074	105	135	166	196	227	258	288	319	349	15
16	016	047	075	106	136	167	197	228	259	289	320	350	16
17	017	048	076	107	137	168	198	229	260	290	321	351	17
18	018	049	077	108	138	169	199	230	261	291	322	352	18
19	019	050	078	109	139	170	200	231	262	292	323	353	19
20	020	051	079	110	140	171	201	232	263	293	324	354	20
21	021	052	080	111	141	172	202	233	264	294	325	355	21
22	022	053	081	112	142	173	203	234	265	295	326	356	22
23	023	054	082	113	143	174	204	235	266	296	327	357	23
24	024	055	083	114	144	175	205	236	267	297	328	358	24
25	025	056	084	115	145	176	206	237	268	298	329	359	25
26	026	057	085	116	146	177	207	238	269	299	330	360	26
27	027	058	086	117	147	178	208	239	270	300	331	361	27
28	028	059	087	118	148	179	209	240	271	301	332	362	28
29	029		088	119	149	180	210	241	272	302	333	363	29
30	030		089	120	150	181	211	242	273	303	334	364	30
31	031		090		151		212	243		304		365	31

FOR LEAP YEAR, USE NEXT PAGE

JULIAN DATE CALENDAR

[FOR LEAP YEARS ONLY]

(USE IN 1992, 1996, 2000, ETC.)

Day	Jan	Feb	Mar	Apr	May	Jun	July	Aug	Sept	Oct	Nov	Dec	Day
1	001	032	061	092	122	153	183	214	245	275	306	336	1
2	002	033	062	093	123	154	184	215	246	276	307	337	2
3	003	034	063	094	124	155	185	216	247	277	308	338	3
4	004	035	064	095	125	156	186	217	248	278	309	339	4
5	005	036	065	096	126	157	187	218	249	279	310	340	5
6	006	037	066	097	127	158	188	219	250	280	311	341	6
7	007	038	067	098	128	159	189	220	251	281	312	342	7
8	008	039	068	099	129	160	190	221	252	282	313	343	8
9	009	040	069	100	130	161	191	222	253	283	314	344	9
10	010	041	070	101	131	162	192	223	254	284	315	345	10
11	011	042	071	102	132	163	193	224	255	285	316	346	11
12	012	043	072	103	133	164	194	225	256	286	317	347	12
13	013	044	073	104	134	165	195	226	257	287	318	348	13
14	014	045	074	105	135	166	196	227	258	288	319	349	14
15	015	046	075	106	136	167	197	228	259	289	320	350	15
16	016	047	076	107	137	168	198	229	260	290	321	351	16
17	017	048	077	108	138	169	199	230	261	291	322	352	17
18	018	049	078	109	139	170	200	231	262	292	323	353	18
19	019	050	079	110	140	171	201	232	263	293	324	354	19
20	020	051	080	111	141	172	202	233	264	294	325	355	20
21	021	052	081	112	142	173	203	234	265	295	326	356	21
22	022	053	082	113	143	174	204	235	266	296	327	357	22
23	023	054	083	114	144	175	205	236	267	297	328	358	23
24	024	055	084	115	145	176	206	237	268	298	329	359	24
25	025	056	085	116	146	177	207	238	269	299	330	360	25
26	026	057	086	117	147	178	208	239	270	300	331	361	26
27	027	058	087	118	148	179	209	240	271	301	332	362	27
28	028	059	088	119	149	180	210	241	272	302	333	363	28
29	029	060	089	120	150	181	211	242	273	303	334	364	29
30	030		090	121	151	182	212	243	274	304	335	365	30
31	031		091		152		213	244		305		366	31

APPENDIX J

UNIT OF ISSUE CODES*

Code	Term	Definition
AM	Ampoule	A small glass tube sealed by fusion after filling.
AT	Assortment	A collection of a variety of items that fall into a category or class packaged as a small unit constituting a single item of supply. Use only when the term "assortment" is a part of the item name.
AY	Assembly	A collection of parts assembled to form a complete Unit, constituting a single item of supply, e.g., hose Assembly. Use only when the term "assembly" is a Part of the item name.
BA	Ball	A spherical-shaped mass of material such as twine or thread
BE	Bale	A shaped unit of compressible materials bound with cord or metal ties and usually wrapped, e.g., paper or cloth rags.
BF	Board Foot	A unit of measure for lumber equal to the volume of a board 12" X 12" X 1".
BG	Bag	A flexible container of various sizes and shapes which is fabricated from such materials as paper, plastic or textiles. Includes "sack" and "pouch".
BK	Book	A book-like package, such as labels or tickets, fastened together along one edge, usually between protective covers.
BL	Barrel	A cylindrical container, metal or wood, with sides that bulge outward and flat ends or heads of equal diameter. Includes "keg".
BD	Bundle	A quantity of the same item tied together without compression.
BO	Bolt	A flat fold of fabric having a stiff paperboard core.
BR	Bar	A solid piece or block of various materials, with its length greater than its other dimensions, e.g., solder. Not applicable to items such as soap, beeswax, buffing compound.

Code	Term	Definition
BT	Bottle	A glass, plastic, or earthenware container of various sizes, shapes, and finishes such as jugs but excluding jars, ampoules, vials, and carboys, with a closure for retention of contents.
BX	Box	A rigid three dimensional container of various sizes and material. Includes :case", "carton", "tray", and "crate".
CA	Cartridge	Usually a tubular receptacle containing loose or pliable material and designed to permit ready insertion into an apparatus for dispensing the material. Usually associated with adhesives and sealing compounds.
CB	Carboy	A heavy duty, bottle-type container used for transportation and storage of liquids. Usually designed to be encased in a rigid protective outer container for shipment.
CD	Cubic Yard	A unit of cubic measure.
CE	Cone	A cone-shaped mass of material wound on itself such as twine or thread, wound on a conical core.
CF	Cubic Foot	A unit of cubic measure.
CK	Cake	A block of compacted or congealed matter. Applicable to such items as soap, buffing compound.
CL	Coil	An arrangement of material such as wire, rope and tubing wound in a circular shape.
CN	Can	A rigid receptacle made of fiber, metal, plastic or a combination thereof. Cans may be cylindrical or any number of irregular shapes. Restricted to items which cannot be issued in less than container quantity. Includes "pail" and "canister". Do bot use when the packaged quantity equates to a unit of measure, i.e., pint, quart, gallon, pounce or pound.
CO	Container	A general term for use only when an item is permitted to be packaged for issue in optional containers, e.g., bottle or tube for a single National Stock Number.
CY	Cylinder	A rigid, cylindrical, metal container designed as a portable container for storage and transportation of compressed gasses, generally equipped with protected valve closure and pressure relief safety device.

Code	Term	Definition
CZ	Cubic Meter	A unit of cubic measure expressed in the metric system of measurement. Limited in application to locally assigned stock numbers used in the local procurement of items such as ready-mix concrete and asphalt in oversea areas where the metric system prevails.
DR	Drum	A cylindrical container designed as an exterior pack for storing and shipping bulk materials, e.g., fuels, chemicals, powders, etc.. Drums may be made of metal, rubber, polyethylene or plywood, or fiber with wooden, metal or fiber ends.
DZ	Dozen	Twelve (12) of an item of supply.
EA	Each	A numeric quantity of one item of supply. Do not use if a more specific term applies, such as kit, set, assortment, assembly, group, sheet, plate, strip or length.
FT	Foot	Unit of linear measure sometimes expressed as "linear foot".
FV	Five	Five (5) of an item.
FY	Fifty	Fifty (50) of an item.
GL	Gallon	Unit of liquid measure.
GP	Group	A collection of related items issued as a single item of supply, e.g., test set group. Use only when the term "group" is a part of the item name.
GR	Gross	One hundred forty four (144) of an item.
HD	Hundred	One hundred (100) of an item.
HK	Hank	A loop of yarn or roping, containing definite yardage, e.g., cotton, 840 yards; worsted, 560 yards. See "skein" for comparison.
IN	Inch	Unit of linear measurement, equivalent to 1/12 of a foot and sometimes expressed as "linear inch".
JA	Jar	A rigid container having a wide mouth and often no neck, typically made of earthenware or glass. Excludes "bottle".

Code	Term	Definition
KT	Kit	A collection of related items issued as a single item of supply, such as the tools, instruments, repair parts, instruction sheets and often supplies typically carried in a box or bag. Also includes selected collections of equipment components, tools, and/or materials for the repair, overhaul or modification of equipment. Use only when the term "kit" is a part of the item name.
LB	Pound	A unit of avoirdupois weight measure equivalent to 16 ounces.
LG	Length	Term applied to items issued in fixed or specific linear measurement, without deviation. This term no longer applies to random lengths which will be expressed in definitive units of linear measure such as foot or yard. Excludes "strip".
LI	Liter	A unit of liquid measure expressed in the metric system of measurement.
MC	Thousand Cubic Feet	A unit of cubic measure expressed in one thousand (1,000) increments.
ME	Meal	The measure of food generally taken by an individual at one time.
MR	Meter	A unit of linear measure expressed in the metric system of measurement, equivalent to 39.37 inches.
MX	Thousand	One thousand (1,000) of an item.
OT	Outfit	A collection of related items issued as a single item of supply, such as the tools, instruments, materials, equipment, and/or instruction manual(s) for the practice of a trade or profession or for the carrying out of a particular project or function. Use only when the term "outfit" is a part of the item name.
OZ	Ounce	A unit of liquid or avoirdupois weight.
PD	Pad	Multiple sheets of paper that are stacked together and fastened at one end by sealing.
PG	Package	A form of protective wrapping for two or more of the same item of supply. To be used only when a unit of measure or container type term is not applicable. Includes "envelope".

Code	Term	Definition
PM	Plate	A flat piece of square or rectangular-shaped metal of uniform thickness, usually 1/4 inch or more. Use only when "plate" (Federal Supply Classes (FSGs) 9515 and 9535) is used in an item name to denote shape.
PR	Pair	Two similar corresponding items, e.g., gloves, shoes, bearings; or items integrally fabricated of two corresponding parts, e.g., trouser, shears, goggles.
PT	Pint	A unit of liquid or dry measure.
PZ	Packet	A container used for subsistence items. Use only when "food packet" is part of the item name (Federal Supply Group (FSG) 89).
QT	Quart	A unit of liquid or dry measure.
RA	Ration	The food allowance of one person for one day. Use only when "ration" (FSC 8970) is a part of the item name.
RL	Reel	A cylindrical core on which a flexible material, such as wire or cable, is wound. Usually has flanged ends.
RM	Ream	A quantity of paper varying from 480 to 516 sheets, depending upon grade.
RO	Roll	A cylindrical configuration of flexible material which has been rolled on itself such as textiles, tape, abrasive paper, photosensitive paper and film, and may utilize a core with or without flanges.
SD	Skid	A pallet-like platform consisting of a load-bearing area fastened to and resting on runner-type supports.
SE	Set	A collection of matched or related items issued as a single item of supply, i.e., tool sets, instrument sets, and matched sets. Use only when the term "set" is a part of the item name.
SF	Square Foot	A unit of square measure (area).

Code	Term	Definition
SH	Sheet	A flat piece of rectangular-shaped material of uniform thickness that is very thin in relation to its length and width, such as metal, plastic, paper and plywood. Use of this term is not limited to any group of items or FSCs. However, it will always be applied when "sheet" is used in the item name to denote shape, e.g., aluminum alloy sheet, except in items in FSC 7210.
SK	Skein	A loop of yarn 120 yards in length, usually wound on a 54-inch circular core. See "hank" for comparison.
SL	Spool	A cylindrical form with an edge or rim at each end and an axial hole for a pin or spindle on which a flexible material such as thread or wire is wound.
SO	Shot	A unit of linear measure, usually applied to anchor chain; equivalent to 15 fathoms (90 ft).
SP	Strip	A relatively narrow, flat length of material, uniform in width, such as paper, wood and metal. Use only when the term "strip" is a part of the item name.
SX	Stick	Material in a relatively long and slender, often cylindrical form for ease of application or use, e.g., abrasives.
SY	Square Yard	A unit of square measure (area).
TD	Twenty-four	Twenty-four (24) of an item.
TE	Ten	Ten (10) of an item.
TF	Twenty-five	Twenty-five (25) of an item.
TN	Ton	The equivalent of 2000 lbs. Includes short ton and net ton.
TO	Troy Ounce	A unit of troy weight measure, based on 12 ounce pound, generally applied to weights of precious metals.
TS	Thirty-six	Thirty-six (36) of an item.
TU	Tube	Normally a squeeze-type container, most commonly manufactured from a flexible type material and used in packaging toothpaste, shaving cream, and pharmaceutical products. Also applicable as form around which items are wound, such as thread. It is not applicable to mailing tube, pneumatic tube or cylindrical containers of a similar type.

Code	Term	Definition
VI	Vial	A small container which is cylindrical in shape and flat bottomed with a variety of neck finishes to accommodate any type of cap, cork or stopper.
YD	Yard	A unit of linear measure, equivalent to 3 feet and sometimes expressed as "linear yard".

* Adopted from DoD 4100.39-M, Volume 10, Chapter 4, Table 53

[This page intentionally left blank.]

J-8

[This page intentionally left blank.]

APPENDIX K

OFFER/RELEASE CODES

Based upon agreement between the DoD component and the FMS purchaser, offer/release codes are used for each line involving defense articles, as follows:

A — Freight and parcel post shipments will be released automatically by the shipping activity without advance notice (Notice of Availability).

Y — Advance notice is required before release of shipment, but shipment can be released automatically if release instructions are not received by shipping activity within 15 calendar days. Parcel post shipments will be automatically released.

Z — Advance notice is required before release of shipment. Shipping activity will follow-up on the notice of availability until release instructions are furnished. Parcel post shipments will be automatically released.

X — The U.S. Service and country representative have agreed that the:
  a. U.S. service will sponsor the shipment to a country address.
  b. Shipments are to be made to an assembly point or staging area.

The Offer/Release Code appears in column (6) of the Letter of Offer and Acceptance and card column 46 of the DD Form 1348 (MILSTRIP) requisition.

[This page intentionally left blank.]

[This page intentionally left blank.]

APPENDIX L

MODE OF SHIPMENT (MOS) CODES

Mode of Shipment Code**	Initial Method of Movement by the Shipper
*	FMS Customer Pilot Pickup
A	Motor, truckload
B	Motor, less truckload
C	Van (unpacked, or uncrated personal or government property)
D	Drive-away, truck-away, tow-away
E	Bus
F	Air Mobility Command (Channel and Special Assignment Airlift Mission)
G	Surface, parcel post
H	Air, parcel post
I	Government truck for shipments outside local delivery area
J	Air, small package carrier
K	Rail, carload includes trailer or container-on-flatcar (excluding SEAVAN)
L	Rail, less than carload includes trailer or container-on-flatcar (incl. SEAVAN)
M	Surface, Freight Forwarder
O	Organic military air (includes aircraft of foreign governments)
P	Through government bill of lading (TGBL)
Q	Commercial air freight;
R	European Distribution System (EDS)/or Pacific Distribution System (PDS)
S	Scheduled Truck Service (applies to contract carriage, guaranteed traffic routings and/or scheduled service)
T	Air freight forwarder
U	QUICKTRANS
V	Sea-van service
W	Water, river, lake, or coastal (commercial)
X	Bearer Walk through (customer pickup of materiels)
Y	Military intra-theater airlift services
Z	MSC (controlled/contract/arranged space)
2	Government watercraft, barge/lighter
3	Roll-on or roll-off (RORO) service
4	Armed Forces Courier Service (ARFCOS)
5	Surface, small package carrier
6	Military official mail (MOM)
7	Express mail
8	Pipeline
9	Local delivery by government or commercial truck including deliveries between air or water terminals and adjacent activities.

** This code is for information only. It is not used by DIFS in any systemic computes.

APPENDIX M

ADJUSTMENT REPLY CODES (ARC)

ARC	DESCRIPTION
AA	DUPLICATE BILLING AND/OR SHIPMENT RESULTED FROM RECEIPT OF DUPLICATE REQUISITION AND DUPLICATE SUPPLY ACTION.
AB	BILL REFLECTED CORRECT UNIT OR EXTENDED PRICE OF MATERIEL SHIPPED.
AE	SUPPLIER ADJUSTED TO UNIT PACK SINCE REQUISITION DID NOT PROHIBIT THIS ACTION; OR SHIPMENT MADE IN ACCORDANCE WITH INSTRUCTIONS IN REQUISTIONS.
AF	AUTHORIZED SUBSTITUTE IN LATEST SUPPLY MANUAL. REQUISITION DID NOT PRO-HIBIT SUBSTITUTIONS.
AG	CLAIMS LESS THAN $100 LOSS OR GAIN TO BE ABSORBED BY CUSTOMER.
AI	LOCAL RECORDS INDICATE PRIOR REVERSAL OF DUPLICATE CREDIT OR CHANGE IN BILL NUMBER CITED.
AJ	CREDIT WAS GRANTED AS A RESULT OF PRIOR REQUEST AND PROCESSING IN BILLING.
AK	SHIPMENT MADE VIA COMMERCIAL BILL OF LADING; U.S. GOVERNMENT NOT RESPONSIBLE FOR DAMAGED SHIPMENTS.
AL	COPIES OF SHIPPING DOCUMENT EVIDENCING PROOF OF SHIPMENT/ACCEPTANCE ARE ATTACHED.
AN	CLAIMS LESS THAN $25 LOSS OR GAIN TO BE ABSORBED BY CUSTOMER.
AO	REQUEST CANNOT BE GRANTED BECAUSE DISCREPANCY REPORT WAS NOT RECEIVED WITHIN ALLOWABLE TIMEFRAME.
AP	REQUEST CANNOT BE GRANTED BECAUSE ITEM WAS PROCURED SPECIFICALLY FOR FMS CUSTOMER. GENERAL CONDITION A2, AS SET FORTH IN ANNEX A OF THE DD FORM 1513, APPLIES.
BA	MATERIEL TO BE DISPOSED OF LOCALLY.
BB	MATERIEL TO BE RETURNED TO ACTIVITY DESIGNATED IN COLUMNS 4-6 FOR SUBSEQUENT CREDIT.
BC	HOLD UNACCEPTABLE SHIPMENT QUANTITY PENDING DISPOSITION INSTRUCTIONS TO BE SUBMITTED VIA SEPARATE COMMUNICATION.

ARC	DESCRIPTION
CA	REQUESTED CREDIT ADJUSTMENT WILL BE MADE AND BILL ISSUED. NO SUPPLY ACTION REQUIRED.
CB	REQUESTED CREDIT ADJUSTMENT WILL BE MADE AND AMENDED BILL ISSUED. NO SUPPLY ACTION REQUIRED.
CF	REQUEST GRANTED FOR FINANCIAL ADJUSTMENT NOT DIRECTLY RELATED TO MATERIEL SHIPMENT, I.E., REPAIR COSTS.
CW	CREDIT ADJUSTMENTS GRANTED ON ACCESSORIAL CHARGES -- FKF CARDS ONLY.
CX	CREDIT ADJUSTMENT GRANTED ON ADMINISTRATIVE CHARGES --FKD CARDS ONLY.
CY	DEBIT ADJUSTMENT GRANTED ON ADMINISTRATIVE CHARGES -- FKC CARDS ONLY.
CZ	DEBIT ADJUSTMENT GRANTED ON ACCESSORIAL CHARGES -- FKE CARDS ONLY.
DA	REQUEST PREVIOUSLY PROCESSED AND CREDIT GRANTED.
DB	REQUEST PREVIOUSLY PROCESSED AND CREDIT NOT GRANTED.
DD	BILLING PREVIOUSLY RENDERED.
DG	DUPLICATED BILLING WILL BE FURNISHED.
DI	LETTER OF EXPLANATION FOLLOWS.
DJ	NO RECORD OF PREVIOUS REQUEST. RESUBMIT.
DK	COPIES OF SHIPPING DOCUMENTS EVIDENCING PROOF OF SHIPMENT AND ACCEPTANCE ARE ATTACHED.
DM	REPLY DELAYED 30 DAYS. MATTER BEING INVESTIGATED.
DX	REQUEST FOR ROD CANCELLATION APPROVED.
EB	DOCUMENT NUMBER INCOMPLETE. RESUBMIT.
EC	BILL NUMBER INCOMPLETE/MISSING.
EF	RECORDS DO NOT INDICATE DUPLICATE SHIPMENT AND/OR BILLING ON BILL NUMBER CITED. IF DUPLICATION OCCURED ON ANOTHER BILL, RESUBMIT CITING BOTH BILL NUMBERS.
EI	CLAIM SHOULD BE SUPPORTED BY APPROPRIATE DOCUMENTATION. PLEASE RESUBMIT.
EJ	CLAIM SHOULD BE SUPPORTED BY CONFIRMATION OF CANCELLATION. PLEASE RESUBMIT

APPENDIX N

TRANSPORTATION BILL CODES AND RELATED CHARGES

TBC DESCRIPTIONS

(Also see note on page N-4)

TBC	APPLICABLE GENERIC CODE(S)	DESCRIPTION
A	L1D	MATERIEL MOVED BY PARCEL POST TO AN INLAND CONUS DESTINATION OR FREIGHT FORWARDER, OR TO AN OVERSEAS DESTINATION THROUGH THE ARMY/AF POSTAL SYSTEM (APO) OR INTERNATIONAL MAIL. ALL SUBSEQUENT ARRANGEMENTS ARE MADE BY THE FMS CUSTOMER.
B	L1E	MATERIEL MOVED BY COMMERCIAL PACKAGE CARRIER TO AN INLAND CONUS DESTINATION OR FREIGHT FORWARDER, WHEN ALL SUBSEQUENT ARRANGEMENTS ARE MADE BY THE FMS CUSTOMER.
C	L1A L2B L1B/L1C[1] L2C	MATERIEL MOVED BY GBL, AMC CHANNEL AIRLIFT, USAF ORGANIZATIONAL AIRLIFT, MSC SEALIFT, AND COMBINATIONS THEREOF, TO AN OVERSEAS POD IN RATE AREA ONE OR TWO INCLUDING OVERSEAS CARRIER DISCHARGE. ALL SUBSEQUENT ARRANGEMENTS ARE MADE BY THE FMS CUSTOMER.
D		ANY FORM OF MATERIEL FOR WHICH THE FMS CUSTOMER IS TOTALLY RESPONSIBLE, E.G., MATERIEL MOVED BY A COLLECT COMMERCIAL BILL OF LADING TO AN INLAND CONUS DESTINA-TION, FREE ALONG SIDE (FAS), OVERSEAS CARRIER CONUS POE, FREIGHT FORWARDER, A CONUS POE, OR AN INLAND OVERSEAS DESTINATION. ALSO USED IF TRANSPORTATION COSTS ARE NOT APPLICABLE.
E	L1A	MATERIEL MOVED BY GBL, AMC CHANNEL AIRLIFT, USAF ORGANIZATIONAL AIRLIFT, MSC SEALIFT, AND COMBINATIONS THEREOF, TO AN INLAND CONUS/CANADA DESTINATION, FREE ALONG SIDE (FAS), OVERSEAS CARRIER CONUS POE, A FREIGHT FORWARDER, OR A CONUS POE, WHEN ALL SUBSEQUENT ARRANGEMENTS ARE MADE BY THE FMS CUSTOMER.
F	L1A L1F L2B L1B/L1C[1]	MATERIAL MOVED BY GBL, AMC CHANNEL AIRLIFT, USAF ORGANIZATIONAL AIRLIFT, MSC SEALIFT AND COMBINATIONS THEREOF TO AN OVERSEAS POD IN RATE AREA ONE OR TWO WHEN OVERSEAS CARRIER DISCHARGE AND ALL SUBSEQUENT ARRANGEMENTS ARE MADE BY THE FMS CUSTOMER.

TBC	APPLICABLE GENERIC CODE(S)	DESCRIPTION
G	L1A L1F L2B L1B/L1C[1] L2C	MATERIAL MOVED BY GBL, AMC CHANNEL, AIRLIFT, USAF ORGANIZATIONAL AIRLIFT, MSC SEALIFT, ARFCOS, MOM, WEAPON SYSTEM POUCH SERVICE, AND COMBINATIONS THEREOF TO THE ULTIMATE FMS CONSIGNEE AT AN OVERSEAS INLAND DESTINATION IN RATE AREA ONE OR TWO.
H	L1A L2B	MATERIAL MOVED BY GBL, AMC CHANNEL AIRLIFT, USAF ORGANIZATIONAL AIRLIFT, MSC SEALIFT AND COMBINATIONS THEREOF TO A CONUS POE WHEN ALL ARRANGEMENTS SUBSEQUENT TO LOADING THE VESSEL ARE MADE BY THE FMS CUSTOMER.
J	L2B L1C L2C	MATERIEL MOVED BY AMC CHANNEL AIRLIFT TO AN OVERSEAS APOD IN RATE AREA ONE OR TWO WHEN THE USE OF INLAND CONUS TRANSPORTATION IS NOT REQUIRED IN EFFECTING DELIVERY TO THE CONUS POE. ALL ARRANGEMENTS SUBSEQUENT TO CARRIER DISCHARGE ARE MADE BY THE FMS CUSTOMER.
K	L1C	MATERIEL MOVED BY AMC SPECIAL ASSIGNMENT AIRLIFT MISSION (SAAM) WITHIN THE CONUS, TO AN OVERSEAS APOD OR INLAND FMS CONSIGNEE BASE, WITHIN AN OVERSEAS AREA OR BETWEEN OVERSEAS AREAS. ANY ARRANGEMENTS SUBSEQUENT TO CARRIER DISCHARGE ARE MADE BY THE FMS CUSTOMER
L		SUBSTITUTE FOR ANY OF THE OTHER STANDARD CODES WHENEVER ACTUAL TRANSPORTATION COSTS WILL BE REPORTED.
M	L40	MATERIEL MOVED BY FMS COUNTRY OWNED AIRCRAFT FROM A US/DOD STAGING AREA.
N	L1A L40	MATERIEL MOVED BY GBL OR OTHER CONUS INLAND MODE TO A CONUS STAGING/AGGREGATION AREA; STAGING/ AGGREGATION OF THE MATERIAL; AND ONWARD MOVEMENT OF THE MATERIEL TO A FREIGHT FORWARDER BY A COLLECT COMMERCIAL BILL OF LADING (CBL), BY COUNTRY-OWNED OR PROVIDED AIRCRAFT, OR BY AMC OR BY COMMERCIAL SAAM.
P	L1A L40 L1A	MATERIEL MOVED BY GBL OR OTHER CONUS INLAND MODE TO A CONUS STAGING/AGGREGATION AREA; STAGING/AGGREGATION OF THE MATERIAL; AND ONWARD MOVEMENT OF THE MATERIEL FROM THE STAGING AREA BY GBL OR OTHER PREPAID (REIMBURSABLE) CONUS TRANSPORTATION TO AN AERIAL/WATER POE, FREE ALONG SIDE (FAS) AN OVERSEAS CARRIER AT A CONUS POE, OR TO ANY OTHER CONUS DESTINATION, WHEN ALL SUBSEQUENT ARRANGEMENTS ARE MADE BY THE FMS CUSTOMER

TBC	APPLICABLE GENERIC CODE(S)	DESCRIPTION
Q	L1A L40 L1A L2B L1B/L1C[1]	MATERIEL MOVED BY GBL OR OTHER CONUS INLAND MODE TO A CONUS STAGING/AGGREGATION AREA; STAGING/AGGREGA-TION OF THE MATERIAL; AND OUT MOVEMENT OF THE MATERIEL FROM THE STAGING AREA BY GBL OR OTHER PREPAID (REIMBURSABLE) CONUS TRANSPORTATION TO AN AERIAL/WATER POE, PORT HANDLING OF THE MATERIEL; AND ONWARD MOVEMENT BY GBL, AMC CHANNEL AIRLIFT, USAF ORGANIZATIONAL AIRCRAFT, MSC SEALIFT, AND/OR COMBINA-TIONS THEREOF TO AN OVERSEAS POD IN RATE AREA ONE OR TWO, WHEN OVERSEAS CARRIER DISCHARGE AND ALL SUBSE-QUENT ARRANGEMENTS ARE MADE BY THE FMS CUSTOMER.
R	L1A L40 L1A L2B L1B/L1C[1] L2C L1F	MATERIEL MOVED BY GBL OR OTHER CONUS INLAND MODE TO A CONUS STAGING/AGGREGATION AREA; STAGING/AGGREGA-TION OF THE MATERIAL; AND OUT MOVEMENT OF THE MATERIEL FROM THE STAGING AREA BY GBL OR OTHER PREPAID (REIMBURSABLE) CONUS TRANSPORTATION TO AN AERIAL/WATER POE, PORT HANDLING OF THE MATERIEL; AND ONWARD MOVEMENT BY GBL, AMC CHANNEL AIRLIFT, USAF ORGANIZATIONAL AIRCRAFT, MSC SEALIFT, AND/OR COMBINA-TIONS THEREOF TO AN OVERSEAS POD IN RATE AREA ONE OR TWO; OVERSEAS PORT HANDLING OF THE MATERIEL, AND ONWARD OVERSEAS INLAND MOVEMENT TO THE ULTIMATE FMS CONSIGNEE AT AN OVERSEAS INLAND DESTINATION IN RATE AREA ONE OR TWO.
S	L1A L40 L1A L2B	MATERIEL MOVED BY GBL OR OTHER CONUS INLAND MODE TO A CONUS STAGING/AGGREGATION AREA; STAGING/AGGREGATION OF THE MATERIAL; OUT MOVEMENT OF THE MATERIEL FROM THE STAGING AREA BY GBL OR OTHER PREPAID (REIMBURSABLE) CONUS TRANSPORTATION TO AN AERIAL/WATER POE; AND LOADING OF THE MATERIEL ABOARD A COUNTRY OWNED OR PROVIDED AIRCRAFT/VESSEL, WHEN ALL ARRANGEMENTS SUBSEQUENT TO LOADING THE AIRCRAFT/ VESSEL ARE MADE BY THE FMS CUSTOMER
U	L1D/L1E L2B	MATERIEL MOVED BY PARCEL POST OR COMMERCIAL PACKAGE CARRIER TO A CONUS POD WHEN ALL ARRANGEMENTS SUBSE-QUENT TO LOADING THE VESSEL ARE MADE BY THE FMS CUSTO-MER. (MODE OF SHIPMENT DETERMINES WHETHER PARCEL POST OR COMMERCIAL PACKAGE CARRIER USED.)
V	L1D/L1E L2B L1B/ L1C[1] L2C	MATERIEL MOVED BY PARCEL POST OR COMMERCIAL PACKAGE CARRIER TO AN OVERSEAS POD IN RATE AREAS ONE OR TWO, INCLUDING OVERSEAS CARRIER DISCHARGE WHEN SUBSEQUENT ARRANGEMENTS ARE MADE BY THE FMS CUSTOMER. (MODE OF SHIPMENT DETERMINES WHETHER PARCEL POST OR COMMERCIAL PACKAGE CARRIER USED.)

TBC	APPLICABLE GENERIC CODE(S)	DESCRIPTION
W	N/A	COST TAKEN FROM LOOKUP TABLE.
X	L1D/L1E L2B L1B/L1C[1]	MATERIEL MOVED BY PARCEL POST OR COMMERCIAL PACKAGE CARRIER TO AN OVERSEAS POD IN RATE AREAS ONE OR TWO, WHEN OVERSEAS CARRIER DISCHARGE AND SUBSEQUENT ARRANGEMENTS ARE MADE BY THE FMS CUSTOMER. (MODE OF SHIPMENT DETERMINES WHETHER PARCEL POST OR COMMERCIAL PACKAGE CARRIER USED.)
Y	L1D/L1E L2B L1B/L1C[1] L2C L1F	MATERIEL MOVED BY PARCEL POST OR COMMERCIAL PACKAGE CARRIER TO THE ULTIMATE FMS CONSIGNEE AT AN OVERSEAS INLAND DESTINATION IN RATE AREAS ONE OR TWO. (MODE OF SHIPMENT DETERMINES WHETHER PARCEL POST OR COMMERCIAL PACKAGE CARRIER USED.)
Z	L1A	MATERIEL MOVED WITHIN THE CONUS BY COMMERCIAL CARRIER WITH A PUBLISHED MAXIMUM RATE OF $25.00 (FOR EXAMPLE, AS PUBLISHED BY UNITED PARCEL SERVICES).

NOTE: Generic Codes L1A, L1D, and L1E when used in conjunction with Delivery Source Codes AA, AB, AC, AD, AH, AJ, AK, CA, EF, or EG are no longer applicable to DWCF assets.

1. WHEN THE TRANSPORTATION COMPUTE IS BASED ON A TBC AND THE PORT OF EXIT (POE) IS EQUAL TO AIR, "A," DFAS-DE WILL COMPUTE L1C; IF THE POE IS OTHER THAN "A," DFAS-DE WILL COMPUTE L1B

TBC RELATED CHARGES

TBC	APPLICABLE GENERIC CODE	PERCENTAGE BY GENERIC CODE [3]	TOTAL
A	L1D PARCEL POST	3.75[3]	3.75
B	L1E COMMERCIAL PKG CARRIERS	3.75[3]	3.75
C	L1A INLAND TRANSPORT CONUS	3.75	
	L2B CONUS PORT HANDLING	2.5	
	L1B/L1C OCEAN/AIR TRANSPORTATION	4.0/6.0[1,4]	
	L2C OVERSEAS PORT HANDLING	1.0	11.25/13.25
D	N/A	0.0	0.0
E	L1A INLAND TRANSPORT CONUS	3.75	3.75
F	L1A INLAND TRANSPORT CONUS	3.75	
	L2B CONUS PORT HANDLING	2.5	
	L1B/L1C OCEAN/AIR TRANSPORTATION	4.0/6.0[1,4]	10.25/12.25
G	L1A INLAND TRANSPORT CONUS	3.75	
	L1F INLAND TRANSPORT OVERSEAS	3.0	
	L2B CONUS PORT HANDLING	2.5	
	L1B/L1C OCEAN/AIR TRANSPORTATION	4.0/6.0[1,4]	
	L2C OVERSEAS PORT HANDLING	1.0	14.25/16.25
H	L1A INLAND TRANSPORT CONUS	3.75	
	L2B CONUS PORT HANDLING	2.5	6.25
J	L2B CONUS PORT HANDLING	2.5	
	L1C AIR TRANSPORTATION	4.0/6.0[1,4]	
	L2C OVERSEAS PORT HANDLING	1.0	7.5/9.5
K	L1C AIR TRANSPORTATION	N/A	Actual amount billed by AMC
L	AS APPLICABLE	N/A	Actual amount computed by shipper
M	L40 STAGING	3.0[3]	3.0
N	L1A INLAND TRANSPORT CONUS	3.75	
	L4O STAGING	3.0[3]	6.75
P	L1A INLAND TRANSPORT CONUS	3.75	
	L4O STAGING	3.0[3]	
	L1A INLAND TRANSPORT CONUS	3.75	10.5
Q	L1A INLAND TRANSPORT CONUS	3.75	
	L4O STAGING	3.0[3]	
	L1A INLAND TRANSPORT CONUS	3.75	
	L2B CONUS PORT HANDLING	2.5	
	L1B/L1C OCEAN/AIR TRANSPORTATION	4.0/6.0[1,4]	17.0/19.0

TBC	APPLICABLE GENERIC CODE	PERCENTAGE BY GENERIC CODE [3]	TOTAL
R	L1A INLAND TRANSPORT CONUS	3.75	
	L4O STAGING	3.0[3]	
	L1A INLAND TRANSPORT CONUS	3.75	
	L2B CONUS PORT HANDLING	2.5	
	L1B/L1C OCEAN/AIR TRANSPORTATION	4.0/6.0[1,4]	
	L2C OVERSEAS PORT HANDLING	1.0	
	L1F INLAND TRANSPORT OVERSEAS	3.0	21.0/23.0
S	L1A INLAND TRANSPORT CONUS	3.75	
	L4O STAGING	3.0[3]	
	L1A INLAND TRANSPORT CONUS	3.75	
	L2B CONUS PORT HANDLING	2.5	13.0
U	L1D/L1E PARCEL POST/COMM PKG	3.75[3]	
	L2D CONUS PORT HANDLING	2.5	6.25
V	L1D/L1E PARCEL POST/COMM PKG	3.75[3]	
	L2B CONUS PORT HANDLING	2.5	
	L1B/L1C OCEAN/AIR TRANSPORTATION	4.0/6.0[1,4]	
	L2C OVERSEAS PORT HANDLING	1.0	11.25/13.25
W	[Only those National Stock Numbers listed in Appendix F, DOD 5105.38-M, will be assessed the transportation charge listed in that table.]		
X	L1D/L1E PARCEL POST/COMM PKG	3.75[3]	
	L2B CONUS PORT HANDLING	2.5	
	L1B/L1C OCEAN/AIR TRANSPORTATION	4.0/6.0[1,4]	10.25/12.25
Y	L1D/L1E PARCEL POST/COMM PKG	3.75[3]	
	L2B CONUS PORT HANDLING	2.5	
	L1B/L1C OCEAN/AIR TRANSPORTATION	4.0/6.0[1,4]	
	L2C OVERSEAS PORT HANDLING	1.0	
	L1F INLAND TRANSPORT OVERSEAS	3.0	14.25/16.25
Z	L1A. Material moved within the CONUS by commercial carrier with a published maximum rate of $25.00 (for example, as published by United Parcel Service).		$25.00/limit

1 OCEAN OR AIR TRANSPORTATION IS COMPUTED AT 4.0% OR 6.0% DEPENDING ON THE DELIVERY AREA (1 OR 2).

2 ABOVE PERCENTAGE RATES ARE APPLIED IN FULL UP TO A UNIT COST OF $10,000. FOR THAT PORTION OF THE UNIT COST IN EXCESS OF $10,000, 25% OF THE RATE IS APPLIED.

3 REIMBURSED TO SHIPPING DEPOT SHOWN ON THE DELIVERY TRANSACTIONS.

4 WHEN THE TRANSPORTATION COMPUTE IS BASED ON A TBC AND THE PORT OF EXIT (POE) IS EQUAL TO AIR "A," DFAS-DE WILL COMPUTE L1C; IF THE POE IS OTHER THAN "A," DFAS-DE WILL COMPUTE L1B

NOTE: Generic Codes L1A, L1D, and L1E when used in conjunction with Delivery Source Codes AA, AB, AC, AD, AH, AJ, AK, CA, EF, or EG are no longer applicable to DWCF assets.

TRANSPORTATION AREA RATE TABLE

COUNTRY	RATE	COUNTRY	RATE
AFGHANISTAN	2	GABON	2
ALBANIA	1	GAMBIA	2
ALGERIA	1	GERMANY	1
ANDORA	1	GHANA	2
ANTIGUA	1	GREECE	1
ARGENTINA	2	GRENADA	1
AUSTRALIA	2	GUATEMALA	1
AUSTRIA	1	GUINEA	2
BAHRAIN	2	GUINEA-BISSAU	2
BANGLADESH	2	HAITI	1
BARBADOS	1	HONDURAS	1
BELGIUM	1	HUNGARY	1
BELIZE	1	ICELAND	2
BENIN	1	INDIA	2
BERMUDA	1	INDONESIA	2
BOLIVIA	2	IRELAND	1
BOLIVIA D1 INT'L NARCOTICS CONTROL	2	ISRAEL	1
BOTSWANA	2	ITALY	1
BRAZIL	2	IVORY COAST	2
BRUNEI	2	JAMAICA	1
BULGARIA	1	JAPAN	2
MYANMAR	2	JORDAN	2
CAMEROON	2	KENYA	2
CANADA	1	KOREA	2
CAPE VERDE	2	KUWAIT	2
CENTRAL AFRICAN REPUBLIC	2	LATVIA	1
CHAD	2	LEBANON	1
CHILE	2	LIBERIA	2
CHINA	2	LICHTENSTEIN	1
COLOMBIA	1	LITHUANIA	1
COLOMBIA D5 INT'L NARCOTICS CONROL	1	LUXEMBOURG	1
COSTA RICA	1	MADAGASCAR	2
CUBA	1	MALAWI	2
CYPRUS	1	MALAYSIA	2
CZECH&SLOVAK	1	MALI	2
DENMARK	1	MALTA	1
DJIBOUTI	2	MAURITANIA	2
DOMINICA ROSEAU	1	MAURITIUS	2
DOMINICAN REPUBLIC	1	MEXICO	1
ECUADOR	2	MOROCCO	1
EGYPT	1	NEPAL	2
EL SALVADOR	1	NETHERLANDS	1
EQUATORIAL GUINEA	2	NEW ZEALAND	2
ESTONIA	1	NICARAGUA	1
ETHIOPIA	2	NIGER	2
EUROPE	1	NIGERIA	2
FIJI	2	NORWAY	1
FINLAND	1	OMAN	2
FRANCE	1	PAKISTAN	2

TRANSPORTATION AREA RATE TABLE

COUNTRY	RATE	COUNTRY	RATE
PANAMA	1	ST CHRISTOPHER-NEVIS	1
PAPUA-NEW GUINEA	2	ST LUCIA	1
PARAGUAY	2	ST VINCENT	1
PERU	2	SUDAN	2
PERU D3 INT'L NARCOTICS CONTROL	2	SURINAME	1
PHILIPPINES	2	SWEDEN	1
POLAND	1	SWITZERLAND	1
PORTUGAL	1	TAIWAN	2
QATAR	2	THAILAND	2
ROMANIA	1	TOGO	2
RUSSIA	1	TRINIDAD	1
RWANDA	2	TUNISIA	1
R/4-ASIA PACIFIC REGION	2	TURKEY	1
SAO TOME & PRINCIPE	2	UKRAINE	1
SAUDI ARABIA	2	UNITED ARAB EMIRATES	2
SENEGAL	2	UNITED KINGDOM	1
SEYCHELLES	2	URUGUAY	2
SIERRA LEONE	2	VENEZUELA	1
SINGAPORE	2	YEMEN	2
SOMALIA	2	YUGOSLAVIA	1
SPAIN	1	ZAIRE	2
SRI LANKA	2		

INTERNATIONAL ORGANIZATIONS

ORGANIZATION	RATE
AFRICA REGION	2
AMERICAN REPUBLIC REGION	1
EAST ASIA/PACIFIC REGION	2
EUROPE REGION	1
EUROPEAN SPACE AGENCY	1
F-16 BELGIUM	1
F-16 DENMARK	1
F-16 NETHERLANDS	1
F-16 NORWAY	1
F-16 ISRAEL (SME)	1
F-18 AUSTRALIA	2
NATO	1
Headquarters	1
Airborne Early Warning & Control Operations & Support Budget (O&S)	1
Prog Mgt Ofc (NAPMO)	1
Commun & Info Sys Agency (NACISA)	1
EURO Fighter Acft Dev, Prod & Log Mgt Agency (NEFMA)	1
HAWK Prod & Log Org (NHPLO)	1
Multi-Role Combat Acft (MRCA) Dev & Prod Agency (NAMMA)	1
NAMSA, F-104	1
NAMSA, General, Nike	1
NAMSA, General, Other	1

INTERNATIONAL ORGANIZATIONS (continued)

ORGANIZATION	RATE
NATO (continued)	
NAMSA, HAWK	1
NAMSA, M60 Series Tank	1
NAMSA, Nike Training Center (NNTC)	1
NAMSA, Patriot	1
NAMSA, Weapons	1
Supr Allied Cdr, Atlantic (SACLANT)	1
Southern Region Signal & Communication	1
Supreme HQ, Allied Powers, Europe (SHAPE)	1
NEAR EAST & SOUTHERN ASIA (NESA) REGION	2
ORGANIZATION OF AMERICAN STATES	1
UNITED NATIONS	1

NOTE: This table does not necessarily indicate that sales/shipments are being made to all countries/organizations listed.

[This page intentionally left blank.]

[This page intentionally left blank.]

APPENDIX O

DELIVERY SOURCE CODES AND
ACCESSORIAL COMPUTATION MATRIX

	DSC 1st Position	DSC 2nd Position
Sale of DoD Articles Under Section 21		
• Working Capital Funds nonexcess items, including technical data packages and publications, from inventory		
1. Matured FMSO	A	A
2. Other than matured FMSO	A	B
• Working Capital Funds nonexcess items diverted from procurement initiated to maintain stock fund inventory		
1. Matured FMSO	A	C
2. Other than matured FMSO	A	D
• Procurement funded item (including technical data packages and publications) from inventory that requires replacement.	A	E
• Procurement funded item (including technical data packages and publications) from inventory that do not require replacement.	A	G
• Excess Working Capital Funds Item		
1. Matured FMSO	A	H
2. Other than matured FMSO	A	J
• Excess Procurement Funded Item from Inventory PC&H computed on original acquisition cost of item and submitted by IA.	A	K
• Any item other than Defense Working Capital Fund Items sold from inventory which are not subject to normal PC&H charge. This code shall only be used when the case contains a transportation line or a packing, crating and handling line, or a pricing exception has been granted by the Office of the Under Secretary of Defense (Comptroller).	A	L

APPENDIX O

DELIVERY SOURCE CODES (DSC) AND
ACCESSORIAL COMPUTATION MATRIX

	DSC 1st Position	DSC 2nd Position
Performance of DoD Services Under Section 21 or 22		
• Training Course		
1. DoD	B	A
2. Contractor	B	B
• Repair or replace customer equipment. IAs shall include actual PC&H and transportation for materiel consumed in overhaul in reported costs	B	C
• Other DoD services. Does not include "above-the-line" transportation or "above-the-line" PCH&T associated with the repair or modification of customer-owned equipment that is included in repair cost reported using code "BC".	B	D
• Storage charge (for other than FMSO cases)	B	E
• Leases		
1. Depreciation	B	F
2. LOA sales of articles and services in connection with lease, prior to, during, or after lease period (includes transportation, PC&H, refurbishment)	B	G
• Actual PC&H charge. This report must accompany delivery transactions for items sold from inventory with DSCs AK and AL	B	H
• "Above-the-line" transportation to FMS customers that is included in management line(s). Code includes "high-flight" or special airlift. Code does not include "above-the-line" transportation cost that is included in the selling price of an item or service.	B	T
Unique FMSO Charges		
• FMSO I materiel used to support system obsolete to DoD use (buy out of unique repair parts to support obsolete end-items).	C	A

DELIVERY SOURCE CODES (DSC) AND
ACCESSORIAL COMPUTATION MATRIX

	DSC 1st Position	DSC 2nd Position
• Annual inventory maintenance and storage cost. Charge annually on current FMSO II case. The FMSO I case manager shall input the FMS detail delivery transaction. There is no annual charge for Working Capital Fund items for CLSSAs, as the Working Capital Fund standard stabilized) price recoups all costs.	C	B
• Normal inventory loss on procurement appropriation funded secondary items (physical inventory gain or loss, expiring shelf life, and damage of stored parts). Charge assessed annually on current FMSO II case. The FMSO I case manager shall input the delivery transactions.	C	C
• Cash advances for on-hand portion of FMSO I.	C	D

Procurement for FMS Customers Under Section 22

Codes DE through DL represent Work-in-Process (WIP) transactions. The break-down of these charges provides audit trail visibility for pricing purposes. The DFAS-DE shall treat them as progress payments and report them as such to the FMS customer. These charges shall be liquidated by one of the contract delivery codes DA through DD in combination with reimbursement code "N".

	DSC 1st Position	DSC 2nd Position
1. Contractor Services (other than training)	D	A
2. DWCF item, TDP, or publications from contractor	D	B
3. Procurement appropriation funded secondary item from contractor	D	C
4. Procurement funded principal or major item from contractor	D	D
5. Progress payment to contractor	D	E
6. DoD services in support of procurement. (This code was applied to actual CAS hours prior to establishment of the charge. It now applies to other than CAS services).	D	F
7. Nonrecurring Cost Recoupment Charge (R&D and Production).	D	G
8. Government-furnished materiel (GFM) a. Shipped from inventory	D	J

	DSC 1st Position	DSC 2nd Position
b. Shipped from another contractor	D	K
c. PCH&T applicable to procurement funded GFM	D	L
9. Contractor effort in overseas locations which is is supported by an FMS management line rather than through normal CAS effort.	D	X

	DSC 1st Position	DSC 2nd Position
Miscellaneous Charges		
1. Royalty Charge (USG TDP)	E	E
2. Other federal agency shipment		
a. From stock	E	F
b. From contractor	E	G
3. NATO POL	E	H
4. Redistributable MAP property	E	J
5. Collection on nonrecurring production charge or license fee on behalf of a third country	E	K
6. Prepositioning costs	E	L
7. Interest on arrearage computed in accordance with Volume 6, Chapter 12, DoD 7000.14-R, Volume 15. (Collecting and Reporting of Foreign Indebtedness Within the Department of Defense. Restricted to use by the DFAS-DE)	E	M
8. Nonrecurring cost recoupment charges	E	N

Special Defense Acquisition Fund

The SDAF shall use Delivery Source Codes as follows:

	DSC 1st Position	DSC 2nd Position
• This code shall be used for SDAF sales of items originally purchased from DoD DWCF inventories.	S	A
• This code shall be used for SDAF sales of items originally purchased from DoD inventories other than Defense Business Operations Fund.	S	B
• This code shall be used for SDAF sales of items procured from contractors for the fund.	S	D
• This code shall be used for SDAF sales of items procured from contractors and shipped directly from the contractor to the FMS customer, providing there is no requirement for any special packing, crating, or handling.	S	E

- **ACCESSORIAL COMPUTATION MATRIX**
  [N = No; Y = Yes]

DSC	CONTRACT ADMINISTRATION[1]	PCH[2]	ADMIN[4]	TRANSPORTATION PARCEL POST[5,6]
AA	N	N	Y	Y
AB	N	N	Y	Y
AC	N	N	Y	Y
AD	N	N	Y	Y
AE	N	Y	Y	Y
AG	N	Y	Y	Y
AH	N	N	Y	Y
AJ	N	N	Y	Y
AK	N	N	Y	Y
AL	N	N	Y	Y
BA	N	N	Y	N
BB	Y	N	Y	N
BC	N	N[3]	Y	N[3]
BD	N	N	Y	N
BE	N	N	Y	N
BF	N	N	N	N
BG	N	N	Y	N
BH	N	N	Y	N
BT	N	N	Y	N
CA	N	N	N	Y
CB	N	N	Y	N
CC	N	N	Y	N
CD	N	N	N	N
DA	Y	N	Y	N
DB	Y	N	Y	Y
DC	Y	N	Y	Y
DD	Y	N	Y	Y
DE	Y	N	Y	N
DF	N	N	Y	N
DG	N	N	Y	N
DJ	N	N	Y	N
DK	Y	N	Y	N
DL	N	N	Y	N
DX	N	N	Y	N
EE	N	N	Y	N
EF	N	Y	Y	Y

- ## ACCESSORIAL COMPUTATION MATRIX
  ### [N = No; Y = Yes]

DSC	CONTRACT ADMINISTRATION[1]	PCH[2]	ADMIN[4]	TRANSPORTATION PARCEL POST[5,6]
EG	N	N	Y	Y
EH	N	N	Y	N
EJ	N	Y	Y	Y
EK	N	N	Y	N
EL	N	N	N	N
EM	N	N	N	N
EN	N	N	Y	N
SA	N	N	Y	Y
SB	N	Y	Y	Y
SD	N	Y	Y	Y
SE	N	N	Y	Y

[1] DFAS-DE will compute CAS (unless statutory waiver of contact administration has been made) if price code is "N" and reimbursement code is other than "N."

[2] PC&H does not apply to stock fund/Defense Working Capital Fund items with ship dates from 1 October1990.

[3] Included in actual or estimated actual repair cost.

[4] Administrative costs will be computed unless administrative costs have been waived pursuant to statute.

[5] Transportation costs will be computed using the Transportation Bill Code in position 59 of the Delivery Transaction. However, if this position is blank, transportation costs will be computed using the Delivery Term Code (position 34).

[6] The Inland CONUS Transportation charge of 3.75% does not apply to Defense Working Capital Fund shipments with shipping dates subsequent to 1 October 1990. Computation for Generic Codes L1D and L1E for DWCF items was discontinued on items with shipping dates from 1 October 1991. See DoD 7000.14-R for additional information regarding transportation charges.

Appendix P

Part 1
Abbreviations and Acronyms

	A

AAA	Army Audit Agency or Authorization Accounting Activity (U.S. Navy)
AAC	Acqusition Advice Code
ACC	Air Combat Command (USAF)
ACCT	Account
ACO	Administrative Contracting Officer
AECA	Arms Export Control Act
AFAA	Air Force Audit Agency
AFIT	Air Force Institute of Technology
AFM	Air Force Manual
AFMC	Air Force Materiel Command
AFR	Air Force Regulation
AFSAT	Air Force Security Assistance Training (Group)
AFSC	Armed Forces Staff College
AIS	Automated Information System (Defense Automated Addressing System)
ALC	Air Logistics Center (under AFMC) or American Language Course
AMARC	Aerospace Maintenance and Regeneration Center
AMC	Army Materiel Command or Air Mobility Command (USAF)
AMCOM	Aviation Missile Command (U.S.Army)
AMDF	Army Master Data File
AMEMB	American Embassy
AMRAAM	Advanced Medium Range Air-to-Air Missile
AO	Action Officer
AOG	Aircraft on the Ground (Grounded Aircraft)
AOR	Area of Responsibility
APL	Allowance Parts List (U.S. Navy)
APOD	Aerial Port of Debarkation (Delivery)
APOE	Aerial Port of Embarkation
AR	Army Regulation
ARC	Adjustment Reply Code

ASD	Aeronautical Systems Division (USAF/AFMC) or Assistant Secretary of Defense
ASD(C)	Assistant Secretary of Defense (Comptroller)
ASD(ISA)	Assistant Secretary of Defense (International Security Affairs)
ASL	Authorized Supply Level (U.S. Army)
ASN	Assistant Secretary of the Navy
ASO	Aviation Supply Office (U.S. Navy)
ATC	Air Training Command (U.S. Air Force)
ATMG	Arms Transfer Management Group
AWACS	Airborne Warning and Control System
AWC	Air War College or Army War College

B

B/L	Bill of Lading
BA	Budget Authorization
BAC	Billing Advice Code
BO	Back Order (Supply) or Blanket Order (FMS Case)
BOE	Blanket Open End (FMS Case)
BY	Budget Year or Base Year

C

C3CM	Command,Control, and Communications Countermeasures
C3I	Command, Control, Communications, and Intelligence
CA	Contract Authority
CAD/PAD	Cartridge Actuated Device/Propellant Actuated Device
CAO	Contract Administration Office or Case Administering Office
CAS	Contract Administrative Services or Cost Accounting Standard
CASEUR	Contract Administration Service -Europe (U.S.Air Force)
CAT	Conventional Arms Transfers
CBL	Commercial Bill of Lading
CC	Country Code
CCBL	Collect Commercial Bill of Lading
CCCI	Case Closure Certificate Inventory
CCM	Central Case Manager
CD	Case Designator

CDO	Country Desk Officer
CECOM	Communications Electronics Command (U.S. Army)
CET	Civilian Engineering Team
CETS	Contractor Engineering Technical Services
CETSP	Contractor Engineering Technical Services Program
CFE	Contractor Furnished Equipment
CFM	Contractor Furnished Materiel
CFMW	Case Financial Management Worksheet
CFS	Contract Field Services
CFSP	Contractor Field Services Personnel
CGSC	Command and General Staff College (U.S. Army)
CGSEL	Common Ground Support Equipment List
CI	Case Identifier
CIP	Component Improvement Program (Engines)
CIS	Contractor Initial Support or Commonwealth of Independent States
CISIL	Centralized Integrated System International Logistics (U.S. Army)
CJCS	Chairman, Joint Chiefs of Staff
CLA	Cross Leveling Agreement
CLO	Country Liaison Officer (Foreign Country Representative)
CLSSA	Cooperative Logistics Supply Support Arrangement
CM	Configuration Management, Case Manager
CMCRL	Consolidated Master Cross Reference List
CMCS	Case Management Control System
CMI	Classified Military Information
CMS	Contractor Maintenance Services
CN	Counter Narcotics
CNATRA	Chief of Naval Air Training (U.S. Navy)
CNET	Chief of Naval Education and Training
CNO	Chief of Naval Operations
CNTECHTRA	Chief of Naval Technical Training (U.S. Navy)
CO	Contracting Officer or Change Order or Commanding Officer
COCO	Contractor Owned/Contractor Operated (Facilities)
COCP	Customer Order Control Point (U.S. Army)
COE	Corps of Engineers (U.S. Army)
COG	Navy Material Cognizance Symbol

COGARD	U.S. Coast Guard
COM	Chief of Mission (U.S. Embassy)
COMNAVSUP	Commander, Naval Supply Systems Command
COMSEC	Communications Security (NSA)
CONUS	Continental United States
COOPLOG	Cooperative Logistics
COR	Contracting Officer's Representative
CPM	Country Program Manager
CSP	Concurrent (initial) Spare Parts
CSS	Contractor Support Services
CWA	Cash with Acceptance
CY	Calendar Year or Current Year

D

DA	Department of the Army
DAAS	Defense Automatic Addressing System
DAASC	Defense Automatic Addressing System Center
DAC	Defense Acquisition Circular or Department of the Army Civilian
DAF	Department of the Air Force
DAO	Defense Attaché Office or Disbursing Accounting Office
DARPA	Defense Advanced Research Projects Agency
DASD(ISA)	Deputy Assistant Secretary of Defense (International Security Affairs)
DASD(ISP)	Deputy Assistant Secretary of Defense (International Security Policy)
DATT	Defense Attaché
DCA	Defense Cooperation in Armaments
DCAA	Defense Contract Audit Agency
DCM	Deputy Chief of Mission (U.S. Embassy)
DCMAO	Defense Contract Management Area Operation
DCMD	Defense Contract Management District
DCN	Document Control Number or Design Change Notice
DCS	Deputy Chief of Staff or Direct Commercial Sales
DCSLOG	Deputy Chief of Staff for Logistics (U.S. Army)
DD Form 250	Department of Defense Material Inspection and Receiving Report
DD Form 645	Department of Defense FMS Quarterly Billing Statement
DDN	Defense Data Network

DELP	Defense English Language Program
DEPSECDEF	Deputy Secretary of Defense
DESC	Defense Electronic Supply Center
DFARS	Defense Federal Acquisition Regulation Supplement
DFAS	Defense Accounting and Finance Service-five centers

> HQ Washington DC
> Cleveland Center, Ohio
> Columbus Center, Ohio
> Indianapolis Center, Indiana—DFAS-IN
> Kansas City Center, Kansas

DIA	Defense Intelligence Agency
DIC	Document Identifier Code or Defense Industrial Cooperation
DIFS	Defense Integrated Financial System
DIS	Defense Investigative Service
DISAM	Defense Institute of Security Assistance Management (Wright-Patterson AFB, OH)
DISC	Defense Industrial Supply Center
DLA	Defense Logistics Agency
DLIELC	Defense Language Institute English Language Center (Lackland AFB, TX)
DLIFLC	Defense Language Institute Foreign Language Center (Presidio of Monterey, CA)
DLSC	Defense Logistics Services Center
DO	Defined Order (FMS Case)
DoC	Department of Commerce
DoD	Department of Defense
DoDAADS	Department of Defense Activity Address Directory System
DoDAC	Department of Defense Address Code
DoDD	DoD Directive
DoDI	DoD Instruction
DoDIG	DoD Inspector General
DoDIP	Department of Defense Informational Program
DOD	*Department of Defense Transportation Regulation Part II Cargo Movement* (DoD 4500.9-R)
DoE	Department of Energy
DoS	Department of State
DoT	Department of Transportation
DPACT	Defense Policy Advisory Committee on Trade

DPRO	Defense Plant Representative Office
DRMO	Defense Reutilization Marketing Office
DRMS	Defense Reutilization Marketing Service
DRP	Direct Requisitioning Procedure (U.S. Navy)
DRSA	Office of Defense Relations and Security Assistance (Dept. of State)
DS	Direct Support Level of Maintenance
DSCA	Defense Security Cooperation Agency
DSAM	Directorate of Security Assistance Management (U.S. Army)
DSC	Defense Supply Center or Delivery Source Code
DSMC	Defense Systems Management College (Ft Belvoir, VA)
DT&E	Development, Test, and Evaluation
DTC	Delivery Term Code or Office of Defense Trade Controls (Dept. of State)
DTP	Office of Defense Trade Policy (Dept. of State)
DTS	Defense Transportation System
DU	Dependable Undertaking
DV	Distinguished Visitor

E

EA	Expenditure Authority or Each
EAA	Export Administration Act
ECL	nglish Comprehension Level
ECP	Engineering Change Proposal
EDA	Excess Defense Articles
EDD	Estimated Delivery Date
EI	End Item
ELT	English Language Training
EOQ	Economic Order Quantity
ESD	Estimated Shipment Date or Electronics Systems Division (Air Force)
ESF	Economic Support Fund
ETSS	Extended Training Services Specialist

F

FAA	Foreign Assistance Act of 1961
FAD	Force Activity Designator

FAO	Foreign Area Officer (U.S. Army)
FAR	Federal Acquisition Regulation
FAS	Free Alongside Ship
FC	Fixed Cost
FF	Freight Forwarder
FFP	Firm Fixed Price
FICS	FMS Integrated Control System
FLO	Foreign Liaison Office or Foreign Liaison Officer (located within CONUS)
FM	Financial Management
FMCS	Foreign Military Construction Sales
FMFP	Foreign Military Financing Program
FMS	Foreign Military Sales
FMSO	Fleet Material Support Office (U.S. Navy)
FMSO I	Foreign Military Sales Order No. I (stock level sales case)
FMSO II	Foreign Military Sales Order No. II (requisition/consumption sales case)
FOB	Free On Board
FOIA	Freedom of Information Act
FORSCOM	Forces Command (Specified Command)
FRB	Federal Reserve Bank
FSC	Federal Supply Classification
FSCM	Federal Supply Code for Manufacturers
FSG	Federal Supply Group
FSN	Federal Stock Number or Foreign Service National (local hire overseas)
FSO	Foreign Service Officer (Department of State)
FST	Field Service Team
FTD	Field Training Detachment or Foreign Technology Division (U.S. Air Force)
FTS	Field Training Service
FWE	Foreign Weapons Evaluation
FY	Fiscal Year

G	

G&A	General and Administrative Expense (e.g., overhead)
GA	Grant Aid [obsolete) or General Authority
GAO	General Accounting Office
GATT	General Agreement on Tariffs and Trade

GBL	Government Bill of Lading
GC	Generic Code
GCC	Gulf Cooperation Council
GFE	Government Furnished Equipment
GFI	Government Furnished Information
GFM	Government Furnished Materiel
GFP	Government Furnished Property
GO_	Government of (country name)
GOCO	Government-Owned, Contractor Operated
GOGO	Government-Owned, Government-Operated
GPC	Government Procurement Code
GS	General Support Level of Maintenance
GSA	General Services Administration
GSE	Ground Support Equipment

H

HC	Host Country
HLDBK	Contractor Holdback
HNS	Host Nation Support

I

IA	Implementing Agency
ICP	Inventory Control Point or International Cooperative Programs
IDB	Interdepartmental Bill
IF	Industrial Fund
IFB	nvitation For Bid
IL	International Logistics
ILC I	nternational Logistics Center (U.S. Air Force)
ILCO	International Logistics Control Office
ILCS	International Logistics Communication System
ILOSS	International Logistics Overseas Support System
ILP	International Logistics Program
ILS	Integrated Logistics Support
ILSP	Integrated Logistics Support Plan

IM	Item/Inventory Manager
IMET	International Military Education and Training
IMS	International Military Student
IMSM	International Military Student Manager
IMSO	International Military Student Officer (Office) (Organization)
IMT	International Military Trainee or International Military Training
INS	Immigration and Naturalization Service (Dept. of Justice)
IP	Informational Program (DOD)
IPD	Issue Priority Designator or Implementing Project Directive
ISA	International Security Affairs [Assistant Secretary of Defense (International Security Affairs)]
ISP	International Security Policy [Assistant Secretary of Defense (International Security Policy)]
ISSL	Initial Spares Support List (See CSP)
ITAR	International Traffic in Arms Regulations
ITMO	International Training Management Officer
ITO	Invitational Travel Order

J

JCS	Joint Chiefs of Staff
JFM	Joint Forces Memorandum
JS	Joint Staff
JSAT	Joint Security Assistance Training (Regulation)

K

[None at this time.]

L

LCC	Life Cycle Cost
LCM	Life Cycle Management
LIC	Low-Intensity Conflict
LLI	Long Lead Item
LM	Logistics Management or Local Manufacture
LOA	Letter of Offer and Acceptance (synonymous with DD Form 1513)
LOR	Letter of Request

LSC	Logistics Support Charge

M

MAAG	Military Assistance Advisory Group
MACOM	Major Army Command
MAG	Military Assistance Group
MAGTEC	Marine Corps Air Ground Training and Education Center
MAJCOM	Major Command (U.S. Air Force)
MANPADS	Man-Portable Air Defense System
MAPAC	Military Assistance Program Address Code
MAPAD	Military Assistance Program Address Directory
MASL	Military Articles and Services List(s) (for materiel and training)
MCL	Munitions Control List
MCRL	Master Cross Reference List
MCSATFA	Marine Corps Security Assistance Training Field Activity
MCTL	Military Critical Technologies List
MDA(A)	Mutual Defense Assistance Agreements
MDAO	Mutual Defense Assistance Office
MDE	Major Defense Equipment
MET	Mobile Education Team
MICAP	Mission Capability
MILDEPS	Military Departments
MILGP	Military Group
MILPERS	Military Personnel
MILSBILLS	Military Standard Billing System
MILSPEC	Military Specification
MILSTEP	Military Supply and Transportation Evaluation Procedures
MILSTRAP	Military Standard Transaction Reporting and Accounting Procedures
MILSTRIP	Military Standard Requisitioning and Issue Procedures
MIRR	Material Inspection and Receiving Report (DD Form 250)
MIS	Management Information System
MISIL	Management Information System International Logistics (U.S. Navy)
MLA	Manufacturing License Agreement
MMC	Material Management Code
MOA	Memorandum of Agreement

MOD	Ministry of Defense (international equivalent of U.S. DoD)
MOU	Memorandum of Understanding
MRI	MILSTRIP Routing Identifier
MRO	Materiel Release Order
MRRL	Materiel Repair Requirements List
MSC	Military Sealift Command (U.S. Navy) or Major Subordinate Command (U.S. Army) or Mess Specialist, Chief (U.S. Navy). Medical Service Corps (U.S. Army and U.S. Air Force)
MSG	Message
MTCR	Missile Technology Control Regime
MTMC	Military Traffic Management Command
MTT	Mobile Training Team
MWO	Modification Work Order

N	

NAD	Navy Aviation Deport
NADEP	Naval Aviation Depot
NAF	Non-Appropriated Fund(s)
NAMSA	NATO Maintenance and Supply Agency
NAMSO	NATO Maintenance and Supply Organization
NAPR	NATO Armaments Planning Review
NATO	North Atlantic Treaty Organization
NAVAIR	Naval Air Systems Command
NAVCOMPT	Navy Comptroller
NAVEDTRACOM	Naval Educational and Training Command
NAVFAC	Naval Facilities Engineering Command
NAVILCO	Navy International Logistics Control Office (Philadelphia, Pennsylvania)
NAVPRO	Naval Plant Representative Office
NAVSEA	Naval Sea Systems Command
NAVSUP	Naval Supply Systems Command
NAVY IPO	Navy International Programs Office
NC	Nonrecurring Cost
NCB	National Codification Bureau
NDI	Non-Developmental Items
NDP-1	National Disclosure Policy

NDPC National Disclosure Policy Committee

NETSAFA Naval Education and Training Security Assistance Field Activity

NICP National Inventory Control Point (U.S. Army)

NIIN National Item Identification Number

NIPARS Nonstandard Item Parts And Repair Support (U.S. Air Force)

NMCS Not Mission Capable Supply

NMDE Non-Major Defense Equipment

NMDL Navy Management Data List

NOA New Obligation Authority or Notice of Availability

NPC Nonrecurring Production Costs

NPFC Naval Publications and Forms Center

NRC Nonrecurring Cost

NSA National Security Agency

NSADS Navy Security Assistance Data System

NSC Naval Supply Center or National Security Council

NSD Naval Supply Depot

NSI Nonstandard Item

NSN National Stock Number (replaces FSN)

NSS National Supply System

NSY Naval Shipyard

NTSC Naval Training Systems Center

NWC National War College or Naval War College

O

O&M Operation and Maintenance

OA Obligational Authority

OAC Operating Agency Code

OASD/ISA Office of Assistant Secretary of Defense/International Security Affairs

OBT Observer Training

OC-ALC Oklahoma City Air Logistics Center (U.S. Air Force - AFMC)

OCONUS Outside of the Continental United States

ODC Office of Defense Cooperation

ODTC Office of Defense Trade Controls (Dept. of State)

OECD Organization for Economic Cooperation and Development

OED Offer Expiration Date (LOA)

OJCS Office of the Joint Chiefs of Staff

OJT On-the-Job Training

OMA Operations and Maintenance (U.S. Army)

OMB Office of Management and Budget

OMC Office of Military Cooperation

OO-ALC Ogden Air Logistics Center (U.S. Air Force-AFMC)

OPNAV Office of the Chief of Naval Operations

OPR Office of Primary Responsibility

OSD Office of the Secretary of Defense

OT Orientation Tour

OVHL Overhaul

P

P&A Price and Availability Data

P/N Part Number

PACOM U.S. Pacific Command

PBAS Program, Budget, & Accounting System (U.S. Army)

PC&H Packaging, Crating, & Handling

PCH&T Packaging, Crating, Handling, and Transportation

PCS Permanent Change of Station

PD Presidential Determination

PDO Property Disposal Officer

PHS&T Packaging, Handling, Storage, and Transportation

PICA Primary Inventory Control Activity

PIP Product Improvement Program

PKO Peacekeeping Operations

PL Public Law

PLT Procurement Lead Time

PM Bureau of Political-Military Affairs (Dept. of State)

PME Professional Military Education or Precision Measuring Equipment

PMR Program Management Review

POC Point of Contact

POD Port of Debarkation

POE Port of Embarkation or Port of Entry

POL Petroleum, Oil, and Lubricants

PPBS Planning, Programming, and Budgeting System

PR Procurement Request

PTC Positive Transaction Control

PWD Program Work Directive

PWRMS Prepositioned War Reserve Materiel Stocks

PY Program Year

Q

QA Quality Assurance

QAT Quality Assurance Team

QBR Quarterly Billing Report

QC Quality Control

QDR Quality Deficiency Report

QRR Quarterly Requisition Report

QTY Quantity

R

R&D Research & Development

R&M Replacement and Modernization

R&R Repair and Return or Repair and Replace

RAD Required Availability Date

RCN Record Control Number

RCS Report Control Symbol

RDD Required Delivery Date

RDT&E Research, Development, Test, and Evaluation

RIC Routing Identifier Code

RIK Replacement in Kind

RIM Retainable Instructional Material

RMS Resource Management Systems

ROM Rough Order of Magnitude

RSI Rationalization, Standardization, and Interoperability

RSN Record Serial Number

SA-ALC San Antonio Air Logistics Center (U.S. Air Force - AFMC)

SAMD Security Assistance Management Directorate (U.S. Army)

SAMIS Security Assistance Management Information System

SAMM Security Assistance Management Manual (DOD 5105.38-M)

SAMR Security Assistance Management Review

SAN Security Assistance Network

SAO Security Assistance Organization/Office

SAPRWG Security Assistance Program Review Working Group

SATFA Security Assistance Training Field Activity (U.S. Army)

SATMO Security Assistance Training Management Organiztion (U.S. Army)

SATP Security Assistance Training Program

SCN Student Control Number

SCR System Change Request

SDAF Special Defense Acquisition Fund

SDR Supply Dificiency Report

SECDEF Secretary of Defense

SECNAV Secretary of the Navy

SECSTATE Secretary of State

SET Specialized English Training

SF 364 Standard Form 364, Report of Discrepancy

SFRC Senate Foreign Relations Committee

SII Special Instructions Indicator

SM-ALC Sacramento Air Logistics Center (U.S. Air Force - AFMC)

SME Significant Military Equipment

SNUD Stock Number User Directory

SOFA Status of Forces Agreement

SOP Standard Operating Procedure

SOW Statement of Work

SPAWAR Space & Naval Warfare Systems Command (U.S. Navy)

SPD System Program Director (U.S. Air Force)

SPM System Program Manager

SPO System Program Office (U.S. Air Force)

SPOD Surface (Sea) Port of Debarkation

SPOE Surface (Sea) Port of Embarkation

SSBO System Support Buy-out

SSC System Sales Case or Supply Status Code

SSP Single Stock Point

SST Site Survey Team

STARS Standard Accounting and Reporting System (U.S. Navy)

STARR/PC Supply Tracking and Repairable Return/Personal Computer

STL Standardized Training Listing

STRICOM Simulation, Training and Instrumentation Command

SVI Single Vendor Integrity

T

T&E Test and Evaluation

TA Type Assistance

TAA Technical Assistance Agreement or Trade Agreement Act

TAC Type of Address Code

TACOM Tank, Automotive and Armaments Command (U.S. Army)

TAFT Technical Assistance Field Team

TAPR Training Activity Program/Report

TASA Television-Audio Support Activity (U.S. Army)

TAT Technical Assistance Team

TBC Transportation Bill Code

TCN Transportation Control Number

TCP Technical Coordination Program

TD Technical Data

TDP Technical Data Package

TECOM Test and Evaluation Command (U.S. Army)

TL Termination Liability

TL/TLW Termination Liability/ TL Worksheet

TLA Travel and Living Allowance

TLR Termination Liability Reserve

TMDE Test Measurement & Diagnostic Equipment

TO Technical Order

TOA Total Obligational Authority or Transportation Operating Agency

TOEFL Test of English as a Foreign Language

TPA Total Package Approach

TPC Total Program Concept

TPMR Training Program Management Review

TRACS Training Control System

TRADOC Training and Doctrine Command (U.S. Army)

TRANSCOM U.S. Transportation Command

TRNG Training

TSASS TRADOC Security Assistance Supporting System

TTA Tailored Training Approach

U

U/I Unit of Issue

U/P Unit Price

UCMD Unified Commands

UCOM Unified Command

ULO Unliquidated Obligations

UMMIPS Uniform Materiel Movement and Issue Priority System

UN United Nations

UND Urgency of Need Designator

USA U.S. Army

USACOM United States Atlantic Command

USAF U.S. Air Force

USAFE U.S. Air Forces, Europe

USAID United States Agency for International Development

USAMC U.S. Army Materiel Command

USAREUR U.S. Army, Europe

USARSA U.S. Army School of the Americas

USASAC U.S. Army Security Assistance Command

USC U.S. Code (as in law)

USCENTCOM U.S. Central Command

USCG U.S. Coast Guard

USDLO U.S. Defense Liaison Office

USDP U.S. Disclosure Policy or Under Secretary of Defense for Policy

USEUCOM U.S. European Command

USG U.S. Government

USLO U.S. Liaison Office

USMC U.S. Marine Corps

USML U.S. Munitions List

USMTM U.S. Military Training Mission

USN U.S. Navy

USPACOM U.S. Pacific Command

USSOCOM U.S. Special Operations Command

USSOUTHCOM U.S. Southern Command

USTRANSCOM U.S. Transportation Command

V

[None at this time.]

W

WCN Worksheet Control Number

WCF Working Capital funds

WFO Washington Field Office (SATFA, U.S. Army)

WIMMS Weapons Integrated Material Management System

WIP Work In Process

WPOD Water Port of Discharge

WR-ALC Warner-Robins Air Logistics Center (U.S. Air Force - AFMC)

WRSA War Reserve Stocks for Allies

WSD Weapon System Designator

WSLO Weapon System Logistics Office

WSP Weapon System Package

X Y Z

[None at this time.]

APPENDIX P

Part 2
Glossary of Selected Terms

	A

above-the-line-cost [obsolete terminology] Cost identified as specific FMS line items or as part of a specific line on an [obsolete form] DD Form 1513 (see Table 200-1, DoD 7290-3-M). Applicable costs are added to arrive at estimated cost (line 21 of the DD Form 1513).

acceptance The act of an authorized representative of the government by which the government assumes for itself, or as agent of another, ownership of existing and identified supplies tendered, or approves specific services rendered, as partial or complete performance of the contract on the part of the contractor.

acceptance date The date which appears in the acceptance portion of the LOA and indicates the calendar date on which a foreign buyer agrees to accept the items and conditions contained in the FMS LOA.

accepted case An LOA that has been signed by the designated representative of the eligible recipient before the expiration date and has been received by DFAS-IN with any required initial deposit.

accessorial cost The value of expenses incidental to issues, sales, and transfers of materiel which are not included in the standard price or contract cost of materiel; also, any expenses incidental to the performance of services, training, etc. May be commonly referred to by the higher level generic code "LOO" for all types of accessorial costs.

accrued costs The financial value of delivered articles and services and incurred costs reported to DFAS-IN via

Delivery Transactions. Incurred costs represent disbursements for which no physical deliveries have yet occurred. Examples are: progress payments to contractors, GFM/GFE provided to contractors, and nonrecurring costs.

action officer (AO) The person responsible for taking action on a project, for coordination of all staff activities, and for assembling an action package for decision by higher authority.

actual cost A cost sustained in fact, on the basis of costs incurred, as distinguished from forecasted or estimated costs.

actual cost of work performed The costs actually incurred and recorded in accomplishing the work performed within a given time period.

actual dollars Expenditures as recorded in prior time periods.

adjustment reply code (ARC) A code which identifies the type of action being taken in reply to the FMS customer

Supply Discrepancy Report (SDR). ARCs are transmitted to DFAS-IN by an FMS case implementing agency in Delivery Transactions.

administrative contracting officer (ACO) The U.S. government contracting officer who is assigned the responsibility for the administration of USG contracts.

administrative agency The military department charged with the responsibility for the provision of logistical and administrative support to a DoD element either in the U.S. or in a foreign country or international organization.

administrative cost The value of costs associated with the administration of the FMS Program. The prescribed administrative percentage cost for a case appears in the United States of America Letter of Offer and Acceptance (LOA). May be commonly referred to by the generic code "L6A" for administrative costs.

administrative leadtime The time interval between the initiation of procurement action and the letting of a contract or the placing of an order.

agency Any department, office, commission, authority, administration, board, Government-owned corporation, or other independent establishment of any branch of the Government of the United States.

allotment [FMS] authority issued to a DoD Component to incur commitments and obligations within a specified amount. In the FMS program there are two types of allotments:

- Allotment for actual administrative expenses - All of the actual cost incurred by DoD Components in administering the FMS program are funded by this allotment. The allotment is issued on a quarterly basis and may not be exceeded.
- Allotment for program implementation - An allotment of FMS case contract authority for use on a direct cite basis, citing the allotment holder's accounting station. This type of allotment is made when DFAS-IN determines it does not have the accounting capability to support detailed accounting requirements below the FMS case level, i.e., commitments, obligations and disbursements resulting from contract award to implement individual FMS case line items. The amount released on each FMS case is a specific limitation and the monthly status-ofallotment report must show the status of each case.

anticipated reimbursements A term which refers to the dollar value of reimbursable orders that has been included in a DoD component's budget. Applicable amounts are not available for obligation until an actual customer order has been received.

Armed Services Board of Contract Appeals A board established to act as the authorized representative of theSECDEF or department Secretaries, in deciding appeals under the provisions of the disputes clause contained in USG contracts.

Arms Export Control Act **(AECA)** The basic U.S. law providing the authority and general rules for the conduct of FMS and commercial sales of defense articles, defense services, and training. The AECA came into existence with the passage of the Foreign Military Sales Act (FMSA) of 1968. An amendment in the *International Security Assistance and Arms Export Control Act of 1976* changed the name of FMSA to the AECA.

arms transfers Involves the sale, lease, loan, or other transfer of defense articles and defense services such as arms, ammunition, and implements of war, including components thereof, and the training, manufacturing licenses, technical assistance, and technical data related thereto, provided by the USG under the authority of the *Foreign Assistance Act of 1961*, as amended, or the *Arms Export Control Act*, as amended, or other statutory authority, or directly by commercial firms to foreign countries, foreign private firms, or to international organizations. See also conventional arms transfers.

attrition The loss of a resource due to natural causes in the normal course of events such as a turnover of employees or spoilage and obsolescence of materiel.

audit The systematic examination of records and documents to determine:

- the adequacy and effectiveness of budgeting, accounting, financial, and related policies and procedures

- compliance with applicable statutes, regulations, policies, and prescribed procedures
- the reliability, accuracy, and completeness of financial and administrative records and reports
- the extent to which funds and other resources are properly protected and effectively used

auditor [procurement] A term used to represent the cognizant audit office designated by the Defense Contract Audit Agency (DCAA) or Military Service audit activities for conducting audit reviews of the contractor's accounting system policies and procedures for compliance with the criteria.

B

---

back order (BO) The quantity of an item requisitioned by ordering activities that is not immediately available for issue but is recorded as a stock commitment for future issue.

base price The standard price or contract cost of materiel. Does not include surcharges

base year (BY) A reference period which determines a fixed price level for comparison in economic escalation calculations and cost estimates. The price level index for the base year is 1.000.

below-the-line-costs [obsolete terminology] Costs identified on the DD Form 1513 on lines 22 through 25. Applicable costs are added to estimated costs to arrive at estimated total costs. Normally, DFAS-IN retains the obligational authority necessary to execute applicable costs.

bill (or billing) code This is a DFAS-DI Country assigned code which divides FMS customer country billings into management levels lower than a U.S. Implementing Agency or in-country service. This code often correlates to an FMS customer paying office. It appears in Block 3 of the DD Form 645.

billing statement The DD Form 645 Billing Statement represents the official claim for payment by the U.S. Government referred to in the LOA. It also furnishes an accounting to the FMS purchaser for all costs incurred on his behalf under each agreement.

blanket order FMS case An agreement between a foreign customer and the U.S. Government for a specific category of items or services (including training) with no definitive listing of items or quantities. The case specifies a dollar ceiling against which orders may be placed.

budget authority Authority provided by law to enter into obligations which generally result in immediate or future outlays of federal funds. The basic forms of budget authority are appropriations, contract authority, and borrowing authority. Budget authority may be classified by
- The period of availability (one-year, mutiple-years, or without a time limitation)
- The timing of congressional action (current or permanent)
- The manner of determining the amount available (definite or indefinite)

budget year The fiscal year following the current fiscal year, and for which the new budget estimate is prepared.

cancelled case An FMS case (LOA) which was not accepted or funded within prescribed time limitations, or was accepted and subsequently cancelled by the requesting country or the U.S. government. In the latter case, the U.S. government or purchaser electing to cancel all (or part) of a case prior to the delivery of defense articles or the performance of services shall be responsible for all (or associated) termination costs.

case An FMS contractual sales agreement between the United States of America. and an eligible foreign country or international organization documented by an LOA. An FMS case identifier is assigned for the purpose of identification, accounting, and data processing for each LOA.

case amendment An amendment of an FMS case documented by an LOA amendment which constitutes a contracted scope change to an existing LOA.

case description A short title specifically prepared for each FMS case by the implementing agency.

case designator A unique designator assigned by the implementing agency to each FMS case. The designator originates with the offer of a sale, identifies the case through all subsequent transactions, and is generally a threeletter designation, comprising the last element of the Case Identifier.

case identifier A unique six digit identifier assigned to an FMS case for the purpose of identification, accounting, and data processing of each accepted LOA. The case identifier consists of the two-letter country code, a one letter designator for the DoD implementing agency, and a three-letter case designator.

case modification Modification of a case documented by an LOA modification which constitutes an administrative or price change to an existing LOA, without revising the scope of the case.

cash case [FMS] An FMS case for which the source of funding is directly provided by the purchaser, i.e., not through a credit or grant agreement with the USG.

cash in advance [FMS] Payment in U.S. dollars.

cash prior to delivery [FMS] A term of sale in which the USG collects cash in advance of the delivery of defense articles and/or the performance of defense services from DoD resources.

cash sales [FMS] An FMS case financed with purchaser funds other than non-repayable credit funds.

cash with acceptance [FMS] A term of sale indicating that the purchaser forwards by check or wire transfer the full amount shown as the estimated total cost on the LOA.

closed case An FMS case for which all materiel has been delivered, all services have been performed, all financial transactions, including all collections, have been completed, and the customer has received a final statement of account. If additional costs are identified at a later date, the FMS case can be re-opened.

collections [FMS financial] Receipts in U.S. dollars from a purchasing country to pay for defense articles, services, or military training based on accepted FMS cases.

commercial sale A sale of defense articles or defense services made by U.S. industry directly to a foreign buyer, and which is not administered by DoD through FMS procedures. Also referred to as a direct commercial sale.

commercial-type items Any items, including those expended or consumed in use which, in addition to military use, are used and traded in normal civilian enterprise and which are, or can be, imported/exported through normal international trade channels.

commitment Any communication between a responsible United States of America official and a representative foreign official (including officials of any international organization or supra-national authority) which reasonably could be interpreted as being a promise that the U.S. will provide a foreign government (including international organizations or supra-national authorities) with either funds (including long term credit assignments), goods, services, or information.

commitment [financial] A firm administrative reservation of funds based upon firm procurement directives, orders, requisitions, authorizations to issue travel orders, or requests which authorize the recipient to create obligations without further recourse to the official responsible for certifying the availability of funds. The act of entering into a commitment is usually the first step in the process of spending available funds. The effect of entering into a commitment and the recording of that commitment on the records of the allotment is to reserve funds for future obligations. A commitment is subject to cancellation by the approving authority if it is not already obligated. Commitments are not required under Operation and Maintenance appropriations.

commodity group A grouping or range of items which possess similar characteristics, have similar applications, or are susceptible to similar supply management methods.

competitive proposals A method for awarding a United States of America government contract on a basis other than low bid, whereby the best and final offer may be obtained after discussions are concluded.

completed case An FMS case for which all deliveries and collections have been completed, but for which a final accounting statement (DD Form 645) has not been furnished to the purchaser.

concurrent spare parts (CSP) These are spare parts programmed as an initial stockage related to a major item or system. CSPs are normally shipped in advance of the release of the major item or system.

constant year dollars A method of relating dollar values for various years by removing the annual effects of inflation and showing all dollars at the value they would have had in a selected base year. See also current year dollars.

constructive delivery [FMS] Completion of delivery of materiel to a carrier for transportation to a consignee, or delivery to a U.S. post office for shipment to a consignee. Delivery is evidenced by completed shipping documents or listings of delivery at the U.S. post office. The delivery of materiel to the customer or the customer's designated freight forwarder at a point of production, testing, or storage at dockside, at staging areas, or at airports constitutes actual delivery. Also referred to as physical delivery.

Continental United States (CONUS) United States of America territory, including the adjacent territorial waters, located within the North American Continent between Canada and Mexico.

contract An agreement between two or more legally competent parties, in the proper form, on a legal subject matter or purpose, for a legal consideration.

contract administration All the activities associated with the performance of a contract from pre-award to closeout.

contract administration surcharge [FMS] A surcharge applied to all FMS purchases from procurement to cover the cost of contract administration, quality assurance and inspection, and contract audit. The surcharge percentage depends upon any contract administrative reciprocal agreements with a particular purchasing country.

contract authority Budget authority contained in an authorization bill that permits an agency of the federal government to enter into contracts or other obligations for future payments from funds not yet appropriated by Congress. The assumption is that the necessary funds will be made available for payment in a subsequent appropriations act.

contract/budget authority [FMS] Authority provided by law to enter into obligations in support of FMS cases without all of the cash necessary to liquidate the obligations. There are two basic types of budget authority resulting from the operation of the FMS program:

- contract/budget authority in the trust fund. This authority represents that portion of an FMS case which will be implemented in a current fiscal year. That portion of an FMS case that may not be implemented in a current fiscal year but is scheduled for a future year(s) is an uncommitted acceptance. Uncommitted acceptances are not budget authority but are reported in schedules attached to the "Report on Budget Execution."
- contract/budget authority in DoD appropriation/fund account. In the direct program portion of the budget, this authority results from the appropriation process. For the reimbursable portion of the budget, the authority results from the receipt of customer orders. In the case of the FMS program, the customer order (and hence budget authority) results from receipt by the implementing agency of a reimbursable order issued by the DFAS-IN for all or a portion of an FMS case.

contracting activity Each service designates certain commands as contracting activities. The subordinate command is that in which a principal contracting office is located. It may include the program office, related functional support offices, and contracting offices. DoD FAR Supplement 2.1 lists the contracting activities. The Head of the contracting activity has certain approval and authority responsibilities.

conventional arms transfers (CAT) The transfer of nonnuclear weapons, aircraft, equipment, and military services from supplier states to recipient states. The USG views arms transfers as a useful foreign policy instrument to strengthen collective defense arrangements, maintain regional military balances, secure U.S. bases, and compensate for the withdrawal of troops. U.S. arms may be transferred by grants, leases, loans, direct commercial sales, or government-to-government sales under FMS.

cooperative logistics The logistics support provided a foreign government/agency through its participation in a United States Department of Defense logistics system, with reimbursement paid to the USG for the support provided. [JCS Pub 1]

cooperative logistics sales Sales pursuant to arrangements wherein continuing support is provided a foreign government through its participation in a U.S. Department of Defense logistics system with reimbursement to the USG for the support performed.

cooperative logistics supply support arrangements (CLSSA) Military logistics support arrangements designed to provide responsive and continuous supply support at the depot level for U.S.-made military materiel possessed by foreign countries and international organizations. The CLSSA is normally the most effective means for providing common repair parts and secondary item support for equipment of U.S. origin which is in allied and friendly country inventories.

cooperative logistics support arrangement Procedural arrangements (cooperative logistics arrangements) and implementing procedures (supplementary procedures) which together support, define, or implement cooperative logistics understandings between the United States and a friendly foreign government.

coproduction A program implemented by a government-to-government or commercial licensing arrangement which enables a foreign government or firm to acquire the "know-how" to manufacture or assemble, repair, maintain and operate, in whole or in part, a defense item.

cost estimate A judgment or opinion regarding the anticipated cost of an object, commodity, or service. A cost estimate is the result of an estimating procedure which specifies the expected dollar cost required to perform a stipulated task or to acquire an item. A cost estimate may constitute a single value or a range of values.

Country Liaison Officer (CLO) An officer or non-commissioned officer (NCO) of a foreign military establishment selected by his or her government and attached to a MILDEP or DoD agency for the primary purpose of helping administer IMSs from his or her home country. For administrative purposes, the CLO is considered in a student status.

country team Senior members of USG agencies assigned to a U.S. diplomatic mission overseas, and subject to the direction and supervision of the Chief, U.S. Mission (Ambassador). Normally, such members meet regularly (i.e., weekly) to coordinate USG political, economic, and military activities and policies in the host country.

credit Transactions approved on a case-by-case basis by the Departments of State, Treasury, and Defense, which allow repayment of military export sales for periods beyond 120 days after delivery of materiel or performance of service. [Sections 23 and 24, AECA]

credit arrangement An arrangement with a foreign government that the USG will advance a stipulated amount of credit for the financing of an FMS or a DCS to that government.

credit case The use of USG appropriated funds from the Foreign Military Sales Financing Program (FMFP) account to finance a foreign country's FMS purchases of U.S. defense articles or services. Credit funds may be in the form of repayable loans or non-repayable grants.

credit guaranty A guaranty to any individual corporation, partnership or other judicial entity doing business in the United States (excluding USG agencies other than the Federal Financing Bank) against political and credit risks of nonpayment arising out of their financing of credit sales of defense articles and defense services to eligible countries and international organizations.

cross-leveling An accounting technique by which DFAS-IN transfers funds (cash receipts) from one FMS case to another FMS case.

cross-servicing That function performed by one military service in support of another military service for which reimbursement is required from the service receiving support.

current fiscal year See also fiscal year .

current year The fiscal year in progress.

current-year dollars Dollar values of a given year that include the effects of inflation or escalation for that year, or which reflect the price levels expected to prevail during the year at issue. Also referred to as escalated dollars or then-year dollars.

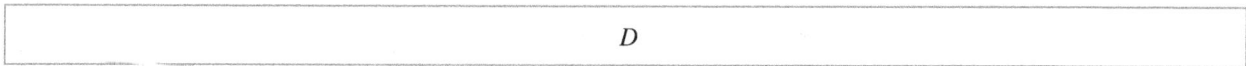

D

defense article As defined in Section 644(d), FAA and Section 47(3), AECA, includes any weapon, weapons system, munition, aircraft, vessel, boat, or other implement of war; any property, installation, commodity, materiel, equipment, supply, or goods used for the purposes of furnishing military assistance or making military sales; any machinery, facility, tool, material, supply, or other item necessary for the manufacture, production, processing, repair, servicing, storage, construction, transportation, operation, or use of any other defense article or any component or part of any articles listed above, but shall not include merchant vessels, or as defined by the *Atomic Energy Act of 1954*, as amended (42 U.S.Code 2011), source material, by-product material, special nuclear material, production facilities, utilization facilities, or atomic weapons or articles involving Restricted Data.

Defense Automatic Addressing System [DAAS] The DAAS functions as an automated system for routing logistics data traffic and provides document processing and data information services.

Defense Contract Management Command [DCMC] An agency under the direction of the Director of the Defense Logistics Agency, which provides unified contract administration services to DoD components and NASA, for all contracts except those specifically exempted. In 1990, DCMC superseded the Defense Contract Administration Service (DCAS).

defense information As defined in Section 644(e), FAA, the term defense information includes any document, writing, sketch, photograph, plan, model, specification, design, prototype, or other recorded or oral information relating to any defense article or defense service, but shall not include Restricted Data as defined by the *Atomic Energy Act of 1954*, as amended, or data removed from the Restricted Data category under Section 142d of that Act.

Defense Institute of Security Assistance Management [DISAM] The centralized DoD school for the consolidated professional education of personnel involved in security assistance management. DISAM is located at Wright- Patterson AFB, Ohio, and provides an array of resident and non-resident instruction for both USG and foreign government military and civilian personnel as well as for defense contractor and industry personnel.

Defense Security Cooperation Agency [DSCA] The agency that performs administrative management, program planning, and operations functions for U.S. military assistance programs at the DoD level under the policy direction of the Assistant Secretary of Defense (International Security Affairs).

defense service As defined in Section 644(f), FAA and Section 47(4), AECA, the term defense service includes any service, test, inspection, repair, training, publication, technical or other assistance, or defense information used for the purpose of furnishing military assistance or FMS, but does not include military education and training activities or design and construction services under Section 29, AECA.

defense stock The term defense stock includes defense articles on hand which are available for prompt delivery. It also includes defense articles under contract and on order which would be available for delivery within a reasonable time from the date of order by an eligible foreign government or international organization without increasing outstanding contracts or entering into new contracts. Any orders received from an eligible foreign government or international organization which cannot be filled in this manner fall within the provisions of Section 22 of the *Arms Export Control Act* which requires such orders to be filled under new procurement contracts.

defined order case These are FMS cases characterized by orders for specific defense articles and services which are separately identified line items on the LOA.

delivered case See completed case.

delivery Includes constructive or actual delivery of defense articles; also, includes the performance of defense services for the customer or requisitioner, as well as surcharges, when they are normally recorded in the billing and collection cycle immediately following performance.

delivery forecasts Periodic estimates of contract production deliveries used as a measure of the effectiveness of production and supply availability scheduling and as a guide to corrective actions to resolve procurement or production bottlenecks. These forecasts provide estimates of deliveries under obligation against procurement from appropriated or other funds.

dependable undertaking [FMS] A firm commitment by a foreign government or international organization to pay the full amount of a contract for new production or for the performance of defense services which will assure the U.S. against any loss on such contract and to make funds available in such amounts and at such times as may be required by the contract, or for any damages and costs that may accrue from the cancellation of such a contract, provided that in the judgment of the DoD there is sufficient likelihood that the foreign government or international organization will have the economic resources to fulfill the commitment.

depot level maintenance Maintenance performed on material requiring a major overhaul or a complete rebuilding of parts, assemblies, subassemblies, and end items, including the manufacture of parts, modification, testing, and reclamation as required. Provides more extensive shop facilities and equipment and personnel of higher technical skill than are normally available at the lower levels of maintenance, i.e., organizational and intermediate level maintenance.

designated country representative A person or persons duly authorized by a foreign government to act on behalf of that government to negotiate, commit, sign contractual agreements, and/or accept delivery of materiel.

direct cite Citation of the FMS Trust Fund as the financing source on documents. Also see reimbursable financing DCS. See commercial sale.

direct cost Any cost that is specifically identified with a particular final cost objective. Such costs are not necessarily limited to items that are incorporated into the end product as labor or materiel.

disbursements [gross and net] Gross disbursements represent the amount of checks issued, cash, or other reimbursable transactions processed, payments made, less refunds received. Net disbursements represent gross disbursements less income collected and credited to the appropriation of fund account, such as amounts received for goods and services provided. Also see outlays and expenditures disclosure authorization an authorization by an appropriate U.S. military department authority which is required prior to the disclosure of classified information to foreign nationals who are cleared by their governments to have access to classified information.

distributed costs Costs which have been identified or allocated to an FMS case or cases.

DoD acquisition system A single uniform system whereby all equipment, facilities, and services are planned, designed, developed, acquired, maintained, and disposed of within the DoD. The system encompasses establishing and enforcing policies and practices that govern acquisitions, to include documenting mission needs and establishing performance goals and baselines; determining and prioritizing resource requirements for acquisition programs; planning and executing acquisition programs; directing and controlling the acquisition review process; developing and assessing logistics and implications; contracting; monitoring the execution status of approved programs; and reporting to Congress.

DoD Activity Address Directory System [DODAADS] The DODAADS provides data elements, identification codes, and clear text addresses of organizational activities needed for materiel requisitioning, marking, shipping document preparation, billing and similar applications.

DoD components These include all of the following: the Office of the Secretary of Defense (OSD); the Military Departments; the Joint Chiefs of Staff (JCS); the Unified and Specified Commands; the Office of the Inspector General, Department of Defense (OIG/DoD); the Defense Agencies, to include the Strategic Defense Initiative Organization (SDIO); and DoD Field Activities.

DoD direct credit [FMS] A long-term credit for an FMS purchase which is directly financed from an appropriation or account available for that purpose. Authority is Section 23 of the AECA, as amended, or pertinent earlier legislation.

earmarking of stocks The arrangement whereby nations agree, normally in peacetime, to identify a proportion of selected items of their war reserve stocks to be called for by specified NATO commanders under emergency conditions.

economic lot size That number of units of material or a manufactured item that can be purchased or produced within the lowest unit-cost range. Its determination involves reconciling the decreasing trend in unit preparation cost and the increasing trend in unit costs of storage, interest, insurance, depreciation, and other costs incident to ownership, as the size of the lot is increased.

economic order quantity [EOQ] The most economical quantity of parts to order at one time to support a defined production rate, considering the applicable procurement and inventory costs.

Economic Support Fund [ESF] A USG Program through which economic assistance is provided on a loan or grant basis, to selected foreign governments having unique security problems, which are of strategic concern to the U.S. The funds may be used to finance imports of commodities, capital, or technical assistance in accordance with the terms of a bilateral agreement; counterpart funds thereby generated may be used as budgetary support. These funds enable a recipient to devote more of its own resources to defense and security purposes than it otherwise could do without serious economic or political consequences. [Formerly termed "Security Supporting Assistance."]

economies of scale Reductions in the unit cost of output resulting from the production of additional units. Such economies stems from:

- an increased specialization of labor as the volume of output increases
- decreased unit costs of materials
- better utilization of management
- the acquisition of more efficient equipment
- a greater use of by-products

eligible recipient [security assistance] Any friendly foreign country or international organization determined by the President to be eligible to purchase or receive (on a grant basis) U.S. defense articles and defense services, unless otherwise ineligible due to statutory restrictions.

end item [EI] A final combination of end products, component parts, and/or materials which is ready for its intended use, e.g., aircraft, ship, tank, mobile machine shop.

engineering change proposal [ECP] A proposal to a responsible authority recommending that a change to an original item of equipment be considered, and the design or engineering change be incorporated into the article to modify, add to, delete, or supersede original parts.

English Comprehension Level [ECL] examination A test of the overall proficiency of foreign military students in English language listening and reading. A minimum entry level for each DoD course of instruction is set by the military departments on the basis of course level difficulty and hazard factors.

equipment A major subdivision of a weapon system or subsystem that performs a function impacting the operational capability and readiness of the weapon system/subsystem. It is grouped into two general categories, mission equipment and support equipment. Equipment does not denote bit-part pieces, components, or elements that comprise an equipment entity.

estimated actual charges A systematic and documented estimate of actual costs. The procedure is used in the absence of an established cost accounting system and the procedure is sometimes referred to as a cost finding technique.

excess defense articles [EDA] Defense articles owned by the United States Government which are neither procured in anticipation of military assistance or sales requirements, nor procured pursuant to a military assistance or sales order. EDA are items which are in excess of the Approved Force Acquisition Objective and Approved Force Retention Stock of all Department of Defense Components at the time such articles are dropped from inventory by the supplying agency for delivery to countries or international organizations.

execution The operation of carrying out a program as contained in the approved budget. Often referred to as budget execution.

Executive Order A rule or regulation, issued by the President, a governor, or some other administrative authority, that has the effect of law. Executive orders are used to implement and give administrative effect to provisions of the Constitution, to treaties, and to statutes. They may be used to create or modify the organization or procedures of administrative agencies or may have general applicability as law. Under the national *Administrative Procedure Act of 1946*, all executive orders must be published in the *Federal Register*.

expendable supplies and material Supplies which are consumed in use, such as ammunition, paint, fuel, cleaning and preserving materials, surgical dressings, drugs, medicines, etc., or which lose their identity, such as spare parts, etc. Sometimes referred to as consumable supplies and material.

expenditure authority [EA, as used in FMS] A document or authority from DFAS-IN to an FMS case implementing DoD component which allows expenditures against obligations previously recorded against an FMS case. The disbursing activity must ensure that cash is available prior to processing the disbursement.

expenditures The actual spending of money as distinguished from the appropriation of funds. Expenditures are made by the executive branch; appropriations are made only by Congress. The two rarely are identical in any fiscal year. In addition to some current budget authority, expenditures may represent prior budget authority made available one, two, or more years earlier. See also disbursements.

extended offer [FMS] An FMS offer for which a reply from the buyer has not been received within the time limit specified on the LOA but which remains in effect pending clarification of its status.

F

Federal Acquisition Regulation **[FAR]** The FAR is the primary regulation for use by federal executive agencies for the acquisition of supplies and services with appropriated funds.

field training services [FTS] A generic term that refers to either engineering and technical services, contract field services, or both.

financing appropriation The appropriation account originally increased as a result of the performing DoD Component's acceptance of a reimbursable order from DFAS-IN. This activity is reflected as "FMS reimbursables." (See reimbursable financing.)

financing, type of [FMS] The method by which the U.S. Government is authorized to sell defense articles and services under the *Arms Export Control Act* (e.g., cash with acceptance, dependable undertaking, credit etc.). The type of financing is reflected through an entry of the proper term(s) of sale on the LOA.

fiscal year Accounting period beginning 1 October and ending 30 September of the following year. The fiscal year is designated by the calendar year in which it ends. Fiscal year 1991 begins on 1 October 1990 and ends 30 September 1991.

fixed costs Costs that do not vary with the volume of business, such as property taxes, insurance, depreciation, security, and minimum water and utility fees.

flyaway costs The costs related to the production of a useable end item of military hardware. Flyaway cost include the cost of procuring the basic unit (airframe, hull, chassis, etc.), a percentage of basic unit for changes allowance, propulsion equipment, electronics, armament, and other installed government-furnished equipment, and nonrecurring production costs. Flyaway cost equates to Rollaway and Sailaway costs.

follow-on training Sequential training following an initial course of training.

Foreign Assistance Act **[FAA]** *of 1961* The basic law providing the authority and the general rules for the conduct of foreign assistance grant activities/programs by the USG.

foreign liaison officer [FLO] An official representative, either military or civilian, of a foreign government or international organization stationed in the United States normally for the purpose of managing or monitoring security assistance programs.

foreign military sales [FMS] That portion of U.S. security assistance authorized by the AECA as amended, and conducted on the basis of formal contracts or agreements between the USG and an authorized recipient government or international organization. FMS includes government-to-government sales of defense articles or defense services, from DoD stocks or through new procurements under DoD-managed contracts, regardless of the source of financing.

foreign military sales [FMS] case United States of America Letter of Offer and Acceptance (LOA) which has been accepted by a foreign country.

Foreign Military Sales Order [FMSO] A terms used to describe LOAs which implement Cooperative Logistics Supply Support Arrangements. Two LOAs are written: a FMSO I and a FMSO II.

Foreign Military Sales Order No. I [FMSO No. I] Provides funding for the pipeline capitalization of a cooperative logistics support arrangement, which consists of stocks on hand and replenishment of stocks on order in which the participating country buys equity in the U.S. supply system for the support of a specific weapons system. Even though stocks are not moved to a foreign country, delivery (equity) does in effect take place when the country pays for the case.

Foreign Military Sales Order No. II [FMSO No. II] Provides for the replenishment of withdrawals of consumption-type items (repair parts, primarily) from the DoD supply system to include charges for accessorial costs. A cutomer buying an item on a FMSO II case creates the funds source for buying another item in the FMSO I pipeline

Foreign Military Sales Planning Directive [DD Form 2061] A working paper that provides an identification of the cost elements included in the prices on an LOA; provides a time-phased plan for the execution of an LOA; and, identifies procurement/ reimbursement appropriations/ funds.

formal training [military] Training (including special training) in an officially designated course. It is conducted or administered according to an approved program of instruction. This training generally leads to a specific skill in a certain military occupational specialty.

General Accounting Office [GAO] An agency of the legislative branch, responsible solely to the Congress, which functions to audit all negotiated government contracts and investigate all matters relating to the receipt, disbursement, and application of public funds. The GAO determines whether public funds are expended in accordance with appropriations, and recommends to Congress various policies and procedures to be enacted into law to provide oversight and governance of government spending.

generic code [GC] A three-digit code identified in the *Military Articles and Services List* (MASL) which represents the type of materiel or services to be furnished according to a specific budget activity/project account classification. May related to the federal supply class (1st four positions of the NSN).

government furnished equipment [GFE] Items in the possession of, or acquired by the USG, and delivered to or otherwise made available to a contractor.

government furnished materiel [GFM] USG property which may be incorporated into, or attached to an end item to be delivered under a contract or which may be consumed in the performance of a contract. It includes, but is not limited to, raw and processed material, parts, components, assemblies, small tools, and supplies.

government furnished property [GFP] Property in the possession of, or acquired directly by the USG, and subsequently delivered to or otherwise made available to the contractor.

government-owned, contractor-operated [GOCO] facility A manufacturing plant that is owned by the Government and operated under contract by a non-government, private firm.

government-owned, government-operated (GOGO) facility A manufacturing plant that is both owned and operated by the Government.

grant A form of assistance involving a gift of funds, equipment, and/or services which is furnished by the USG to selected recipient nations on a free, non repayable basis.

H

holding account An account established for each country/international organization for the purpose of recording and safeguarding unidentified and certain earmarked funds for future use.

I

implementation date [FMS] The date when supply action on an FMS case is initiated or directed by an implementing agency.

implementing agency [IA] The U.S. Military Department or Defense Agency responsible for the execution of military assistance programs. With respect to FMS, the Military Department or Defense Agency assigned responsibility by the Defense Security Assistance Agency to prepare an LOA and to implement an FMS case. The implementing agency is responsible for the overall management of the actions which will result in delivery of the materials or services set forth in the LOA which was accepted by a foreign country or international organization.

indirect cost Costs which are incurred for common or joint objectives, and which are not as readily subject to treatment as direct costs. See also direct costs.

indirect offset A general type of industrial or commercial compensation practice required of a contractor by a purchasing government as a condition for the purchase of defense articles/services. The form of compensation, which generally offsets a specific percentage of the cost of the purchase, is unrelated to the items purchased, and may include contractor purchases of commodities and manufactured goods produced in the purchasing country.

Informational Program [IP] The DoD Informational Program (IP) that affords an opportunity for IMSs to become familiar with the United States, the social, cultural, and political institutions of the U.S., and its people and their ways of life. The IP further increases IMSs' awareness of the U.S. commitment to basic principles of internationally-recognized human rights.

initial deposit [FMS] Money transferred to the credit of the Treasurer of the United States or other authorized officer at the time of acceptance of an FMS case (LOA) as full or partial payment for defense articles, services, or training contracted for by an eligible foreign country.

interfund billing system [IBS] (reimbursable) Under IBS, a selling activity will credit the appropriation or fund which owns the materiel and/or finances the accessorial charges at the time of billing the ordering activity, and will charge the appropriations/funds of the ordering activity. IBS normally encompasses all supply system sales and purchases of materiel, including perishable substances, bulk petroleum, oil, lubricants, and aviation fuel. Reimbursable sales will be billed at the time items are dropped from inventory except that billings for sales under FMS will be based on constructive delivery. [DODI 7420.12]

international logistics support The provision of military logistics support by one participating nation to one or more participating nations, whether with or without reimbursement.

international military education and training [IMET]) order A document issued by the Defense Security Cooperation Agency (DSCA) to authorize and direct the delivery of defense articles or the furnishing of defense services (including military training) to designated grant aid (IMET) recipients. The IMET order identifies the funding source for each program line of a country program (IMET program).

international military education and training [IMET] program The portion of the U.S. security assistance program which provides training to selected foreign military and defense associated civilian personnel on a grant basis. Training is provided at U.S. military facilities and with U.S. Armed Forces in the U.S. and overseas, and through the use of Mobile Training Teams. Training also may be provided by contract technicians, contractors (including instruction at civilian institutions), or by correspondence courses. The IMET Program is authorized by the FAA, as amended.

International Military Student [IMS] A national of a foreign government, with military or civilian status of that government, who is receiving education or training or is touring USG activities under the sponsorship of the security assistance training program (SATP).

inventory control That phase of military logistics which includes managing, cataloging, requirements determinations, procurement, distribution, overhaul, and disposal of materiel.

inventory control point [ICP] The organizational element within a DoD system which is assigned responsibility for materiel management of a group of items including such management functions as the computation of requirements, the initiation of procurement or disposal actions, distribution management, and rebuild direction.

investment cost The cost of equipment, supplies and services that improve the capability of a force, including initial unit equipment, war reserves of equipment and ammunition, concurrent spare parts, and initial spare parts stockage levels. Also includes replacement costs for obsolescent and attrited equipment, rebuild and modernization costs for newly provided equipment, projects programmed as dollar value lines to facilitate administration, and training costs associated with the introduction of new equipment or an improved capability.

invitational travel order [ITO] A written authorization for international military students to travel to, from, and between U.S. activities for the purpose of training under an approved and funded IMET or FMS program.

item identification number A seven-character identifier assigned to each line of training in the MASL. The first character is a letter which identifies the MILDEP offering the training (B-Army, P-Navy, D-Air Force). The following six characters are numbers that identify the specific item of training. The identification number is used in all FMS and IMET training programs and implementation documents.

item manager [IM] An individual within the organization of an inventory control point or other such organization assigned management responsibility for one or more specific items of materiel.

item number See line item number.

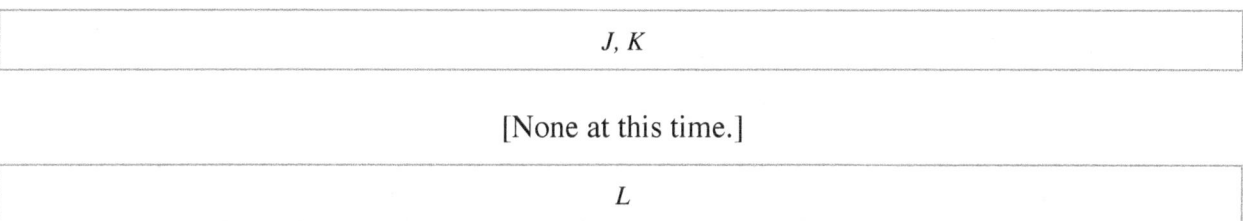

J, K

[None at this time.]

L

lease [security assistance] An agreement for the temporary transfer of the right of possession and use of a nonexcess defense article or articles to a foreign government or international organization, with the lessee agreeing to reimburse the USG in U.S. dollars for all costs incurred in leasing such articles, and to maintain, protect, repair, or restore the article(s), subject to and under the authority of Section 61, AECA (Title 22 U.S.C 2796).

letter of offer and acceptance [LOA] the United States of America Letter of Offer and Acceptance (LOA) by which the USG offers to sell to a foreign government or international organization U.S. defense articles and defense services pursuant to the AECA, as amended. The LOA lists the items and/or services, estimated costs, and the terms and conditions of sale; it also provides for the signature of an appropriate foreign government official to indicate acceptance.

letter of request [LOR] The term used to identify a request from an eligible FMS participant country for the purchase of U.S. defense articles and services. The request may be in message or letter format.

liabilities Amounts of money owed to others for goods and services received, or for assets acquired. Liabilities include accrued amounts earned but not yet due for payment, and progress payments due to contractors.

life cycle The total phases through which an item/system passes from the time it is initially developed until disposal.

life cycle cost The total costs to the government of acquisition and ownership of a system over its useful life. It includes the costs of development, acquisition, support, and, where applicable, disposal.

limited rights Involves the rights to use, duplicate, or disclose technical data (TD) in whole or in part, by or for the Government, with the express written permission of the party furnishing the TD to be

- released or disclosed outside the Government

- used by the Government for manufacture (or if software documentation, for preparing the same or similar software)
- used by a party other than the Government except under certain restricted circumstances

line item number A code which identifies a detail line item on the LOA. This code is perpetuated on the FMS customers' bill.

loan An agreement for the temporary transfer of the right of possession and use of a defense article or articles not acquired with military assistance funds to a foreign government or international organization, at no rental charge to the transferee, subject to and under authority of the FAA, Section 503. Also, applies to loans to a NATO or major non-NATO ally of materials, supplies, or equipment for the purpose of carrying out a program of cooperative research, development, testing, or evaluation subject to and under the authority of Section 65, AECA. Also involves the transfer of funds from one economic entity to another (e.g., government to government, individual to individual, or bank to individual) which must be repaid with interest over a prescribed period of time.

logistics The science of planning and carrying out the movement and maintenance of forces. In its most comprehensive sense, involves those aspects of military operations which deal with:
- design and development, acquisition storage, movement, distribution, maintenance, evacuation, and disposition of materials
- movement, evacuation, and hospitalization of personnel; (c) acquisition or construction, maintenance, operation, and disposition of facilities
- acquisitioning or furnishing of services

logistics support charge (LSC) A charge based on the Arms Export Control Act (AECA) requirement for full cost recovery. This charge is intended to recover the cost of logistics support involved in providing the spares and other items required to maintain a weapon system. These support costs are associated with production control, requisition processing, inventory maintenance, administration of Reports of Discrepancy (ROD), and logistics management. The LSC is applied by the DFAS-IN to delivery costs for those lines in FMS cases which have been identified assupport lines based on the generic code included in the LOA.

long-lead items/long-lead time materiels Those components of a system or piece of equipment for which the times to design and fabricate are the longest, and therefore, to which an early commitment of funds may be desirable in order to meet the earliest possible date of system completion. Might be ordered during full scale development (FSD) to arrive in time for production start.

M

---

maintainability The ability of an item to be retained in or restored to specified conditions when maintenance is performed by personnel having specified skill levels, using prescribed procedures and resources, at each prescribed level of maintenance and repair.

maintenance The upkeep of property, necessitated by wear and tear, which neither adds to the permanent value of the property nor appreciably prolongs its intended life, but keeps it in efficient operating condition. Normally includes "repair" but in Defense, in the case of real property, is distinguished from repair through being limited to the recurrent, day-to-day periodic, or scheduled work required to preserve or restore a real-property facility to such condition that it may be effectively utilized for its designated purpose. The term "preventive maintenance" involves deterring something from going wrong; the term "corrective maintenance" involves restoring something to its proper condition.

major defense equipment [MDE] Any item of significant military equipment on the *United States Munitions List* having a nonrecurring research and development cost of more than $50 million or a total production cost of more than $200 million.

major line item A program line for which the requirement is expressed quantitatively as well as in dollars. These lines are identified in the military articles and services list(s) (MASL) by a unit of issue (XX) other than dollars.

materiel management Direction and control of those aspects of logistics which deal with materiel, including the functions of identification, cataloging, standardization, requirements determination, procurement, inspection, quality control, packaging, storage, distribution, disposal, maintenance, mobilization planning, industrial readiness planning, and item management classification; encompasses materiel control, inventory control, inventory management, and supply management.

memorandum of agreement [MOA] or memorandum of understanding [MOU] A written agreement between governments or a government and international organization signed by authorized representatives and signifying an intent to be legally bound.

***military articles and services list* (MASL)** A catalogue of materiel, services, and training used in the planning and programming of Military Assistance Program (MAP), IMET, and FMS. Separate MASLs are maintained for IMET and FMS training which provide data on course identification, course availability, price, and duration of training.

Military Assistance Advisory Group [MAAG] A joint service group based overseas which primarily administers United States military assistance planning and programming in a host country. The term MAAG encompasses Joint U.S. Military Advisory Groups, Military Missions, Military Assistance Groups, U.S. Military Groups, and U.S. Military Representatives exercising responsibility within a U.S. Diplomatic Mission for security assistance and other related DoD matters. Defense Attachés are included only when specifically designated as having security assistance functions. See also security assistance organization.

Military Assistance Program Address Directory [MAPAD] The MAPAD provides clear text addresses of country representatives, freight forwarders, and customer-within-country required for releasing FMS and MAP shipments processed in accordance with military standard requisitioning and issuing procedures (MILSTRIP), and addresses required for the forwarding of related documentation.

military export sales All sales of defense articles and defense services made from U.S. sources to foreign governments, foreign private firms, and international organizations, whether made by DoD or by U.S. industry directly to a foreign buyer. Such sales fall into two major categories: FMS and Commercial Sales.

military standard billing system [MILSBILLS] This system provides data elements, codes, standard mechanized]procedures, and formats for use by DoD Components for billing, collecting and related accounting for sales from]system stocks, including direct deliveries. The mechanized procedures apply to FMS as outlined in DODI 7420.12 (regarding Interfund Billing System).

military standard contract administration procedures [MILSCAP] Provides uniform procedures, rules, formats, time standards and standard data elements and codes for the interchange of contract-related information between and among DoD components and contractors.

military standard requisitioning and issue procedures [MILSTRIP] A uniform procedure established by the DoD to govern the requisition and issue of materiel within standardized priorities.

military standard transaction reporting and accounting procedures [MILSTRAP] Prescribes uniform procedures, data elements, codes, documents, and time standards for the flow of inventory accounting information pertaining to receipt, Issue, and adjustment actions, between inventory control points, stock control/activities, storage sites, and posts or bases.

military supply and transportation evaluation procedures [MILSTEP] Provides a standard method for the preparation and collection of basic data necessary to measure supply system performance and transportation effectiveness.

mobile education team [MET] A team of U.S. DoD personnel on temporary duty in a foreign country for the purpose of training foreign personnel in resource management. Teams normally funded from E-IMET Program.

mobile training team [MTT] A team of U.S. DoD personnel on temporary duty in a foreign country for the purpose of training foreign personnel in the operation, maintenance, or other support of weapon systems and support equipment, as well as training for general military operations. MTTs may be funded from either FMS or IMET Programs.

munitions list The *U.S. Munitions List* is an enumeration of defense articles and defense services and is published in the Department of State's *International Traffic in Arms Regulations*.

N

---

national stock number A 13-digit stock number consisting of a 4-digit Federal Supply Classification and a 9-digit National Item Identification Number.

net case value Amount of the estimated cost reflected on the LOA and its amendments/modifications.

nonrecurring costs [NRC or NC] Those costs funded by an RDT&E appropriation to develop or improve a product or technology either through contract or in-house effort. Also, those one-time costs incurred in support of previous production of a specified model and those costs incurred in support of a total projected production run.

nonrecurring demands A one-time requisition from a customer which is not used to compute demand-based requirements.

nonrepayable credits/loans Grant funds appropriated by the Congress of the United States of America for use in the Foreign Military Financing Program under Title III of the annual *Foreign Operations Appropriations Act*. Formerly termed" forgiven credits/loans," these grant funds are allocated to selected countries for their use in financing FMS acquisitions of defense articles, defense services, and training under the authority of Section 23, AECA. Additionally, certain countries may be authorized these grant funds to finance DCS.

nonstandard article For FMS purposes, a nonstandard article is one that the DoD does not manage, either because an applicable end item has been retired or because it was never purchased for DoD components.

nonstandard item An item of supply determined by standardization action as not authorized for procurement.

nonstandard service For FMS purposes a nonstandard service is a service that the DoD does not routinely provide for itself or for purchase.

obligation A duty to make a future payment of money. The duty is incurred as soon as an order is placed, or a contract is awarded for the delivery of goods and the performance of services. It is not necessary that goods actually be delivered, or services actually performed, before the obligation is created; neither is it necessary that a bill, or invoice be received first. The placement of an order is sufficient. An obligation legally encumbers a specified sum of money which will require an outlay or expenditure in the future.

obligational authority [OA] Authority, from DFAS-IN to the implementing agency, allowing obligations to be incurred against a country's Trust Fund in an amount not to exceed the DFAS-IN established value.

obligations Amounts of orders placed, contracts awarded, services received, and similar transactions during a given period requiring the future payment of money. Such amounts include adjustments for differences between obligations previously recorded and accrued expenditures of actual payments.

offer date The date which appears on the offer portion of an LOA and which indicates the date on which an FMS offer is made to a foreign buyer.

Office of Defense Cooperation (ODC) A Security Assistance Organization limited to three U.S. military and DoD civilian members for the performance of security assistance functions. Where necessary, the Chief of the Diplomatic Mission may request up to three additional members to perform such functions. See also security assistance organization.

omnibus billing statement of account A statement of additional charges or credits to cases that have been recategorized from active to inactive status.

open sales case A n FMS case which is designated as open as long as any portion of the transaction is incomplete, i.e., delivery of materiel, performance of services, financial transactions, or rendering of the final statement of accounts.

open sales offer An FMS offer made to a foreign purchaser which is pending acceptance.

operation & maintenance [O&M] costs Costs associated with equipment, supplies, and services required to train, operate, and maintain forces in a recipient country, including the cost of spare parts other than concurrent spares and initial stockages, ammunition and missiles used in training or replacements for such items expended in training or operations, rebuild and overhaul costs (excluding modernization) of equipment subsequent to initial issue, training and other services that do not constitute investment costs, and administrative costs associated with overall program management and administration.

ordering activity An activity which originates a requisition or order for procurement, production, or performance of work or service by another activity.

outlays Actual expenditures. Checks issued, interest occurred on the public debt, or other payments. Total budget outlays consist of the sum of the outlays from appropriations and other funds in the budget, less receipts (i.e., refunds and reimbursements).

outside CONUS All geographic areas not within the territorial boundaries of the continental United States of America. OCONUS includes Hawaii and Alaska.

overhead costs See indirect costs.

overseas training Training provided foreign nationals at training installations outside the U.S.

packing, handling, storage, & transportation [PHS&T] The resources, processes, procedures, design considerations, and methods to ensure that all system, equipment, and support items are preserved, packaged, handled, and transported properly, including: environmental considerations, equipment preservation requirements for short-and-long-term storage, and transportability. One of the principle elements of integrated logistics support (ILS).

payment on delivery [FMS] An FMS term of sale in which the USG issues a bill to the FMS purchaser at the time of delivery of defense articles or the rendering of defense services from DoD resources. This term may only be used pursuant to a written statutory determination by the Director, DSCA, who may find it in the national interest to authorize such payment. Based on Presidential action, this term may also be modified to read "Payment 120 Days After Delivery."

payment schedule List of dollar amounts and when they are due from the foreign customer. The payment schedule supplements the LOA presented to the customer. After acceptance of the LOA, the payment schedule generally serves as the basis for billing to the customer. Changes in the estimated costs of an FMS case may require changes in the accompanying payment schedule.

performing activity An activity which is responsible for performing work or service, including the production of material and/or the procurement of goods and services from other contractors and activities.

pipeline That portion of accepted security assistance program orders for defense articles and services, for which delivery, either constructive or actual, has not occurred, or services have not been rendered.

price and availability [P&A] data Prepared by the MILDEPs, DSCA, and other DoD components in response to a foreign government's request for preliminary data for the possible purchase of a defense article or service. P&A data are not considered valid for the preparation of an LOA. Furnishing of this data does not constitute a commitment for the USG to offer for sale the articles and services for which the data are provided.

procuring activity See contracting activity.

procurement lead time The interval in months between the initiation of procurement action and receipt into the supply system of the production model (excluding prototypes) purchased as the result of such actions; procurement leadtime is composed of two elements, production lead time, and administrative lead time.

procuring contracting officer [PCO] The individual authorized to enter into contracts for supplies and services on behalf of the government by detailed bids or negotiations and who is responsible for overall procurement under such contracts.

production lead time The time interval between the placement of a contract and receipt into the supply system of materiel purchased.

professional military education [PME] Career training designed to provide or enhance leadership and the recipient force's capabilities to conduct military planning, programming, management, budgeting, and force development to the level of sophistication appropriate to that force.

program management review [PMR] A management level review held by a Systems Program Office or Systems Program Manager for the purpose of determining the status of an assigned system. PMRs are designed as tools to identify problems, if any, and to develop appropriate follow-up actions as required.

progress payments Those payments (disbursements) made to contractors or DoD industrial fund activities as work progresses under a contract; payments are made on the basis of cost incurred or percentage of work completed, or of a particular stage of completion accomplished prior to actual delivery and acceptance of contract items.

Q

quality assurance [QA[A planned and systematic pattern of all actions necessary to provide confidence that adequate technical requirements are established, that products and services conform to established technical requirements, and that satisfactory performance is achieved.

R

rationalization, standardization & interoperability (RSI) Any action that increases the effectiveness of NATO Forces through more efficient or effective use of defense resources committed to the Alliance.

reciprocal defense procurement Procurement actions which are implemented under memoranda of understanding/memoranda of agreement (MOU/MOA) between the U.S. and various participating nations whereby the participants agree to effect complementary acquisitions of defense articles from each other's country.

reimbursable transactions Transactions utilized on internal U.S. DoD documents whereby no check is drawn. Funds are moved from one fund cite to another without the cost of writing check, thus, no check drawn procedure. See also direct citation.

reimbursements Amounts received by an activity for the cost of material, work, or services furnished to others, for credit to an appropriation or their fund account.

reorder point The point at which time a stock replenishment requisition is submitted to maintain the predetermined stock age objective.

repair and replace [FMS] Programs by which eligible Cooperative Logistics Supply Support Arrangement (CLSSA) customers return repairable carcasses to the U.S. and receive a serviceable item without awaiting the normal repair cycle timeframe. The concept is that the replacement involves an exchange of CLSSA customer owned stocks in the customer's hands and the CLSSA customer-owned stocks in the USG inventory in the U.S. Countries are initially charged the estimated repair cost, with adjustment to the actual repair cost upon completion of repair of the carcass.

repair and return Programs by which eligible foreign countries return unserviceable repairable items for entry into the U.S. Military Department repair cycle. Upon completion of repairs, the same item is returned to the country and the actual cost of the repair is billed to the country.

reparable item An item that can be reconditioned or economically repaired for reuse when it becomes unserviceable replenishment The purchase of item following the initial purchase, whether bought for the initial support of additional end items, stock replenishment, or other purposes.

reprogramming The transfer of funds between program elements or line items within an appropriation.

research and development Those program costs primarily associated with research and development efforts, including the development of a new or improved capability to the point where it is ready for operational use. These costs include equipment cost funded under the RDT&E

appropriation and related military construction appropriation costs. They exclude costs which appear in the military personnel, operation and maintenance, and procurement appropriations.

S
---

security assistance [SA] A group of programs authorized by the Foreign Assistance Act of 1961, as amended, and the AECA, as amended, or other related statutes by which the United States provides defense articles, military training, and other defense related services, by grant, credit, cash sale, lease, or loan, in furtherance of national policies and objectives.

Security Assistance Management Manual [DOD 5105.38M] A manual published by the DSCA under authority of DoD Directive 5105.38. It sets forth the responsibilities, policies, and procedures governing the administration of security assistance within the DOD.

Security Assistance Management Review [SAMR] A management review led by a security assistance organization, for the purpose of determining the status of one or more specific problems. Such reviews may include the entire range of a purchaser's security assistance program.

security assistance organization/office [SAO] The generic term SAO encompasses all DoD elements, regardless of actual title, located in a foreign country with assigned responsibilities for carrying out security assistance management functions.

Security Assistance Policies and Procedures (Volume 15 to DoD 7000.14-R). A manual published by the DFAS under the authority of DODI 7290.3. It establishes basic financial procedures for security assistance activities involving management, fiscal matters, accounting, pricing, budgeting for reimbursements to DoD appropriations accounts and revolving funds, auditing, international balance of payments, and matters affecting the DoD budget.

services Includes any service, test, inspection, repair, training, publication, technical or other assistance, or defense information furnished as military assistance under the FAA of 1961, as amended, or furnished through FMS under the U.S. AECA of 1976, as amended.

significant military equipment [SME] Those defense articles and services on the *U.S. Munitions List* in the *International Traffic in Arms Regulation* (ITAR) which are preceded by an asterisk. SME are articles which require special export controls "because of their capacity for substantial utility in the conduct of military operations."

spares/spare parts An individual part, subassembly, or assembly supplied for the maintenance or repair of systems or equipment.

specialized English training [SET] Instruction conducted at DLIELC for IMSs who have attained the required ECL to develop vocabulary skills for entry into both hazardous and highly technical courses.

staging cost The cost incurred by the Department of Defense in consolidation of materiel before shipment to an FMS customer. Includes costs incident to storage and control of inventory, consolidation of incoming articles into a single shipment, and a break in CONUS transportation.

standardization The process by which DoD achieves the closest practicable cooperation among the Services and Defense Agencies for the most efficient use of research, development, and production resources, and agrees to adopt on the broadest possible basis the use of
- Common or compatible operational, administrative, and logistic procedures
- Common or compatible technical procedures and criteria
- Common, compatible, or interchangeable supplies, components, weapons, or equipment

- Common or compatible tactical doctrine with corresponding organizational compatibility

As applied to NATO and to non-NATO countries, standardization involves the process of developing concepts, doctrines, procedures and designs to achieve and maintain the most effective levels of compatibility, interoperability, interchangeability and commonality in the fields of operations, administration, and materiel.

surcharge Expenses incident to issues, sales, and transfers of materiel that are not included in the standard price or contact cost of materiel. Elements of surcharges are (but not limited to):—

- Packing, Crating, Handling (PCH)
- Transportation (2nd destination)
- Administrative Fee
- Logistics Support Change
- Contract Administrative Service
- Storage Costs
- Staging

system program office The office of the program manager and the single point of contact with industry, Government agencies, and other activities participating in the system acquisition process.

technical assistance field team [TAFT] A team of U.S. DoD personnel deployed on PCS status, normally for one year or longer, to a foreign country to provide technical assistance and training to foreign military personnel in the operation, maintenance, and employment of specific equipment, technology, weapons, supporting systems, or in other special skills related to military functions.

T

---

technical assistance team (TAT) A team of U.S. DoD personnel deployed to a foreign country on TDY status (i.e., up to 179 days) to place into operation, operate, maintain, and repair equipment provided under the FMS programs.

technical data [TD] Recorded information, regardless of form or characteristic, of a scientific or technical nature. Examples of technical data packages include research and engineering drawings and associated lists, specifications, standards, process sheets, manuals, technical reports, catalog item identifications, and related information and computer software documentation.

technical data package [TDP] Normally includes technical design and manufacturing information sufficient to enable the construction or manufacture of a defense item component modification, or to enable the performance of certain maintenance or production processes. It may include blueprints, drawings, plans, or instructions that can be used or adapted for use in the design, production, manufacture, or maintenance of defense items or technology.

technical manual A publication containing instructions designed to meet the needs of personnel responsible for (or being trained in) the operation, maintenance, service, overhaul, installation, and inspection of specific items of equipment and materiel.

training/training support Formal or informal instruction of IMSs in the United States or overseas by officers or employees of the United States, contract technicians, contractors (including instruction at civilian institutions), or by correspondence courses, technical, educational or information publications and media of all kinds, training aids, orientations, training exercises, and military advice to foreign military units and forces. [Sec. 47(5), AECA]

travel and living allowance (TLA) Those costs associated with transportation, excess baggage, and living allowances (per diem) of IMSs which are authorized for payment under the IMET Program.

trust fund (FMS) A fund established for each FMS customer country for recording all financial transactions for use in carrying our specific purposes and programs in accordance with an agreement. The Trust Fund does not include monies on deposit in an approved Federal Reserve Bank New York (FRBNY) account or, Commercial interest bearing account, until withdrawn by DFAS-IN. (FRBNY funds can only be withdrawn by DFAS-IN) type of address code One of several codes used in the MAPAD to identify a plain language address to which to ship a specific category of documents or material.

type of assistance code A code used to reflect the terms of sale and the planned source of supply for items/services identified on LOA. Also knows as a type of finance code.

U

unaccepted case An FMS letter of offer which was not accepted or funded within the prescribed time shown on the LOA.

unearned advance Monies collected/received that are greater than accrued costs.

undistributed cost An identified cost which has not been allocated to a specific case.

United States Code [U.S.C.] A consolidation and codification of the general and permanent laws of the United States of America arranged according to subject matter under 50 title headings. The USC sets out the current status of the laws, as amended. It presents the laws in a concise and usable form without requiring recourse to the many volumes of the Statutes at Large containing the individual amendments.

unlimited rights Rights to use, duplicate, release, or disclose technical data or computer software in whole or in part in any manner and for any purpose, and to have or permit others to do so.

V

[None at this time]

W

weapon system life cycle cost A time period divided into phases, ranging from the first consideration of the need for a weapon system through the development and in-service stages down to system phase-out and disposal.

work in process The costs of the materiel, labor and indirect costs used in producing customized items. Includes DoD organizations and contracts. A cost accounting system that supports the summary changes (progress payments) must be utilized.

X, Y, Z

[None at this time]

www.ingramcontent.com/pod-product-compliance
Lightning Source LLC
Chambersburg PA
CBHW081207280526
45787CB00006B/2363